To all your magical
dinner parties to come!

xo Tara

The
Dinner Party
Project

The Dinner Party Project

A NO-STRESS GUIDE TO FOOD WITH FRIENDS

Natasha Feldman

Photographs by Alana Kysar
Illustrations by Becky Simpson

HARVEST
An Imprint of WILLIAM MORROW

THE DINNER PARTY PROJECT. Copyright © 2023 by Natasha Feldman.
All rights reserved. Printed in Canada. No part of this book may
be used or reproduced in any manner whatsoever without written
permission except in the case of brief quotations embodied in critical
articles and reviews. For information, address HarperCollins Publishers,
195 Broadway, New York, NY 10007.

HarperCollins books may be purchased for educational, business, or
sales promotional use. For information, please email the Special Markets
Department at SPsales@harpercollins.com.

FIRST EDITION

Designed by Melissa Lotfy and Moses Aipa

Photographs copyright © 2023 Alana Kysar

Art direction by Moses Aipa

Illustrations and cover design © 2023 Becky Simpson

Library of Congress Cataloging-in-Publication Data has been applied for.

ISBN 978-0-358-72299-1

23 24 25 26 27 TC 10 9 8 7 6 5 4 3 2 1

To anyone in search of a big, full life
fueled by friends and food

CONTENTS

Friendsday Wednesday: Or How I Became a (Dinner) Partier xii
How to Make a Dinner Party: The Basics xviii
Menus xxiv
How to Navigate Each Recipe xxix

Cocktails   1

Agua Fresca	2
Sparkling Ginger Limeade	2
Campari Lemonade	3
Xtra-Limey Piña Colada	3
Paper Plane	3
Negroni	4
Extra-Fun French 75	4
Manhattan	4
Not-So-Sweet Strawberry Daiquiri	5
The Versatile Margarita	5

Noshes/Apps   7

Snackies—by Aristotle	8
Spiced Herby Yogurt Sauce	11
Fancy Marinated Olives with Warm Feta	12
Hot Dog Soup (but Really Sausage)	14
Athena's Dip Situation	16
Lemony Paprika Lentil Soup	20
Cheese Board Cheese Chat	22
Radishes Dipped in Honey-Fennel Butter	25
Ridiculously Smooth and Hilariously Easy Hummus	26
Smoked Paprika Potato Crisps with Aioli	29
Tart Apple Butternut Squash Soup	30

Mains   33

Roasted Tomato and Burrata Eggplant Parm   34

Braised Garlicky Eggplant with Chickpeas and Tomatoes   39

Be-Your-Own-Bubbe (BYOB) Jewish Brisket   41

Cacio e Pepe Mac and Cheese   45

Cozy Winter Night Borscht   47

Pan-Crisped Sausage with Lemon Herb Veggies   51

Diner-Style Smash Burgers   53

Peel 'n' Eat Shrimp with "I'd Eat This on a Shoe"
Basil Dipping Magic   57

Foolproof Lemon and Fennel Branzino   61

Glorious Spicy Sausage Pasta   65

Juicy Kofta with Lemon Coriander Yogurt   67

Pan-Seared Salmon for Any Mood   71

Crispy-Crispy Turkey Thighs with Caramelized Onion Jam   73

Rigatoni with Confit Tomatoes and Burrata   76

Perfect Seared Rib Eye   79

Veggie Pot Pie with Parm and Black Pepper Phyllo   81

Your New Favorite Herby Meatballs   85

Salads/Sides 89

A Simple Bistro Salad   90

That Salad with the Herby Dressing (a.k.a. A Chopped Salad)   93

Carole King Salad   95

Roasted Carrot Babies   99

Sour Cream Mashed Potatoes   100

Super-Crunchy Green Salad   103

Andy-Approved Kale Salad   104

Fluffy Everything Pita Clouds   106

Garlicky Cabbage with Whole-Grain Mustard   110

Golden Coconut and Apricot Rice   113

Brown Rice That Doesn't Suck   114

Latke-Style Smashed Potatoes with Dilly Crème Fraîche   116

Charred Lemon Broccolini   119

Roasted Squash with Sage Yogurt   122

Olive Oil–Drenched Sourdough   125

Party Pesto   127

Roasted Veg Parade   128

Shallot Compote Green Beans   131

Veg Stock   132

A Very Adult Salad (a.k.a. Grapies and Greenies)   135

World's Best Oven Fries with Parsley and Parm   138

Honey-Drizzled Zucchini Fritters   141

Pizza Night 143

Same-Day Dough 147

Spicy Soppressata Pizza 151

Wine-Drunk Onion and Fennel Pizza 152

Pizza Sprinkles™! 153

Tacos Get Their Own Chapter 155

Fish-Fry Tacos with Smoky Mayo 156

Smoky Spicy Seared Fish Tacos 158

Sort-of-Kind-of Cochinita Pibil 160

Smoky Chipotle Mayo 164

Avocado Crema 165

Quickled Onions 166

Honey-Jalapeño Black Beans 167

Breakfast for Dinner 169

Bagels and Lox with Homemade Cream Cheese 170

Anything Goes Buttermilk Pancakes
and Crispy Oven Bacon 173

A Frittata for All Seasons 177

Sweet Things   181

Babka-*ish* Monkey Bread   185

Clara's Coffee Cake   187

Brown Butter and Sage RKTs   191

Oops, I Forgot Dessert! Choco-Dipped Fruit   192

Churro Hot Chocolate   195

Orange Dream Granita   196

Sisterhood of the Traveling Lemon Cake   199

Not Your Grandma's Pinwheel Cookies   201

Juicy Fruit Greek Yogurt Panna Cotta   205

Pink Lemonade Bars   206

Fudgy Chocolate Cake with Salted Caramel Frosting   209

Floofy Funfetti Cake   213

Rainbow Cookie Icebox Cake   215

The Messiest Ice Cream Sundaes   219

Thin Mint Pudding Pie   220

Acknowledgments 223
Tools for Your Kitchen 226
Common Ingredients 229
Index 231

FRIENDSDAY
WEDNESDAY

Or, How I Became a (Dinner) Partier

I've met most of my favorite people at dinner parties.

My closest pal of ten years, Julianna? Collected her at a dinner party I hosted to find a new roommate. The night ended in sticky cinnamon buns.

My friend Phi? I met her at a dinner party I was invited to when I ran into a guy I did theater with as a kid.

The guy I did theater with? Well, we aren't tight, but the woman he was dating at the time, the one who threw the dinner party where I met Phi? She is a very close friend of mine now too.

The photographer for this book? Wanna guess how I met her? Yup. At a dinner party.

My husband, Andy? I knew it was the real deal after I brought him to a dinner party hosted by my two best friends. There was risotto involved.

My dog, Malone? Well, she used to be my friend's dog until we fell in love at a dinner party, and the rest is history.

I could regale you all day with stories about people I've met at dinner parties and clung to like a baby koala. Dinner parties bring people together. There's just something about having dinner and drinks at a friend's house that is 1,000x more memorable than going to a restaurant. So as a believer in the power of dinner parties, I spent my mid-twenties attending as many as humanly possible.

But then, as my friends and I got busy with careers, dating lives, families, and general garbage, the dinner parties got further and further apart. One day, I was sitting on the couch feeling unsettled, thinking about what had shifted, and it became really obvious. I knew what I needed. Enter Friendsday Wednesday.

Friendsday Wednesday (n.): A Wednesday when your friends come over for dinner so your week doesn't suck.

It began with a Google Sheet where people could sign up for one of six open spots per week. I thought just a few people would sign up, and that maybe some weeks no one would sign up, and I would have to deal with the existential question that all humans ask themselves in their darkest moments: "DO ALL MY FRIENDS HATE ME?"

But right away the entire month was booked! I was incredibly excited.

I used the first Friendsday Wednesday as a chance to dust off cookbooks I'd been meaning to crack open. I'd pick one recipe I was really excited about and make simple sides to serve with it. I made things like Moroccan stewed lamb with cherry rice, extra-gooey butternut squash mac and cheese, grilled kebabs with fluffy homemade pitas, and cochinita pibil tacos. On occasion, if the day exploded, I would just order takeout. Guests always brought the booze.

Friendsday Wednesday quickly became the best day of the week, not just for me and my partner (hi, Andy!), but for all of our friends. People started texting me to find out what we ate on nights they weren't there, or to ask if they could bring a plus-one, and to get ideas about how they could host their own version of Friendsday Wednesday.

The act of gathering and feeding people allowed me to maintain sanity, support my community, and have some fun. Being an adult can be sort of a drag a lot of the time, and gathering around food is the greatest antidote.

Am I saying that becoming a regular dinner partier will necessarily lead you to a fulfilling career and the love of your life? I'm not <u>not</u> saying it.

Why You Should Become a (Dinner) Partier Too

Who benefits from more dinner parties? Everyone.

I'm not a social scientist, but I do have a theory. Here it goes . . .

You know Maslow's Hierarchy of Needs, the theory that our most basic needs must be met so that we can start to address our more complex needs like self-esteem, confidence, and creativity? Well, I think we're screwing it up.

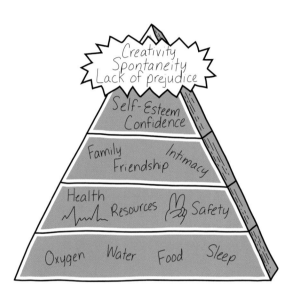

Today, we're not getting our most basic needs met. Statistically, millennials are more burnt out and isolated than any other generation. The General Social Survey found that the number of Americans without any close friends has tripled since 1985. We eat out 30 percent more than any other generation. We're less confident in the kitchen. (Someone close to me, who I will not out in this public forum—cough *Andy*—once asked me how to heat up soup.) We're about half as likely to have someone over for dinner—even just once a month.

Our shortcuts to food, health, and friendship—drinking cereal-milk-flavored meal replacements alone at our desks, taking gummy vitamins that promise magic, and responding to group texts with ridiculous TikTok videos—may trick our brains into thinking we've checked each of Maslow's boxes, but they don't actually form a stable foundation. We have optimized ourselves into oblivion, and it's isolating us, chipping away at our sense of self, and making us anxious and unhappy. Our need for authentic community is impossible to ignore.

Preparing and eating dinner with your family or framily (that's your friend-family) makes your life better. The sense of accomplishment you'll get from creating an opportunity for people to sit around a table while stuffing their faces and laugh-crying is unparalleled. You'll get closer with your friends and make new ones. **And the basic act of cooking is so good for your mental state that studies have shown it de-stresses and grounds you in the same way that meditation does.** In other words, it's basically free therapy.

The DPP Solution

Now, I know what you're thinking: "That sounds fun. But also I'm a tired person, and I don't know if I'll actually do it."

Our overworked and overstressed brains can always come up with reasons not to do things, so let me take a minute to knock down some of those fake excuses now.

"I work till 8 on Wednesdays. Wednesdays are bad for me."

Well, guess what? Friendsday Wednesdays don't have to be on Wednesdays! They can be on Saturdays. You will have to call them Friendsday Saturdays, which is an objectively worse name, but if it fits your lifestyle better, go for it!

"I don't know how to boil water."

First off, I'm sure that's an exaggeration. Second off, that's what this book is for. Each of these recipes was tested by friends of mine who have next to no experience in the kitchen. If they can make my eggplant parmesan with blistered tomatoes and burrata—and they did, and it was good!—then you can too. Plus, the recipes are full of tips to help you work through them, including what you can make in advance (and how to reheat it). There are also suggestions in the menu section for stuff you can just buy prepared at your grocery store (helloooo, frozen cheesecake).

"Look, Natasha, I'm no mid-'90s Martha Stewart. I'm much closer to 2020s Martha Stewart, who posts blurry photos of chickens and close-up pics of her dental work on her Instagram. I don't have time to prepare a meal, do some intricate napkin-fold, arrange a candle-lit tablescape, and then cook and clean. That's too much for me."

Okay, well, look, that was really specific. But the bottom line is that you don't have to make a multicourse meal and show off your mid-'90s Martha skills if you don't want to. You can order pizza and make one of my delicious salads to pair it with, and that's a dinner party too.

So if you're up to it, I propose a challenge: *one dinner party a month for a year.*

If that sounds like a lot, don't panic; it's only twelve dinners out of 365! Just do it. Find your Julianna, your Andy, or your Malone!

Start right now. Commit. Just grab your phone, text two friends, and ask them to come over for dinner two weeks from now. Get it on the books, and then flip to the next page and I'll walk you through the rest.

You didn't text them, did you?
I'll give you one more chance.
Text them now, then read on.

Okay, I trust you!
Now let's get to it!

The Dinner Party Project is here to revive and democratize the dinner party for you, by reminding you to make dinner parties a creative practice rather than a stressful performance. This simple shift in perspective around "hosting" will change your life for the way, way better.

This thing should be fun, low-stress, and leave you feeling connected, relaxed, and excited to eat your leftovers. If not, scale back your efforts: your mid-'90s Martha is showing. No matter what, you gotta have a few gatherings before it feels like second nature.

How Can I Help You Become a Dinner Partier?

If you're looking for proper hand-holding, I've got you! There's a flowchart to help you pick a meal that fits your vibe for any given day (page 22), an illustrated timeline to guide you through the entire dinner party process (page xx), twenty-five predetermined menus (page xxiv) to select from, and tons of other goodies.

If you want to freestyle, the recipes in this book are divided into four categories: noshes and apps; main events; sides and salads; and sweet things. Pick one recipe from each category, and—BAM!—you've got a full-blown dinner party.

More than anything, *The Dinner Party Project* is about helping you establish a central point of connection and belonging in your life. It'll ensure you get quality time with all your friends, new and old. Let this bring you joy, friendship, and a place where you can let your freak flag fly.

Happy cooking.
Love, Tash

How to Make a Dinner Party: The Basics

After a decade of doing private chef work, teaching approximately one zillion cooking classes, and throwing a few hundred dinner parties, I've accumulated a lot of thoughts on hosting, de-stressing dinner parties, and making easy dishes taste really good—all of which I'm very excited to share with you. I'm here to remove the anxiety of entertaining and to help you find a hosting style that works for you.

If you're a person who likes rules and guidance, welcome to this delicious breakdown of how to use this book. If your eyes are bugging out of your head looking at the quantity of words on this page—skip to the next section.

There are four steps to getting your dinner party on.

Step 1: Pick Your Peeps

Most of the recipes in this book are for six humans. So let's do some simple math: if you have six people, all the food will be gobbled up, but if you have a more intimate group of three, then hooray for you, you'll get leftovers! Find a group of people (close friends, fun neighbors you want to get to know better, cousins you just found out you have via genetic testing, friends of friends, coworkers—you get the idea) who want to dinner party regularly, knowing some will tag in and out, and get on a schedule. Dinner party people are everywhere.

Step 2: Pick Your Place

Your house? Do you have a big enough table? The beach? A neighbor's porch? A stoop? Everyone takes a turn? Your location may dictate the kinds of food you serve. If you're going to be in a park, you'll want foods that are all easy to transport and good at room temp; if you're gathering around a coffee table, you'll want a meal that can be eaten on one plate, and so on.

Step 3: Pick Your Style

There are three ways to do this:

THE SOLO
Cook before your friends arrive

THE COLLAB
Cook together

THE POTLUCK
Divvy up recipes

Step 4: Pick Your Menu

This book has lots of ways to help you decide what to make for dinner. You can . . .

- Use the "What Should I Make for Dinner?" flowchart (page 22) to take you from "What the fork should I make?" to "Your New Favorite Herby Meatballs" in under two minutes.

- Go to page xxiv for the full list of preplanned menus.

- Check out the table of contents to mix and match recipes from four categories: noshes/apps; mains; salads/sides; and sweet things.

Here's a little advice for how to approach
the three different cooking styles:

SOLO

- If you're at all nervous, pick a few dishes
  that are great at room temp so you can prep
  them ahead of time and not stress during the
  party. All the salads and vegetable dishes in
  this book are great at room temp.

- DDD: Delegate Drinks and Desserts to your
  guests.

- Remember: Having a dinner party is about
  connecting with your people, having a good
  time, and not being rushed—it's not a Top
  Chef audition. Take the pressure off by
  making a meal that feels manageable and fun.
  If that means making one dish from this book
  and getting everything else premade, that's
  A-OK.

COLLAB COOKING

- Make sure everyone gathers at least 2 hours
  before dinner to account for cooking time.

- Decide ahead of time whether you'll be
  providing all the ingredients yourself, or
  whether people will shop for the dish they'll
  be making.

- Divvy up the recipes and tasks based on
  people's skill sets:

The Person Who Lives There: This person will
put out the ingredients and necessary tools
before everyone arrives. They'll also be
responding to the inevitable questions about
where knives, sugar, and olive oil live.
And they'll play sous chef to the Speedy/
Experienced Cook (see below).

The Organized One: This person might not be
the greatest cook, but they're a scheduling
wizard. They'll read through all the recipes
for timing and transitions and make a master
schedule for the night. They track when
something needs to go in or come out of the
oven, and they keep everything moving. You
got a type-A freak show in your crew? This is
their jam.

The Speedy/Experienced Cook(s): Give them the
most complex dish—in many cases this will
be the main because it has the most moving
parts, but take a look at the recipes in your
menu to decide. If this person needs help,
pull in the sous chef, a.k.a. the Person Who
Lives There.

The Nervous/Newer Cook(s): Give them the
salads, easy appetizers, drink mixing,
vegetable washing, herb chopping, and any
other odd jobs.

The Person Who Doesn't Know How to Boil
Water: This person has two critical roles to
fill:
1. Making sure everyone is well-hydrated with
   beverages (adult and otherwise) at all
   times, and
2. Cleaning up. Ideally, this human washes,
   dries, and puts dishes away immediately,
   so they're not taking up space and can be
   used again.

HELLO
I am on
drink duty

POTLUCK

While you can easily send a text or email and
let people self-assign, here are a few tips
to make your potlucking experience easy-
breezy.

- It's best if the person who lives where the
  dinner party is prepares the recipes that are
  best served hot or are clumsy to transport.

- Appetizers, salads, sides, and room temp
  desserts are great things to ask people to
  bring.

- DDD.

Ingredients for a Successful Night

You've got your people, place, cooking style, and menu—let's finish with how to prep.

Enter: The dinner party timeline. Your new best friend. Curious what you should be doing a week, two days, or thirty minutes before your guests arrive? The timeline has your answer.

SUN	MON	TUES	WED	THURS	FRI	SAT

2 to 4 Weeks Before

TIMELINE
1.
2.
3.
4.
5.

4 Days Before | 2 to 3 Days Before | The Day Before | DINNER PARTY

2 to 4 Weeks Before

Invite guests. Finalize the menu. Assign dishes as needed.

4 Days Before

Confirm people are coming and what they're bringing.

2 to 3 Days Before

Read through the recipes. Write a shopping list and a simple cooking timeline. The timeline should include the order in which to tackle the recipes and how much time you'll need total. Multiple things in the oven with different temperatures? Just pick the median temp.

If you're collab cooking: share the recipes with the Organized One so they can write the cooking timeline.

The Day Before

Grocery shop, wash and chop everything you can, cook/prep whatever is possible. (All recipes have suggestions for this built in.)

The Day Of

BEFORE YOU START COOKING: Run the dishwasher or wash and put away as many dishes as you can, tidy your space, and set the table (whatever that means to you—can be just putting out a stack of dishes and silverware). Take out ingredients that need to be at room temp. Refrigerate any drinks that should be served cold. Check to see if you have ice. No ice? Ask someone to bring!

COOK! (If you're collab cooking, pull out the tools/shelf-stable ingredients you'll need later.)

1 HOUR BEFORE: Put out snacks! If you get easily stressed when you're finishing cooking, put the snacks, drinks, and glasses in another room; people will migrate to them.

30 MINUTES BEFORE: Pause for sanity: change your dirty clothes if you feel like it, brush your teeth if you forgot today (oh, is that just me?), put on some good tunes, get hydrated, and maybe sit for a second.

PARTY TIME: Tell the first person who arrives that they're on drink duty, and make sure they know there are snacks, ample snacks.

(If you're collab cooking, have the Organized One get everyone on track. If soloing or potlucking, enjoy dinner!)

HOW TO NEVER RUN OUT OF WINE

Plan on each person drinking a half bottle of wine.

Ask someone (or multiple someones) to bring the wine, if you want. I like to inform the person what the meal will be so they can find a fun wine that fits in.

For white wine: Keep it in the fridge and pull it out 15 minutes before drinking.

For red wine: Toss it in the fridge for 15 minutes before opening it.

Have a few bottles of wine at home in case the alcohol bearer is late.

FOR THE DPP OVERACHIEVER

<u>Mood Lighting:</u> Good lighting goes a long way in making a dinner feel cozy. Can you use lamps instead of overhead lights? Can you bring a candle or two to the table?

<u>Table Setting:</u> If you wanna have flowers or decorations on the table, make sure they have a low profile so you can see your friends instead of leaves.

<u>Game Night:</u> If your crew likes a game, you can have one for after dinner if people are in the mood. I am particularly fond of Exploding Kittens, Sushi Go!, Catch Phrase, A Fake Artist Goes to New York, Morphology, Code Names, Drawful, Fibbage, and Salad Bowl.

<u>Bathroom Zen:</u> Completely nonessential, but I like to light a candle in the bathroom. It makes me feel very adult and in charge. (Though one time I did set a piece of art on fire, so be careful out there.)

Throwing a dinner party is about connecting with people, having a good time, and not being rushed. Whatever it takes to make the night fun for you is the right way to proceed.

NOW GO HAVE FUN!

What Should I Make For

START HERE! →

How much time do you have?

Daily

How often do you cook?

All day, baby!

How badly do you want to eat a green thing?

Weekly

LOLZ

Have you had pasta yet today?

"How did you know?!"

Fluffy Everything Pita Clouds (page 106)

Super-Crunchy Green Salad (page 103)

Spiced Herby Yogurt Sauce (page 11)

Braised Garlicky Eggplant with Chickpeas and Tomatoes (page 39)

Juicy Fruit Greek Yogurt Panna Cotta (page 205)

Sort-of-Kind-of Cochinita Pibil (page 160)

Honey-Jalapeño Black Beans (page 167)

Quickled Onions (page 166)

Churro Hot Chocolate (page 195)

Are you feeling fancy or nostalgic?

Nope, but yum!

Your New Favorite Herby Meatballs (page 85)

A Very Adult Salad (page 135)

BUY: A box o' pasta!

Fancy pants

Yeah

Tart Apple Butternut Squash Soup (page 30)

Crispy-Crispy Turkey Thighs with Caramelized Onion Jam (page 73)

Roasted Veg Parade (page 128)

Sisterhood of the Traveling Lemon Cake (page 199)

Regular Fancy

Nostalgic

Caviar fancy

Foolproof Lemon and Fennel Branzino (page 61)

A Very Adult Salad (page 135)

Sour Cream Mashed Potatoes (page 100)

Juicy Fruit Greek Yogurt Panna Cotta (page 205)

How equipped is your Kitchen?

Perfect Seared Rib Eye with Pistachio-Date Salsa Verde Sauce (page 79)

BUY: Frozen fries

Radishes Dipped in Honey-Fennel Butter (page 25)

Perfect Seared Rib Eye with Bistro Compound Butter (page 79)

World's Best Oven Fries with Parsley and Parm (page 138)

A Very Adult Salad (page 135)

Juicy Fruit Greek Yogurt Panna Cotta (page 205)

Just what I need

Veggie Pot Pie with Parm and Black Pepper Phyllo (page 81)

A Simple Bistro Salad (page 90)

Thin Mint Pudding Pie (page 220)

Fully equipped

Roasted Tomato and Burrata Eggplant Parm (page 34)

A Very Adult Salad (page 135)   Floofy Funfetti Cake (page 213)

Dinner?: A Flowchart

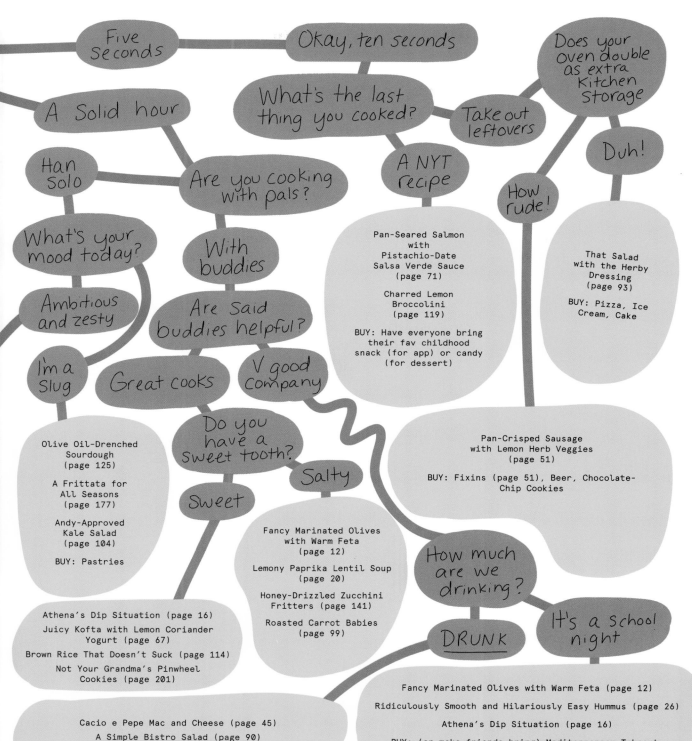

Five Seconds

Okay, ten seconds

Does your oven double as extra Kitchen Storage

A Solid hour

What's the last thing you cooked?

Take out leftovers

Han Solo

Are you cooking with pals?

A NYT recipe

Duh!

How rude!

What's your mood today?

With buddies

Pan-Seared Salmon with Pistachio-Date Salsa Verde Sauce (page 71)

Charred Lemon Broccolini (page 119)

BUY: Have everyone bring their fav childhood snack (for app) or candy (for dessert)

That Salad with the Herby Dressing (page 93)

BUY: Pizza, Ice Cream, Cake

Ambitious and zesty

Are Said buddies helpful?

V good Company

I'm a Slug

Great cooks

Olive Oil-Drenched Sourdough (page 125)

A Frittata for All Seasons (page 177)

Andy-Approved Kale Salad (page 104)

BUY: Pastries

Do you have a sweet tooth?

Salty

Pan-Crisped Sausage with Lemon Herb Veggies (page 51)

BUY: Fixins (page 51), Beer, Chocolate-Chip Cookies

Sweet

Fancy Marinated Olives with Warm Feta (page 12)

Lemony Paprika Lentil Soup (page 20)

Honey-Drizzled Zucchini Fritters (page 141)

Roasted Carrot Babies (page 99)

How much are we drinking?

It's a School night

Athena's Dip Situation (page 16)

Juicy Kofta with Lemon Coriander Yogurt (page 67)

Brown Rice That Doesn't Suck (page 114)

Not Your Grandma's Pinwheel Cookies (page 201)

DRUNK

Fancy Marinated Olives with Warm Feta (page 12)

Ridiculously Smooth and Hilariously Easy Hummus (page 26)

Athena's Dip Situation (page 16)

BUY: (or make friends bring) Mediterranean Takeout, Kebobs and Rice

Cacio e Pepe Mac and Cheese (page 45)

A Simple Bistro Salad (page 90)

The Messiest Ice Cream Sundaes (page 219)

Menus

Each menu also offers ideas on how to integrate store-bought items to make your life easier. Those items are underlined!

Ⓢ = SOLO   Ⓒ = COLLAB   Ⓟ = POTLUCK

Taco Night
Ⓢ Ⓒ

BEV: Margaritas (page 5) or beer

APP: chips with salsa and guac

MAIN (CHOOSE ONE):
- Sort-of-Kind-of Cochinita Pibil (page 160)
- Fish-Fry Tacos with Smoky Mayo (page 156)
- Smoky Spicy Seared Fish Tacos (page 158)
- Honey-Jalapeño Black Beans (page 167) or reheated canned beans

DESSERT: Churro Hot Chocolate (page 195) or chilled cut-up seasonal fruit—melons, mangos, etc.—served with Tajín seasoning (or lime juice, salt, and chile on the side)

Mediterranean Summer Dinner
Ⓢ Ⓒ Ⓟ

BEV: Campari Lemonade (page 3) or Paper Planes (page 3)

APP:
- Fancy Marinated Olives with Warm Feta (page 12) or plain olives
- Ridiculously Smooth and Hilariously Easy Hummus (page 26) or store-bought hummus
- Olive Oil-Drenched Sourdough (page 125) or baguettes warmed in the oven for 5 minutes with salted butter

MAIN:
- Foolproof Lemon and Fennel Branzino (page 61)
- Charred Lemon Broccolini (page 119); can be served room temp
- Roasted Squash with Sage Yogurt (page 122); can be served room temp

DESSERT: Sisterhood of the Traveling Lemon Cake (page 199)

Pizza Night
Ⓢ Ⓒ

BEV: wine

APP: Snackies (page 8)

MAIN:
- Spicy Soppressata Pizza or Wine-Drunk Onion and Fennel Pizza (pages 151 and 152)
- That Salad with the Herby Dressing (a.k.a. A Chopped Salad) (page 93)

DESSERT: Oops, I Forgot Dessert! Choco-Dipped Fruit (page 192)

Bistro Night
Ⓢ Ⓒ

BEV: Extra-Fun French 75s (page 4) or wine

APP: Radishes Dipped in Honey-Fennel Butter (page 25) or cheese and crackers

MAIN:
- Perfect Seared Rib Eye with Bistro Compound Butter (page 79)
- World's Best Oven Fries with Parsley and Parm (page 138) or frozen French fries cooked and tossed in parsley and parmesan just before serving
- A Simple Bistro Salad (page 90)

DESSERT: Juicy Fruit Greek Yogurt Panna Cotta (page 205)

Ideal Burger Night
S **C**

BEV: beer or wine

APP: big bowl of chips

MAIN:
- Diner-Style Smash Burgers (page 53)
- Andy-Approved Kale Salad (page 104)
- World's Best Oven Fries with Parsley and Parm (page 138) or prepared frozen fries

DESSERT: The Messiest Ice Cream Sundaes (page 219); you can buy the sauces if you like

Steakhouse Night
S **C**

BEV: Manhattans (page 4) or wine

APP: bar-style Snackies (page 8)

MAIN:
- Perfect Seared Rib Eye with Pistachio-Date Salsa Verde Sauce (page 79)
- Athena's Dip Situation (page 16)
- Sour Cream Mashed Potatoes (page 100)

DESSERT: pick a "Dessert You Don't Have to Make" (see page 182)

Kofta Platter
S **C** **P**

BEV: Campari Lemonade (page 3) or wine

APP: Ridiculously Smooth and Hilariously Easy Hummus (page 26) or plain hummus with Fluffy Everything Pita Clouds (page 106) or warmed store-bought pitas

MAIN:
- Juicy Kofta with Lemon Coriander Yogurt (page 67)
- Golden Coconut and Apricot Rice (page 113)
- Super-Crunchy Green Salad (page 103)

DESSERT: Sisterhood of the Traveling Lemon Cake (page 199)

Old Jewish Lady Night
S **P**

BEV: red wine

APP: Snackies (page 8)

MAIN:
- Be-Your-Own-Bubbe (BYOB) Jewish Brisket (page 41)
- Latke-Style Smashed Potatoes with Dilly Crème Fraîche (page 116)
- Shallot Compote Green Beans (page 131)

DESSERT: Babka-*ish* Monkey Bread (page 185) or pick a "Dessert You Don't Have to Make" (see page 182)

Summer Shrimp Fest
S **C** **P**

BEV: Xtra-Limey Piña Coladas (page 3)

APP: cheese board (see page 22) or Snackies (page 8)

MAIN:
- Peel 'n' Eat Shrimp with "I'd Eat This on a Shoe" Basil Dipping Magic (page 57)
- Olive Oil–Drenched Sourdough (page 125) or warm baguette
- Carole King Salad (page 95)

DESSERT: Rainbow Cookie Icebox Cake (page 215)

Pretending It's Autumn in LA
S **C** **P**

BEV: Paper Planes (page 3)

APP: Tart Apple Butternut Squash Soup (page 30; optional)

MAIN:
- Crispy-Crispy Turkey Thighs with Caramelized Onion Jam (page 73)
- World's Best Oven Fries with Parsley and Parm (page 138) or prepared frozen fries
- Carole King Salad (page 95)

DESSERT: Brown Butter and Sage Rice RKTs (page 191)

Pi Day

BEV: <u>wine</u>

APP: <u>cheese board (see page 22)</u>

MAIN:
- Veggie Pot Pie with Parm and Black Pepper Phyllo (page 81)
- A Very Adult Salad (a.k.a. Grapies and Greenies) (page 135)

DESSERT: Pink Lemonade Bars (page 206)

The Birthday Dinner

BEV: <u>birthday guest of honor picks</u>

APP: <u>everyone brings their favorite childhood snacks</u>

MAIN:
- Your New Favorite Herby Meatballs (page 85) with spaghetti
- A Very Adult Salad (a.k.a. Grapies and Greenies) (page 135)

DESSERT: Fudgy Chocolate Cake with Salted Caramel Frosting (page 209) <u>or pick a "Dessert You Don't Have to Make" (see page 182)</u>

Midwinter Stew Party

BEV: <u>red wine</u>

APP: <u>olives, chips</u> and Spiced Herby Yogurt Sauce (page 11)

MAIN: Cozy Winter Night Borscht (page 47) or Hot Dog Soup (but Really Sausage) (page 14) with <u>crusty bread and salted butter</u>

DESSERT: Clara's Coffee Cake (page 187)

The Godfather (+ Funfetti)

BEV: Negronis (page 4)

APP: <u>mini cheese board (see page 22)</u>

MAIN:
- Roasted Tomato and Burrata Eggplant Parm (page 34)
- A Simple Bistro Salad (page 90)
- Olive Oil–Drenched Sourdough (page 125) <u>or any crusty bread</u>

DESSERT: Floofy Funfetti Cake (page 213)

Easy Soup Night

BEV: <u>buy something you like</u>

APP: Fancy Marinated Olives with Warm Feta (page 12) <u>or store-bought olives</u>

MAIN:
- Lemony Paprika Lentil Soup (page 20)
- Fluffy Everything Pita Clouds (page 106) <u>or store-bought pitas</u> with Coconut Butter (page 106) <u>or salted butter</u>

DESSERT: Sisterhood of the Traveling Lemon Cake (page 199)

Ugly but Delicious Vegetarian Dinner

BEV: <u>wine</u>

APP: Athena's Dip Situation (page 16) with Fluffy Everything Pita Clouds (page 106) <u>or warmed store-bought pitas</u>

MAIN:
- Braised Garlicky Eggplant with Chickpeas and Tomatoes (page 39)
- Golden Coconut and Apricot Rice (page 113)
- Super-Crunchy Green Salad (page 103)

DESSERT: Thin Mint Pudding Pie (page 220)

Sheet Pan Dinner
Ⓢ Ⓒ

BEV: <u>beer</u>

APP: Snackies (page 8)

MAIN:
- Pan-Crisped Sausage with Lemon Herb Veggies (page 51)
- Garlicky Cabbage with Whole-Grain Mustard (page 110)

DESSERT: Brown Butter and Sage RKTs (page 191)

Mix 'n' Match Pasta Night, a.k.a. Garlic Breath Party
Ⓢ Ⓒ Ⓟ

BEV (CHOOSE ONE OR SERVE BOTH!):
- Negronis (page 4)
- <u>red wine</u>

PASTA (CHOOSE ONE):
- Glorious Spicy Sausage Pasta (page 65)
- Rigatoni with Confit Tomatoes and Burrata (page 76)
- Your New Favorite Herby Meatballs (page 85) with spaghetti
- Cacio e Pepe Mac and Cheese (page 45)

SALAD (CHOOSE ONE):
- A Simple Bistro Salad (page 90)
- That Salad with the Herby Dressing (a.k.a. A Chopped Salad) (page 93)
- Carole King Salad (page 95)
- Super-Crunchy Green Salad (page 103)
- Andy-Approved Kale Salad (page 104)
- A Very Adult Salad (a.k.a. Grapies and Greenies) (page 135)

DESSERT: <u>pick a "Dessert You Don't Have to Make" (see page 182)</u>

BREAKFASTS FOR DINNER (CAUSE YOU'RE WORTH IT)

Pancake Night
Ⓢ Ⓒ

BEV: <u>mimosas or spiked decaf coffee</u>

APP: <u>fruit salad or a bowl of fruit</u>

MAIN: Anything Goes Pancakes <u>(no time? Try the Stonewall brand pancake mix)</u> and Crispy Oven Bacon (page 173)

DESSERT: Clara's Coffee Cake (page 187) <u>or pick a "Dessert You Don't Have to Make" (see page 182)</u>

Frittata Night
Ⓢ Ⓟ

BEV: <u>mimosas or spiked decaf coffee</u>

APP: Smoked Paprika Potato Crisps <u>(or potato chips)</u> with Aioli (page 29)

MAIN:
- A Frittata for All Seasons (page 177)
- Olive Oil–Drenched Sourdough (page 125) <u>or crusty bread</u>
- Carole King Salad (page 95)

DESSERT: Not Your Grandma's Pinwheel Cookies (page 201) <u>or pick a "Dessert You Don't Have to Make" (see page 182)</u>

Lower East Side Night
Ⓢ Ⓒ Ⓟ

BEV: <u>mimosas or spiked decaf coffee</u>

APPS: Radishes Dipped in Honey-Fennel Butter (page 25) <u>or radishes and butter</u>

MAIN: Bagels and Lox with Homemade Cream Cheese (page 170)

DESSERT: Babka-*ish* Monkey Bread (page 185)

SALMON THREE WAYS, A.K.A. SALMON FOR ANY MOOD

Fancy Pants
S C

BEV: Extra-Fun French 75s (page 4)

APP: olive tapenade, cornichons and salami with slices of warmed baguette and salted butter or potato chips with crème fraîche and roe/caviar

MAIN:
- Pan-Seared Salmon for Any Mood with Beurre Blanc (page 71)
- A Very Adult Salad (a.k.a. Grapies and Greenies) (page 135)
- Sour Cream Mashed Potatoes (page 100)

DESSERT: Orange Dream Granita (page 196)

Casual Herby
S P

BEV: Paper Planes (page 3)

APP: Lemony Paprika Lentil Soup (page 20; optional)

MAIN:
- Pan-Seared Salmon for Any Mood with Pistachio-Date Salsa Verde Sauce (page 71)
- Andy-Approved Kale Salad (page 104)
- Brown Rice That Doesn't Suck (page 114)

DESSERT: Fudgy Chocolate Cake with Salted Caramel Frosting (page 209)

Lemon & Dill
S C

BEV: white wine

APP: Fancy Marinated Olives with Warm Feta (page 12) or regular olives

MAIN:
- Pan-Seared Salmon for Any Mood with Lemon and Dill (page 71)
- Honey-Drizzled Zucchini Fritters (page 141) or baked russet/sweet potatoes
- Carole King Salad (page 95)

DESSERT: Brown Butter and Sage RKTs (page 191) or pick a "Dessert You Don't Have to Make" (see page 182)

How to Navigate Each Recipe

ALWAYS READ THE RECIPE ALL THE WAY THROUGH BEFORE STARTING.

Ingredients: They are all presented in order of use, and I often request that ingredients be prepped/chopped (a.k.a. mise en place) before you even preheat your oven. I solemnly swear that it's worth doing this when you're working with a new recipe.

Quantities: Speaking of ingredients, you'll notice lots of the time something will be listed as "½ cup chopped parsley." That's because you measure it once it's chopped. If the recipe says "4 carrots, chopped" that's because the chopping doesn't affect the quantity of the ingredient.

Salt: Unless otherwise specified, I recommend Diamond Crystal kosher or La Baleine fine sea salt. But keep in mind, your ingredients may be sweeter, riper, more flavorless, yada yada yada, than what I used when testing these recipes, so err on the side of less, adding a pinch as you build layers of flavor into your dish, and season it to taste at the end. I like to give a quantity so you're not totally in the dark, but you may need a little less, or a little more. As a warning, Diamond Crystal salt is less dense than regular salt—if you use Morton salt, halve the amount.

Timing: The times indicated on the recipes are guidelines—once you start cooking, the dish will often give visual, aromatic, and textural clues. Use these clues to help determine when a dish is done, or when an ingredient is ready to be flipped. What shade of golden should the garlic be? Has your steak formed a nice crust? Has the sauce thickened to your liking? Your oven, and the ingredients you choose, may necessitate a little more or a little less cooking time.

Total time: Some of the recipes have looonng inactive times, like drying turkey skin overnight for the Crispy-Crispy Turkey Thighs with Caramelized Onion Jam (page 73). I'd hate for you to plan on making something and then realize that you don't have the time.

Tips: Most recipes have tips on how to pick out certain ingredients, ideas for swaps, cutting techniques, how to best prepare ingredients, etc. So, again, be sure to check out those before starting!

Timing: Many things can be made in advance and served at room temp, or kept at a simmer, or easily reheated before dinnertime—the recipe will give you all the details you need.

Things for guests to do: There is nothing more overwhelming than an early bird showing up when you're running behind. Many of the recipes in this book include ingredients specifically allocated for "finishing" the recipe (a squeeze of lemon, a sprinkling of chopped herbs, a finish of salt). So get that guest a lemon or a bunch of herbs and ask them to chop away!

⚠️ Tips for Avoiding Disaster:
A Checklist

The ultimate list of shit you must do (before and during the meal).

☐ **CHECK FOR ALLERGIES**

Ask your guests if they have any dietary restrictions before you plan your menu. Hospital visits are a real dinner party buzzkill.

☐ **READ THE FINE PRINT (BRISKET WASN'T BUILT IN A DAY)**

Peruse each recipe multiple times before you start cooking to get the flow, timing, and ingredients right.

☐ **DON'T SAY YOU'RE GOING TO HAND-MAKE PASTA ON A DAY WITH 17 MEETINGS**

Be realistic about what you can do and delegate as needed.

☐ **PLATES ARE IMPORTANT**

Washing silverware and dishes between courses sucks. If you don't have enough, ask a friend to bring extra.

☐ **YOUR MOM WAS RIGHT, CLEAN AS YOU GO**

The tidier you cook, the less you'll have to clean at the end of the night.

☐ **TAKE OUT THE TRASH**

Especially if it's full or smells, c'mon.

☐ **A.H.S. (ALWAYS HAVE SNACKS)**

Sometimes you burn dinner or it takes an extra hour for _that_ late friend to arrive. Put out cheese, nuts, chips, random vegetables, a six-year-old fruitcake— anything to stave off hanger.

☐ **DON'T FREAK OUT**

The cardinal rule of disaster proofing: if something does go wrong, like your dog eats your steaks off the counter, just keep in mind that it's only dinner. Fix problems that can be fixed, and order takeout for ones that can't.

COCKTAILS

5

Your guests will *always* ask what they can bring to dinner, and the answer will almost *always* be "How about your favorite wine or beer?" To kick it up a notch, ask them to make one of my go-to cocktails or refreshing nonalcoholic drinks. They require few to no tools and have proven themselves to be crowd-pleasers.

1. Agua Fresca 2. Paper Plane 3. The Versatile Margarita 4. Xtra-Limey Piña Colada 5. Not-So-Sweet Strawberry Daiquiri

Pitcher drinks make six 8-ounce drinks; the others make 2 each (multiply by 3 for 6 servings)

Tips + Timing

1. Pitcher drinks can be made (without adding the sparkling water and ice) up to a day in advance and kept in the refrigerator. Just before serving, stir vigorously and add the sparkling water and ice. Cocktails should be made just before serving. But feel free to premeasure all ingredients for ease!
2. No matter the cocktail, freeze the glasses for 10 minutes first. It'll keep the cocktail physically (and metaphorically) cool.

AGUA FRESCA

2 cups water, plus more to taste

4 cups cut-up fresh fruit (try watermelon, pineapple and mango, or cantaloupe)

2 tablespoons sugar, plus more to taste, depending on how sweet the fruit is

2 tablespoons fresh lime juice, plus more to taste

A pinch of salt

4 sprigs of mint

Sparkling water, for the table

POSSIBLE GARNISHES: piece of fresh fruit, lime wedge, Tajín seasoning on rim, salt and sugar (50/50) on rim

Blend 2 cups water, 4 cups fruit, 2 tablespoons sugar, 2 tablespoons lime juice, and a pinch of salt in a blender. Strain out the pulp as you pour the agua fresca into a pitcher. Stir in extra water, sugar, and lime juice to taste. Just before serving, add a lot of ice and the mint sprigs into the pitcher and stir. Give everyone a cold glass garnished as desired, and put out the sparkling water in case people want to add any.

SPARKLING GINGER LIMEADE

3½ cups store-bought limeade, plus more to taste

2½ cups sparkling water, plus more to taste

2 limes, sliced into thin rounds

2-inch piece of fresh ginger, peeled and sliced into thin rounds, plus more to taste

6 sprigs of mint

Vodka (optional)

POSSIBLE GARNISHES: candied ginger, lime wedge

Stir together 3½ cups limeade, 2½ cups sparkling water, lime rounds, ginger, and 6 mint sprigs in a pitcher. Add extra limeade, sparkling water, and ginger to taste. If you are feeling frisky, throw in some vodka. Just before serving, add a lot of ice and stir. Give everyone a cold glass finished with the garnish of your choice.

CAMPARI LEMONADE

1½ cups fresh lemon juice
1½ cups sugar
4½ cups sparkling water
6 ounces Campari aperitif

In a cocktail shaker, shake 1½ cups lemon juice with 1½ cups sugar. Pour the lemon mixture into a pitcher with 4½ cups sparkling water and ice. Stir well. Give everyone a cold glass and finish each drink with 1 ounce of Campari floated on top.

XTRA-LIMEY PIÑA COLADA

3 ounces pineapple juice
3 ounces fresh lime juice
2 ounces Coco Lopez cream of coconut
½ ounce orgeat syrup
2 ounces white rum
2 ounces gold rum
1½ ounces VSOP rum
Pinch of salt
POSSIBLE GARNISHES: plastic monkey, pineapple wedge, cherry, umbrella, toasted coconut on rim

In a cocktail shaker, vigorously shake 3 ounces pineapple juice, 3 ounces lime juice, and 2 ounces Coco Lopez. Add ½ ounce orgeat, 2 ounces white rum, 2 ounces gold rum, 1½ ounces VSOP rum, a pinch of salt, and ice to the shaker. Shake again. Strain into 2 icy cold glasses filled with ice. Finish with a garnish of your choice.
ALT: Add all the ingredients into a blender with 2 cups ice (add more ice as needed) and make blended piña coladas!

PAPER PLANE

2¼ ounces Amaro Nonino liqueur
2¼ ounces Aperol aperitif
2¼ ounces bourbon
2¼ ounces fresh lemon juice
POSSIBLE GARNISHES: origami plane on a toothpick, lemon twist, piece of candied lemon on a tiny paperclip

In a cocktail shaker with lots of ice, shake 2¼ ounces Amaro Nonino, 2¼ ounces Aperol, 2¼ ounces bourbon, and 2¼ ounces lemon juice. Strain, neat, into 2 icy cold glasses. Finish with a garnish of your choice.

NEGRONI

Sometimes the simplest cocktails are the best for a group because they require no thinking. The proportions are all 1-to-1, which makes it impossible to forget, no matter how tipsy you get.

4 ounces dry gin

4 ounces Campari aperitif

4 ounces Carpano Antica Formula vermouth

2 strips of orange peel

POSSIBLE GARNISHES: candied orange wheel, slice of orange

In a mixing glass, stir 4 ounces gin, 4 ounces Campari, and 4 ounces vermouth with lots of ice. Grab 2 icy cold glasses and squeeze a strip of orange peel inside each glass. Rub the peel against the rim, and then drop it into the glass. Fill each glass with ice. Strain the cocktails into the glasses. Finish with additional garnishes of your choice, or keep it simple.

EXTRA-FUN FRENCH 75

3 ounces fresh lemon juice

6 ounces botanical gin

1½ ounces simple syrup*

¾ ounce St. Germain elderflower liqueur

4 ounces champagne

POSSIBLE GARNISHES: lemon twist, a sprig of your neighbor's lavender, cocktail cherry on a toothpick perched on the rim of the glass

In a cocktail shaker with ice, shake 3 ounces lemon juice, 6 ounces gin, 1½ ounces simple syrup, and ¾ ounce St. Germain. Strain, neat, into 2 icy cold glasses. Top each with 2 ounces champagne. Finish with a garnish of your choice.

*Simple syrup can be purchased or made. To make, bring ½ cup sugar with ½ cup water to a boil and stir to dissolve the sugar. Cool before using.

MANHATTAN

6 ounces rye or bourbon, such as Rittenhouse rye or Four Roses Kentucky bourbon

3 ounces Carpano Antica Formula vermouth

6 dashes of Angostura bitters

1 strip of lemon peel

POSSIBLE GARNISHES: cocktail cherry, lemon twist

In a mixing glass, stir 6 ounces rye (or bourbon) with 3 ounces vermouth and 6 dashes bitters. Grab 2 icy cold glasses. Squeeze the lemon peel inside both glasses, rub it against the rims, then discard. Strain the cocktails, neat, into the glasses. Finish with a garnish of your choice.

NOT-SO-SWEET STRAWBERRY DAIQUIRI

3 ounces fresh lime juice

6 ripe, juicy strawberries, hulled (out of season? swap for ⅓ cup different soft ripe fruit)

2 tablespoons turbinado sugar

6 ounces Havana Club Añejo Blanco rum

Pinch of salt

POSSIBLE GARNISHES: lime wheel, small strawberry, plastic flamingo, tiny mermaid

In the bottom of a shaker, muddle together 3 ounces lime juice, 6 strawberries (or other soft fruit), and 2 tablespoons sugar. Shake until the sugar is dissolved. Strain to remove any large bits of strawberry pulp. Add the strawberry juice back into the shaker with 6 ounces rum, a pinch of salt, and ice. Shake feverishly until the cocktail shaker is icy cold, about 2 minutes. Strain, neat, into 2 icy cold glasses. Finish with a garnish of your choice.

ALT: Add all the ingredients into a blender with 2 cups ice (add more ice as needed) and make blended daiquiris!

THE VERSATILE MARGARITA

6 ounces blanco tequila

3 ounces fresh lime juice

2 ounces agave syrup

POSSIBLE GARNISHES: lime wedge, Tajín seasoning on rim, grapefruit slice dipped in chili powder

In a cocktail shaker with lots of ice, shake 6 ounces tequila, 3 ounces lime juice, and 2 ounces agave syrup. Strain into 2 icy cold glasses filled with ice. Finish with a garnish of your choice.

ALT: Add all the ingredients into a blender with 1½ cups ice (add more ice as needed) and make blended margaritas!

Variations

TO MAKE A SPICY MIKA: Shake with sliced jalapeño and finish the glass with a Tajín rim

TO MAKE A TROPICAL ALANA: Swap out half the lime juice for lilikoi (passion fruit) juice.

TO MAKE A NOISY NORA: Float a layer of well-steeped hibiscus tea on top.

Having a snack out when people arrive is a great way to take the pressure off of dinner timing. If there is something to eat at the top, no one is going to get hangry. If it takes longer to pull dinner together or if you burnt everything you were supposed to serve, people will be fine and, most likely, hugely amused. Even if you're cooking the meal as a group, have a snack out for people as they begin to cook. And, yes, it's 100 percent okay if that means opening four bags of assorted chips.

SNACKIES—BY ARISTOTLE

Makes as many as you like
Total time: 5 minutes

Toss a few things that taste good together, *that you didn't have to make,* in a bowl and you've got yourself a snack that looks a lot more festive than the three things in their own bowls. You know, Aristotle's "the whole is greater than the sum of its parts" thing. It's like bar snacks, but better.

The Formula—pick 3 or 4 of the following elements:
something crunchy
something salty
something spicy
something umami
something sweet

Combine all the ingredients in a bowl and serve with little plates or napkins. Be sure to put a spoon in the bowl so people don't have to use their hands like animals.

Examples

Bar Snacks 1: peanuts / mini pretzels / spicy corn nuts

Bar Snacks 2: Goldfish crackers / candied peanuts / pretzel sticks

Tapas-style: Castelvetrano pitted olives (patted dry) / salted roasted almonds / Manchego cubes

Fruity: dried cranberries / sourdough crackers / cheddar cubes

Tropical: unsweetened dried coconut / banana chips / dried spicy mango / salted roasted almonds

Pregnancy Cravings: peanut butter-stuffed pretzels / popcorn / cornichons (on the side)

Classy: sun-dried tomatoes / goat cheese / basil / crackers (on the side) and a knife for slathering

TIMING

Combine snacks up to 24 hours in advance and store in airtight containers. If anything requires refrigeration, keep it separate until serving. Using cheese? Set that out at least an hour before serving so it's as flavorful as possible.

SPICED HERBY YOGURT SAUCE

Makes 1½ cups
Total time: 5 minutes

Whenever I feel like a dish is lackluster, I whip up this sauce. You can thin it out and use it as a salad dressing, you can serve it with grilled meats or kofta (see page 67), you can toss a layer under roasted sweet potatoes, or you can dollop it on top of a frittata. It really can dress up just about any recipe you're feeling whatever about.

I also love it just as it is—an herb-laden, garlic-infused, fresh and lemony yogurt sauce—served as an appetizer, paired with crudités, Olive Oil–Drenched Sourdough (page 125), Fluffy Everything Pita Clouds (page 106), pita chips, or whatever else you've got that can act as a vessel for shoveling more dip into your mouth.

1½ cups plain, full-fat (5%) Greek yogurt

¾ cup finely chopped fresh cilantro

¼ cup fresh lemon juice, plus more to taste

1 garlic clove, minced

2 tablespoons finely chopped mint

½ teaspoon salt, plus more to taste

½ teaspoon black pepper

¼ teaspoon ground coriander

In a medium bowl, whisk together 1½ cups yogurt, the cilantro, ¼ cup lemon juice, garlic, mint, ½ teaspoon salt, ½ teaspoon pepper, and ¼ teaspoon coriander. Taste and add additional salt and lemon juice if desired. Serve at room temperature or chilled.

Tips + Timing

1. Make up to 3 days in advance and store in an airtight container in the fridge. Stir well before serving.
2. Herbs are much easier to chop when they're dry. So after purchasing, wash and dry them well, wrap in a dry paper towel, and store in a resealable plastic bag in the fridge.

FANCY MARINATED OLIVES WITH WARM FETA

Serves 6

Total time: 10 minutes

I find no fault with any olive. They're all unique and I love every one of them. Have I been known to eat canned black olives off of my fingertips like a little baby person? I guess you'll never know. BUT a fancy olive is the best olive, and by "fancy," I mean one that's been given extra flavor and punch via a sultry warm olive-oil bath with herbs and aromatics. But this dish doesn't stop there! The olives are then poured over salty, irresistible feta to make it spreadable, giving the whole nosh an elegant touch. Bread is a very important vessel for enjoying the remaining infused oil once the olives and feta are gone. I like to serve this with a crusty baguette or Olive Oil–Drenched Sourdough (page 125).

½ cup extra-virgin olive oil

2 garlic cloves, thinly sliced

1 bay leaf

Peel of half a lemon (use a vegetable peeler)

Leaves from 4 sprigs of thyme, coarsely chopped

Leaves from 3 sprigs of rosemary, finely chopped

½ teaspoon red pepper flakes

2 (6 ounce) jars of Castelvetrano olives, drained, with pits removed

1 (8 ounce) block of Greek feta cheese packed in brine, room temp

Bread, for serving

In a small pot, combine ½ cup olive oil, the sliced garlic, 1 bay leaf, the lemon peel, thyme, rosemary, and ½ teaspoon red pepper flakes. Bring the mixture to a simmer over medium heat and cook until the lemon peels start to curl in and the herbs begin to wilt, about 4 minutes.

Remove the bay leaf from the oil and add the olives. Stir and simmer until the olives are warm, 3 to 4 minutes.

Crumble, or cube, the 8-ounce block of feta over the bottom of a small serving bowl and pour the warm olives and oil over the top. Serve with bread.

TIPS + TIMING

1. Make up to 2 days in advance and refrigerate in an airtight container. To reheat, put the feta at the bottom of an oven-safe dish and cover with the olives and oil. Bake at 400°F for 10 to 15 minutes to warm the olives and cheese.
2. Castelvetrano, a crisp and buttery olive, is the most popular snacking olive. If you can't find them, try Cerignola, Liguria, or any firm green olive.
3. A crisp white wine is a feta-and-olive snack's best pal!
4. If the olives have pits, remove them by smacking the side of a knife over each olive until you feel the pit. Separate the olive flesh and pull out the pit. Alt: You can make this dish with the pits and put out a small dish for them.

HOT DOG SOUP
(but Really Sausage)

Serves 6
Total time: 1½ hours

I call this "Hot Dog Soup" because one time I ran out of sausage and used hot dogs instead and the name just sort of stuck around. This version doesn't actually have hot dogs in it, but in a pinch, it certainly could. This is my favorite easy, incredibly flavorful soup to throw together. It's so easy, in fact, that my friend who tested this recipe and made it for her parents, sister, and picky bro-in-law said, "Everyone loved it! It was so simple and easy to make! I would, for sure, highlight that in the recipe header."

Here's the real secret: If you want to make a flavorful soup using bits and bobs from your fridge, just throw in a parmesan rind. It adds complexity, salt, and the right amount of "mmmm . . . what's in here?"

½ cup extra-virgin olive oil

4 precooked Italian pork sausages, sliced into ¼-inch rounds

½ yellow onion, finely chopped

2 large carrots, chopped into 1-inch wedges

2 garlic cloves, thinly sliced

1 teaspoon salt, plus more to taste

1 parmesan cheese rind (about 3 ounces)

½ teaspoon red pepper flakes, plus extra for serving

2 (15.5 ounce) cans of white beans of your choice, drained and rinsed

1 (14 ounce) can of whole tomatoes

4 cups vegetable stock, homemade (page 132) or store-bought

¼ cup coarsely chopped parsley leaves

¼ cup grated parmesan cheese

2 teaspoons black pepper

Heat ½ cup olive oil in a large stockpot over high heat.

Once the oil is hot, add the sausage rounds and cook, stirring every minute or so, until they are seared and crispy on both sides, 5 to 7 minutes. Remove them from the oil, trying to take as little oil as possible, and set aside.

Add to the pot the onion, carrots, garlic, and 1 teaspoon salt. Cook, stirring regularly, until the mixture is aromatic and the onion is translucent, 4 to 5 minutes.

Add the parm rind, ½ teaspoon red pepper flakes, 2 cans of white beans, and the can of tomatoes with their juices. Stir well and let the mixture come to a simmer. Break apart the large tomato chunks with a wooden spoon and add the sausages back in, followed by 4 cups stock.

Bring the mixture to a boil. Reduce the heat to medium-low and cook, uncovered, for 1 hour, stirring vigorously every 10 minutes, until the soup is slightly thickened. The more you stir the soup with gusto, the more the starch from the beans will help thicken it.

Remove the parm rind and add salt to taste. Serve each bowl with a sprinkling of parsley, grated parm, and black pepper.

TIPS+TIMING

1. Make up to 3 days before serving and store in an airtight container in the fridge. Reheat on the stove and garnish.
2. I like using half cannellini beans and half chickpeas as the white beans, but feel free to experiment.
3. Sausage is the flavor base for the soup, so it's important to pick a good one. Take a look at its ingredients. A good Italian sausage should have a variety of fun spices like fennel seeds, garlic, oregano, and red pepper flakes. If you can't find Italian pork sausage, try a smoked andouille sausage—different flavor but delicious!
4. If you can't find parmesan rind, no problem. Just throw in a chunk of parm that has a rind on it. It's okay if it gets limp and starts to fall apart. No one has ever been mad because they found a small piece of cheese in their soup . . . unless they're allergic, in which case you should not serve them this soup.
5. If you use store-bought stock, reduce the salt by ½ teaspoon to account for the extra salt!

ATHENA'S DIP SITUATION

Serves 6 to 8
Total time: 30 minutes

When I was growing up, there was a Greek restaurant in my neighborhood called Café Athena, which served an incredibly oily, lemony, garlicky spinach dish that came with a side of fresh pillowy pita and lemon wedges. I used to beg my parents to take me there to get it. I didn't want anything else, only an entire serving of this spinach scooped high atop the pita. They frequently obliged because, honestly, I've never been spinach's #1 fan, so they were happy and amused that I was excited to eat a cold bowl of green anything. I've been obsessed with mastering this quasi dip for years—turns out the dish has three secrets, the *first* of which is just more olive oil. The *second* is cooking the garlic longer than seems reasonable. Usually, a deep golden cooked garlic means burnt-flavored garlic, but in this dish it helps create an extra-bold note. *Third* secret . . . cilantro. Which is crazy because you cannot taste it at all. It's like ninja cilantro.

This is great as an app with crusty bread or pitas but also awesome served as a side to Foolproof Lemon and Fennel Branzino (page 61).

5 (10 ounce) packages of frozen chopped spinach, thawed

1 cup extra-virgin olive oil, divided

12 garlic cloves, minced

2 teaspoons salt, divided, plus more to taste

1 bunch of parsley, finely chopped

1 bunch of fresh cilantro, finely chopped

6 tablespoons lemon juice (about 2 lemons), plus more to taste, and 1 lemon, sliced into wedges, for serving

6 pitas, homemade (page 106) or store-bought, or Olive Oil–Drenched Sourdough (page 125) or another crusty bread, warmed, for serving

Heat a large pan over medium-low heat.

While the pan is heating, wring out the spinach. To do this VERY IMPORTANT STEP, dump the spinach into a large colander over the sink and use your hands to wring it out in ½-cup portions. It takes a little patience, but think of it as a handy edible stress ball. Once each portion of the spinach has been thoroughly dehydrated, toss it into a large bowl. Continue until all the spinach is dry.

Add ¾ cup olive oil to the pan followed by all the minced garlic and ½ teaspoon salt. Stir regularly with a spatula until the garlic is incredibly fragrant and is starting to turn a rich golden hue, about 3 minutes.

Stir in the chopped parsley and cilantro and another ½ teaspoon of salt. Turn the heat off.

Break up and add the squeezed-dry spinach, 1 teaspoon salt, 6 tablespoons lemon juice, and the last ¼ cup olive oil. Mix thoroughly to coat the spinach. Add extra lemon juice and salt to taste. Serve slightly chilled or at room temp, with lemon wedges and warmed bread of choice. My mom also wants me to mention that she loves this served with sliced cucumbers, if that's up your alley.

TIPS + TIMING

1. Can be made up to a day in advance and stored in the fridge in an airtight container. An hour before serving, take the spinach out of the fridge.
2. To get the most out of your lemons, roll them back and forth on the counter with some serious elbow grease a few times to soften the skin and make them easier to juice.
3. I use frozen spinach because it's pre-wilted, so you don't have to buy a metric ton of it to make a reasonable portion. However, if you'd like to steam your own spinach, you're welcome to do so—you'll probably need a truckful (7½ pounds) of it.
4. Best way to thaw the spinach? Leave it in a bowl in the fridge overnight or in a bowl on the countertop for 2 hours. Did you forget and you need to make it ASAP? Defrost in the microwave.
5. Feeling hot? Top with red pepper flakes or serve with a spicy cracker!

LEMONY PAPRIKA LENTIL SOUP

Serves 6 to 8
Total time: 2 hours

Andy likes to tease me because I call this my "mug soup"—he is skeptical of soup as a food group to begin with, and once you start putting it in "unusual vessels," his brain really cannot compute. If you ask me (which you didn't), everything tastes better in a mug. Cereal before bed? Better in a mug. Ice cream sundaes that you can easily eat on the couch? Idyllic in a mug. Chocolate mousse? YES PLEASE. MUG. Soup? Souperb. It's a bowl with a handle—what could be better?! But this isn't about mugs. (OR IS IT?) It's about soup. And this is one of my favorite soups to whip up on a Sunday to enjoy throughout the week or to start off a dinner party.

½ cup extra-virgin olive oil, plus extra to finish

1 yellow onion, finely chopped

2 garlic cloves, minced

1½ teaspoons salt, divided, plus more to taste

1 celery stalk, finely chopped

2 large carrots, peeled and chopped into ½-inch wedges

2 teaspoons paprika (not smoked)

1 teaspoon ground cumin

¼ teaspoon black pepper

¼ teaspoon red pepper flakes, plus more to taste

1 tablespoon tomato paste

1 (14.5 ounce) can of whole tomatoes, drained

1½ cups brown lentils, rinsed

7 cups vegetable stock, homemade (page 132) or store-bought

1 tablespoon red wine vinegar, plus more to taste

¼ cup finely chopped parsley leaves, plus extra to finish

1 lemon, sliced into wedges, for serving

In a large stockpot, heat ½ cup olive oil over medium heat. Once the oil is warm, throw in the chopped onions and cook until translucent, 4 to 5 minutes.

Add in the minced garlic and ½ teaspoon salt. Stir until you can smell the garlic, about 2 minutes.

Toss in the celery, carrots, 2 teaspoons paprika, 1 teaspoon cumin, ¼ teaspoon black pepper, ¼ teaspoon red pepper flakes, ½ teaspoon salt, and 1 tablespoon tomato paste. Stir and cook until the carrots are just beginning to soften and everything has a nice brick-red hue from the paprika, about 4 minutes.

Stir in the can of drained tomatoes, 1½ cups lentils, and the final ½ teaspoon salt. Use a spatula to break up the tomatoes. Cook for a few minutes to reduce any tomato liquid that may have come along with the tomatoes and then add 7 cups stock.

Bring the soup to a boil, then reduce the heat to low and simmer, uncovered, stirring occasionally, for 1 hour and 15 minutes. You want to see small bubbles coming to the surface every few seconds as it simmers. If there is no bubbling, turn the heat up. If it's really active, turn the heat down.

Just before serving, stir in 1 tablespoon vinegar and the parsley. Add extra salt, red pepper flakes, and vinegar to taste.

Serve each portion with a sprinkling of parsley, a drizzle of olive oil, and a lemon wedge on the side to squeeze over the top!

Tips + Timing

1. Make up to 3 days before serving and store in an airtight container in the fridge. Reheat over the stove and garnish before serving.
2. Do not use smoked paprika. It has an incredibly distinct, smoky flavor, which is overpowering for this soup. So look down and make sure that's not the paprika you have in your hand.
3. Adding acid at the end of cooking turbo-boosts the soup's flavor. If you don't have red wine vinegar, try apple cider vinegar or lemon juice.
4. If you can't find brown lentils, substitute green or French lentils.
5. If you use store-bought stock, reduce the salt by ½ teaspoon to account for the extra salt!

CHEESE BOARD CHEESE CHAT

FEATURING:

Sarah Simms Hendrix, co-founder, Lady & Larder
and Lydia Clarke, co-founder, DTLA Cheese and Cheese Cave

ADVICE TO START:

"Don't be a P.P.P. (pre-party panicker) by forcing yourself to make something more complicated than you're comfortable with! Pick a few things you love and go from there." -Sarah

"Looking good isn't nearly as important as tasting great."
—Lydia

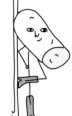

Step 1: Pick Your Cheese

You'll want a total of 2-3 ounces of cheese/meats per person

 Pick three cheeses (Soft, semi-firm, hard)

 Pick two cheeses and a meat (Soft, hard, meat)

 "If all else fails just pick out a big hunk of something you know you'll love." —Lydia

 "An easy way to get a fun variety of cheeses is mixing up the dairy: try a combo of cow, goat, and sheep cheese." —Sarah

"Whatever you select, don't forget the GOLDEN RULE: All cheeses should be put out an hour in advance to be served at room temperature." —Sarah

Step 2: Pick Your Accoutrements

You'll want crackers, honey or jam, and mustard or cornichons (if you're adding meat)

If you want extra credit, try adding: fruit, olives, nuts, dried fruit, crunchy veggies, or a surprise element

SURPRISE ELEMENT! "Add a great salty butter, candy, or chips!" —LYDIA

SURPRISE ELEMENT! "Warm dates in the oven for 10 minutes and drizzle with olive oil and flaky sea salt." —SARAH

Step 3: Put it Together

 Use small bowls to keep ingredients from rolling all over the place.

 "Cut a few slices of any hard cheese so people aren't afraid to dive in." —Sarah

 If using a super-juicy fruit, put it on a side plate so it doesn't leak all over the cheese.

 "Cut the top off of any soft bloomy rinds so they're easy to cut and enjoy." —Lydia

 Make sure there are enough knives/spoons for everything.

RADISHES DIPPED IN HONEY-FENNEL BUTTER

Serves 6 to 8
Total time: 30 minutes

My cousin Nora was the first person who ever offered me a radish sitting next to a mound of heavily salted butter, and while I was confused at first, it was love at first bite. A butter-dipped radish is the perfect combo of cream, crunch, and whimsy.

If you don't have time to coat the radishes in the butter, you can also serve the honey-fennel butter on the side and have everyone dip as they go. When I dip, you dip, we dip.

Honey-Fennel Butter
¾ cup (1½ sticks) European-style salted butter, room temp
1 tablespoon honey
½ teaspoon ground fennel seed

Radishes
21 radishes of your choosing, washed and dried, any wilted greens removed
1 teaspoon ground fennel seed
1 teaspoon flaky sea salt, plus extra to finish

TO MAKE THE HONEY-FENNEL BUTTER: To melt the ¾ cup butter, MacGyver a double boiler by heating 2 inches of water in a small pot over medium heat. Place the butter in a heat-safe bowl that is larger than the pot and set it on top.

Continuously whisk until the butter is half-melted. Remove from heat and continue to whisk until the residual heat finishes melting the butter and the texture is smooth and fluid, like melted chocolate. (If the butter separates or gets too thin, NBD. Just put it in the fridge 'til it solidifies and try again! Alternatively, if it's too solidified, you can give it another minute over the water bath.)

Whisk 1 tablespoon honey and ½ teaspoon fennel into the butter. If you're feeling lazy, stop here and serve the radishes on the side of the butter, or, to be all fancy, continue on.

TO MAKE THE RADISHES: Line a baking sheet with parchment paper.

Dip two-thirds of each radish into the butter a few times to give it a shiny coat. If the radish is hard to hold on to from the top, you can spear it with a toothpick.

Place the radishes onto the baking sheet and sprinkle evenly with 1 teaspoon fennel and 1 teaspoon sea salt.

Refrigerate the radishes to set the butter, about 10 minutes. The butter should be firm enough that if you lightly touch a radish, it doesn't come off on your finger. Serve with extra flaky sea salt on the side.

TIPS + TIMING

1. Make these anytime on the day of; keep in the fridge on a baking sheet, uncovered, until ready to serve.
2. When washing radishes, don't wash the greens if you want to keep them on— they'll wilt. If the greens are dirty, get rid of them.
3. If you can't find ground fennel, crush fennel seeds using a mortar and pestle or quickly blitz them up in a clean coffee grinder.
4. The right butter REALLY makes or breaks this recipe—choose a European-style to ensure a creamy, high-fat-content butter.
5. The longer and thinner the radish, the easier it is to dip. Try looking for French breakfast radishes.

RIDICULOUSLY SMOOTH AND HILARIOUSLY EASY HUMMUS

Serves 6 to 8
Total time: 40 minutes

Hummus has been one of my go-to snacks for as long as I can remember, but it wasn't until I was traveling in Israel in my early twenties that I was introduced to hummus as a component of a meal. It's an incredibly luxurious condiment to fan out under a salad, great alongside kebabs, and ideal on a sandwich. This hummus has my personal favorite texture; it's smooth and creamy but still dense enough to hold its shape.

If you're a true hummus connoisseur, you could soak raw chickpeas the night before, cook them, and then make hummus, but let's be real: most of us want hummus the day we think of it, not tomorrow. So, if you're like me, desiring hummus without a time machine, this is the recipe for you!

3 (15.5 ounce) cans of chickpeas, rinsed

1 cup tahini, well-stirred or shaken

2 garlic cloves, peeled

3 tablespoons fresh lemon juice, plus more to taste

2½ teaspoons salt, plus more to taste

½ cup ice-cold water

4 ice cubes

Topping Options—pick one:

• 2 tablespoons extra-virgin olive oil

• 2 tablespoons extra-virgin olive oil, plus ½ teaspoon paprika and 1 teaspoon chopped parsley leaves

• 2 tablespoons extra-virgin olive oil, ¼ cup chickpeas, ½ teaspoon ground cumin, and 1 teaspoon chopped mint leaves spooned into a small well in the middle of the hummus

• 2 tablespoons extra-virgin olive oil, 2 tablespoons chopped sun-dried tomatoes, and 2 teaspoons crumbled feta spooned into a small well in the middle of the hummus

Put the chickpeas in a small pot and cover with water. Bring to a boil over high heat and then turn down the heat to medium. Cook for 15 minutes. Strain the chickpeas, reserving 1 cup of the cooking liquid.

In a food processor or blender, combine 1 cup tahini, 2 peeled garlic cloves, 3 tablespoons lemon juice, 2½ teaspoons salt, and ½ cup ice-cold water. Blend until very smooth, about 2 minutes. It'll get thick before it gets thin, so have no fear. If, for whatever reason, yours does not thin out, keep adding ice-cold water, 1 tablespoon at a time, until it does.

Add in the chickpeas and blend for 2 minutes. Drop 4 ice cubes in and continue to blend until there are no more visible ice chunks or sounds of ice rattling around. (While the ice is still rattling, feel free to dance.) Scrape the sides down as needed if the hummus starts trailing up the bowl. If you would like a more spreadable texture, add the reserved chickpea cooking liquid 1 tablespoon at a time until you're happy with the texture.

Taste! Add extra salt and lemon juice to make it just right.

Serve with the topping of your choice.

Tips + Timing

1. Make any time up to 3 days before serving. Store in an airtight container in the fridge and give it a good stir before transferring it to a serving bowl and finishing with toppings of your choice.
2. Adding ice-cold water <u>and</u> ice is the trick to great, thick, well-aerated, creamy hummus.
3. The four optional toppings are there for you to get inspired by, but feel free to get as freaky/creative as you like!

SMOKED PAPRIKA POTATO CRISPS WITH AIOLI

Serves 4 to 6
Total time: 30 minutes

Inspired by Spanish patatas bravas, this is a dish of thinly sliced potatoes baked until real crispy, topped with salt and smoked paprika, dipped into garlicky goodness. What's not to love? If you've got all the time in the world and you want to make your own mayo, please, be my guest. But I prefer the quick fix for this one: Make your "aioli" simply by whisking a metric ton of garlic into store-bought mayo. Instant gratification.

Just don't eat all the crisps before your friends come over, or make sure to literally eat all of them to destroy the evidence of their existence . . .

Aioli

1 cup mayo

10 garlic cloves, minced

2 teaspoons white wine vinegar

¼ teaspoon salt, plus more to taste

¼ cup finely minced parsley leaves

Potato Crisps

6 tablespoons extra-virgin olive oil

1 teaspoon salt

½ teaspoon smoked paprika, plus extra to finish

2 very large russet potatoes (about 1½ pounds), sliced into ⅛-inch-thick rounds

Preheat the oven to 425°F.

TO MAKE THE AIOLI: In a medium bowl, whisk together 1 cup mayo, the minced garlic, 2 teaspoons white wine vinegar, ¼ teaspoon salt, and ¼ cup minced parsley. Add extra salt to taste. Refrigerate in a serving bowl until ready to eat.

TO MAKE THE POTATO CRISPS: In a small bowl, whisk together 6 tablespoons olive oil, 1 teaspoon salt, and ½ teaspoon smoked paprika. In a large bowl, toss half of the sliced potatoes with half of the oil mixture. Mix really well and separate the potatoes so each slice gets coated.

Lay the oiled potatoes on a large baking sheet. It's okay if they touch, but *don't overlap* the potatoes or they won't crisp up. This may require two baking sheets.

Once the oiled potatoes are out of the bowl and onto the baking sheets, repeat tossing the rest of the potatoes with the rest of the oil mixture and laying them down on baking sheets. If you don't have enough baking sheets, just cook the first batch and repeat when you're ready!

Bake until the potatoes are visibly golden and crispy, 18 to 20 minutes, rotating the pan every 5 minutes for even cooking. No need to flip the potatoes; they're thin enough that both sides will crisp. If some slices become done sooner than others, just use a spatula to remove them to wire racks or parchment paper.

Put the crisps on a serving platter, sprinkle with extra smoked paprika, and serve with the aioli on the side.

TIPS + TIMING

1. Aioli can be made up to 2 days in advance and stored in an airtight container in the fridge. Crisps can be made an hour before friends come over and left out on a cooling rack.
2. Feeling lazy? Just buy chips and serve them with the aioli—a pretty great snack in about 1 minute.
3. The easiest way to cut the potatoes is with a mandoline, but be careful not to remove your fingertips while getting those perfect slices.

TART APPLE BUTTERNUT SQUASH SOUP

Serves 6

Total time: 1 hour 15 minutes

As a private chef, I've made a lot of variations on butternut squash soup. Lots and lots and lots and lots. But this is the one I always come back to. It just tastes like a big hug. A little sweet, a little tangy, super-creamy, elegant, and very well-balanced. When I make this for a dinner party, I usually double the recipe so I also have soup for the week. :)

1 large butternut squash (2½ pounds), peeled, seeds scooped, and cut into 2-inch pieces (or 4 cups precut squash)

¼ cup extra-virgin olive oil, divided

1 teaspoon salt, divided, plus more to taste

1 teaspoon black pepper, divided, plus more to taste

1 Granny Smith apple, cut into 1-inch slices

2 shallots, chopped

3 garlic cloves, chopped

⅛ teaspoon ground nutmeg

4 cups vegetable stock, homemade (page 132) or store-bought

1½ teaspoons apple cider vinegar, plus more to taste

1 tablespoon unsalted butter

1 tablespoon finely chopped chives, to finish

½ cup plain, full-fat (5%) Greek yogurt, to finish (optional)

Preheat the oven to 425°F.

Grab a baking sheet and cover it with parchment paper. Pile all of your cut squash onto the baking sheet, drizzle with 2 tablespoons olive oil, and sprinkle with ½ teaspoon salt and ½ teaspoon pepper. Mix well with your hands and, once the squash is evenly seasoned, spread it out so there is breathing room between each piece to crisp—if they're looking squished, divide onto two baking sheets.

Roast the squash for 30 minutes and then flip. Continue to cook until both sides are nicely golden with a few little crispy bits, about 15 additional minutes. (If you used precut squash, your time will most likely be shorter, so flip after 15 minutes and keep an eye on them after 30 minutes.)

Meanwhile, in a medium pot, heat the remaining 2 tablespoons olive oil over medium-low heat. Once the

oil is warm, add the apple slices and cook until soft and caramelized, 4 to 6 minutes.

Add the chopped shallots, garlic, ½ teaspoon salt, and ½ teaspoon pepper to the pot and sauté until the shallots are translucent, about 4 minutes.

Transfer the mixture to a blender and add ⅛ teaspoon nutmeg and 4 cups stock. Once the squash is cooked, add it to the blender too. Blend for at least a minute, until smooth and creamy. If your blender is small, you may need to do this in a few batches.

Pour the soup back into the pot over medium heat and stir in the 1½ teaspoons vinegar and 1 tablespoon butter. Season to taste with extra salt, pepper, and vinegar.

Serve topped with chives and a dollop of yogurt, if desired.

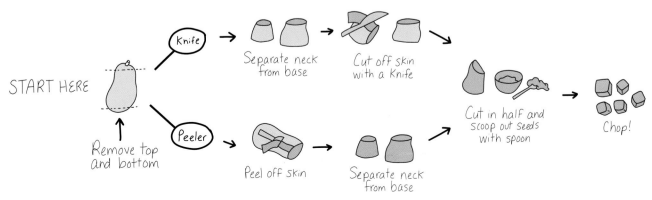

START HERE

Remove top and bottom

Knife → Separate neck from base → Cut off skin with a Knife →

Peeler → Peel off skin → Separate neck from base →

Cut in half and scoop out seeds with spoon → Chop!

TIPS + TIMING

1. Make up to 3 days before serving and store in an airtight container in the fridge. Reheat and garnish before serving.
2. To cut the squash, use a sharp knife to cut off the very top and bottom. Then cut the squash at the point where the neck starts to widen and become circular. Stand both parts up on a cut side and cut away the skin. (Alternatively, you can use a large vegetable peeler to remove the skin.) Slice both parts in half the long way and remove all seeds with a spoon. If you don't feel like cutting the squash, you can also buy it precut.
3. If you prefer a sweeter soup, swap the tart green Granny Smith apple for a sweeter variety, such as Fuji or Pink lady.
4. If you use store-bought stock, reduce the salt by ½ teaspoon to account for the extra salt!

I can chart the milestones of my life through dinner party mains: I fell in love over lobster pasta. I landed my first national cooking show right after having homemade bagels for dinner. I experienced my most devastating breakup before double-decker smash burgers and strawberry milkshakes. (I know everyone talks about the ideal pairing of ice cream and breakups, but let me tell you, for an anxiety-ridden lactose-intolerant person . . . this is not a good idea.) I rang in a quarantine new year with backyard lasagna. I made spaghetti and meatballs to celebrate selling this very book. And, my favorite, I introduced my best friends to Andy over giant bowls of risotto.

ROASTED TOMATO AND BURRATA EGGPLANT PARM

Serves 6
Total time: 1 hour 30 minutes

For me, eggplant parmesan is just about as comforting as it gets. I know some people feel it doesn't compare to its cousin chicken parm, but I'm here to challenge that assumption (though you *can* use chicken in this recipe, if you must). This parm, in particular, has every desirable element: earthy freshness from the eggplant, crispy, crackly edges from the panko, creamy coolness from the burrata, natural sweetness from the roasted tomatoes, and an epic cheese-pull from the mozzarella. Will it inspire you to get an eggplant parm tattoo? Very possibly.

While there are a million ways you can put together an eggplant parm, you're probably most familiar with "the stack," the neighbor of lasagna, in which the eggplant is piled into an amorphous heap. My issue with the stack is that all the crispy bits immediately get soft and soggy. The idea here is to make something more along the lines of a cutlet, one in which the sauce is draped over certain areas and other spots are naked and crispy as ever.

If there are any leftovers, I like to cut them up into bite-size pieces and toss with pasta and butter.

Roasted Tomatoes

1 pint cherry tomatoes (about 25, even better if they're on the vine)

¼ cup extra-virgin olive oil

3 garlic cloves, unpeeled

¼ teaspoon salt

Eggplant

3 large globe eggplants, cut lengthwise into ½-inch-thick slices, ends discarded (see illustration)

6 teaspoons salt

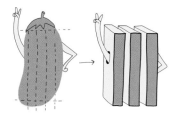

TO MAKE THE ROASTED TOMATOES: Preheat the oven to 350°F. Put the cherry tomatoes into an 8-inch cake pan and cover with ¼ cup olive oil, 3 garlic cloves, and ¼ teaspoon salt. Shake the pan to coat the tomatoes—don't worry about being too precious with them. Bake, without stirring, until the tomatoes are bursting at the seams, plump, and slightly caramelized on the underside, 35 to 45 minutes. Set them aside to cool (but leave the oven on). Once the garlic is cool enough to touch, squeeze out the roasted cloves and toss with the tomatoes to coat them.

TO MAKE THE EGGPLANT: Score all the eggplant slices (see tips for scoring) and lay them out on a dish towel. Sprinkle both sides of the pieces with a total of 6 teaspoons salt, cover with another dish towel, and rest for 10 minutes. Resting the eggplant with salt to draw out moisture (sweating) will reduce splattering while cooking, keep it from tasting bitter, and soften the flesh. After 10 minutes, press on each slice firmly with the dish towel to sop up any extra liquid and wipe off any extra salt.

While the eggplant is sweating, prepare the breading station. Grab 3 large bowls. In the first bowl, whisk together the "flour coat" ingredients (½ cup flour, ½ teaspoon salt, ½ teaspoon red pepper flakes, ½ teaspoon oregano, and ½ teaspoon black pepper). In the second bowl, whisk the "egg coat" ingredients

recipe and ingredients continue

Flour Coat

½ cup all-purpose flour

½ teaspoon salt

½ teaspoon red pepper flakes

½ teaspoon dried oregano

½ teaspoon black pepper

Egg Coat

3 eggs

1½ teaspoons salt

1 teaspoon garlic powder

1 teaspoon onion powder (optional)

Bread Crumb Coat

2½ cups panko or plain bread crumbs

½ cup grated parmesan cheese

Assembly

½ to 1 cup canola oil or other neutral high-heat oil

1 (32 ounce) jar of tomato sauce

8 ounces shredded low-moisture, full-fat mozzarella cheese

2 large balls (8 ounces) of burrata cheese, torn into pieces

½ cup basil leaves, thinly sliced

Red pepper flakes, to finish

Dried oregano, to finish

(3 eggs, 1½ teaspoons salt, 1 teaspoon garlic powder, and, if using, 1 teaspoon onion powder). In the third bowl, mix the "bread crumb" ingredients (2½ cups bread crumbs and ½ cup grated parmesan).

Heat your largest skillet (preferably 12 inches or larger) over medium-high heat. If you have extra kitchen help, you can do multiple pans at once. Grab a rimmed baking sheet and set it next to your three bowls.

You'll notice the first and third bowls are full of dry items and the middle bowl is full of wet ingredients. Use one hand for the dry ingredients and the other for wet so your hands won't be completely coated in goo by the end. Submerge each eggplant slice into the flour first to fully coat, shaking off any excess. Drop the slice into the egg mixture and then hold the slice over the bowl for a few seconds to let any extra egg drip off. Last, cover the slice completely in bread crumbs (as if you were burying it) and press firmly to get as many bread crumbs as possible to adhere. Give it a final shake and lay it out on

the baking sheet. Keep going until all the eggplant slices are coated and ready to fry.

Increase the oven temp to 400°F.

Add ½ cup canola oil into the hot pan. Once the oil is hot, add the eggplant slices, leaving at least ½ inch in between each slice. (Not sure if the oil is ready? Test by dipping a tiny corner of one of the eggplant slices into the oil. If it immediately reacts and there are small bubbles forming and crackling noises, you can toss it in. If it behaves like a still pond, wait another minute and try again!)

Fry each slice, turning once, until both sides are golden brown and crispy, about 3 minutes per side. Transfer the slices back onto the baking sheet, first allowing any excess oil to drip back into the pan.

Continue until all the eggplant slices are perfectly bronzed. If you need to, add more oil to the pan, but wait until it's hot before adding more eggplant. You can bake the eggplant right on the rimmed baking sheet, or transfer to another oven-safe serving vessel (I wipe out and use the same cast-iron skillet that I fried the eggplant in).

Spoon the tomato sauce over the middle of each eggplant slice to keep the edges exposed so that you have some really crispy areas and some crispy-gone-soggy zones (as shown in the illustration). We're looking for each eggplant to be about one-third naked.

Sprinkle the mozzarella on top of the sauce and bake until the cheese is melty and bubbly, about 10 minutes.

To serve, top the hot eggplant slices with the warm, beautiful roasty tomatoes, torn bits of the juicy burrata, and basil leaves, and finish with a little extra dried oregano and red pepper flakes. Put that baking vessel right on your table and you're ready to eat!

TIPS + TIMING

1. The roasted tomatoes can be made up to 3 days in advance and stored in an airtight container in the fridge. The eggplant can be coated in the frying mixture (flour, eggs, and bread crumbs) up to a day in advance and stored in a single layer on a rimmed baking sheet, uncovered, in the refrigerator. Fry, cover in sauce, and bake right before serving.
2. To score an eggplant, take your knife and gently make a hashtag or two on each side of each piece. Scoring the eggplant helps get the crispy, crackly crust.

BRAISED GARLICKY EGGPLANT WITH CHICKPEAS AND TOMATOES

Serves 6
Total time: 1 hour 30 minutes

If you're looking for an easy, make-ahead vegetarian meal that'll charm the pants off of a meat eater, have I got the recipe for you! This braised eggplant comes together really quickly and is incredibly satisfying thanks to the sweetness from the tomatoes, the creaminess of the eggplant, the tart pop from the yogurt, and the freshness of the lemon juice and mint. Prepare it a day in advance and the flavors really meld together. Simply reheat it before serving, top it with the yogurt sauce, and mmmmmm.

¼ cup plus 2 tablespoons extra-virgin olive oil

2 pints cherry tomatoes (about 50), halved

2 teaspoons salt, divided

8 garlic cloves, minced

½ teaspoon dried oregano

1 teaspoon black pepper, divided

3 (15.5 ounce) cans of chickpeas, drained and rinsed

½ cup vegetable stock, homemade (page 132) or store-bought, if needed

3 pounds Japanese or globe eggplants, cut into slices (see illustration on page 40), ends discarded

1 tablespoon coarsely chopped mint leaves, to finish

Red pepper flakes, to finish

½ teaspoon flaky sea salt, to finish

1 lemon, cut into wedges, to finish

Yogurt Sauce

2 tablespoons fresh lemon juice, plus more to taste

1 cup plain, full-fat (5%) Greek yogurt

¼ cup finely chopped mint leaves

½ teaspoon red pepper flakes

Salt to taste

Preheat the oven to 450°F.

In a large skillet, heat the ¼ cup olive oil over medium heat until it is shiny and warm. Add 2 pints cherry tomatoes, sprinkle ½ teaspoon salt on top, and stir with a wooden spoon to coat the tomatoes in the oil. Sauté for about 10 minutes or until the tomatoes are softened and just starting to break down. Add the garlic, ½ teaspoon dried oregano, and ½ teaspoon black pepper and cook until aromatic, about 2 minutes. Add 3 cans of chickpeas and ½ teaspoon salt and cook, stirring occasionally, for another 5 minutes.

Pour the mixture into a 9 x 13-inch baking dish and place the baking dish in the oven. (Depending on the season and the ripeness of the tomatoes, you may end up with lots of liquid, or you may have none. If you have none, add ½ cup stock.)

Wipe the skillet clean and return it to the stovetop over medium-high heat. Add the remaining 2 tablespoons olive oil. Sprinkle the eggplant slices with the remaining 1 teaspoon salt and ½ teaspoon pepper. Place as many slices in the pan as you can fit without crowding and sear until golden brown,

2 to 4 minutes. Flip and repeat. It's important that both sides get a really deep golden sear for the flavor of this dish to sing. Transfer the seared eggplant to a baking sheet and continue with the rest of the slices until they are all seared.

Grab the hot baking dish from the oven and lay the eggplant in 3 tight rows over the top of the chickpea mixture. Bake until the eggplant is caramelized on top and fork-tender, 35 to 45 minutes.

TO MAKE THE YOGURT SAUCE: While the eggplant is cooking, whisk 2 tablespoons lemon juice, 1 cup Greek yogurt, the mint, and ½ teaspoon red pepper flakes in a medium bowl and add salt and extra lemon juice to taste. If the yogurt is so thick it can't be drizzled, add a tablespoon or two of water. Refrigerate until the eggplant is cooked.

Generously drizzle the eggplant with yogurt sauce and sprinkle with the mint, red pepper flakes, and flaky sea salt. Serve with lemon wedges on the side and encourage everyone to squeeze lemon over their portion.

recipe continues

TIPS + TIMING

1. Make both the eggplant and the yogurt sauce up to 3 days in advance and store in <u>separate</u> airtight containers in the fridge. Reheat the eggplant, uncovered, in a 450°F oven until bubbling and hot, about 15 minutes. Just before serving, dollop with the yogurt, mint, and red pepper flakes, and put out lemon wedges for finishing.

2. This makes excellent leftovers for brunch too! Put the leftovers in an oven-safe skillet, create little wells to crack eggs into, and bake in the oven at 350°F for 5 to 8 minutes, until the egg whites are set. Or you can serve it on crusty bread with a fried egg on top.

3. Japanese eggplants are slender with a thin skin and a slightly sweet flesh, while other eggplants have a tendency to be a little more bitter with a meatier texture. If you can't find Japanese eggplant, you can use any variety eggplant; just cut it up into spears that are about 3 x 4½ inches.

Japanese:

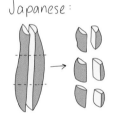

Globe:

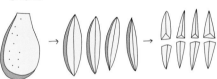

BE-YOUR-OWN-BUBBE (BYOB) JEWISH BRISKET

Serves 6 to 8

Total time: 6½ hours (5 of which are hands-off roasting time) + OVERNIGHT RESTING

People always ask me what my favorite thing to cook is and the answer is always the same: steamed broccoli! I joke. It's brisket. This Eastern European-style fruited brisket reigns supreme in my world. It makes any bad day good, and any good day great. I am, literally, always in the mood for brisket, and I make it at least twelve times a year. My great-grandmother used this recipe, my grandma used this recipe, my mom used this recipe, and, well, you get the picture. The meat is seared and then slowly cooked in the oven with all the usual suspects (carrot, onion, celery, garlic), but what really makes this brisket special is the subtle sweetness from the apricots and prunes.

This recipe is easy easy easy, but it takes a lot of time, as brisket is a cut of meat that comes from the lower chest of the cow, a.k.a. the part that supports most of the cow's weight. You have to let it cook slowly to allow it to break down and do its thing.

5 pounds flat-cut brisket

3 teaspoons salt, divided, plus more as needed

1 teaspoon pepper

1 yellow onion, skins removed, quartered

2 large carrots, peeled and cut into 2-inch pieces

2 celery stalks, cut into 2-inch pieces

1 garlic head, halved lengthwise

1½ cups full-bodied, jammy red wine (I like cabernet sauvignon)

¾ cup dried apricots

¾ cup dried prunes

2 bay leaves

1½ cups beef stock

Preheat the oven to 300°F.

Heat a large skillet over medium-high heat. Pat the meat dry with paper towels and season with 2 teaspoons salt and 1 teaspoon pepper.

If the meat can fit in the skillet in one piece, add it with the fattier side facing down and sear until it's a deep golden hue, about 4 minutes; flip and repeat on side two. If you need to split it in half and do this process twice, that's cool too.

Transfer the brisket to a high-sided 9 x 13-inch baking dish with the fat facing up.

In the skillet with the rendered beef fat, reduce the heat to medium-low and add the onion, carrots, celery, and 1 teaspoon salt. Cook, stirring occasionally, until the onions are translucent and the carrots have

slightly softened, 5 minutes. Add the garlic and 1½ cups wine into the pan. Use a wooden spoon to scrape up any browned bits from the bottom. Cook for 5 minutes to slightly reduce the wine.

Meanwhile, nestle ¾ cup apricots, ¾ cup prunes, and 2 bay leaves around the meat and pour in 1½ cups beef stock. Pour the wine-soaked veggies over the brisket. Cover the baking dish with aluminum foil and place it on a sturdy rimmed baking sheet before sliding into the oven to slowly roast for 5 hours.

Remove the brisket from the oven and open the tinfoil facing away from you (your face will thank me later). Allow the meat to cool for an hour on the counter. Give the meat and cooking liquid a quick taste and add extra salt as needed. At this point you can:

recipe continues

1. Allow the brisket to rest in the fridge overnight; if you'd like, you can re-cover it with the aluminum foil once it has fully cooled in the fridge.
2. OR, if you want to serve the meat on the same day, just proceed, but know it won't be quite as flavorful or as easy to cut as the overnight-rested version.

The next day, preheat the oven to 400°F. Cut off any large, visible fat caps from the brisket, and slice the meat against the grain in ½-inch-thick slices.

Add the meat back into the baking dish and bake, uncovered, until there is light crisping happening at the edges of the meat, about 45 minutes.

Discard the garlic and serve hot, straight from the baking dish, letting people grab whatever smooshed veggies, braising liquid, and stewed fruit they'd like to heap on top of the brisket.

TIPS + TIMING

1. Roast up to 3 days before serving, refrigerate (whole) in the baking dish covered in aluminum foil, and do the final slicing and reheating just before serving.
2. Flat-cut brisket is great for this because it slices really evenly and it's easier to trim the fat once cooked, but point-cut is fine too if that's what you find.
3. Brisket tastes much better after it's had time to rest in the braising liquid, which is why I always cook it a day ahead of serving and slice and reheat before dinner. My friend Molly and I call this "the brisket effect." If you don't have the time, it's still very good on day one, but save some leftovers and you'll see what I mean.
4. If you have a Dutch oven that's big enough for this operation, you're totally welcome to use it! Use the lid instead of foil.
5. WTF IS A BUBBE? It's Yiddish for "grandma." Welcome to your first lesson in training to be a good Jewish grandmother.

CACIO E PEPE MAC AND CHEESE

Serves 6
Total time: 45 minutes

The first time I had cacio e pepe—an Italian pasta dish aptly called "cheese and pepper" because it's made with only pasta, pecorino, and black pepper—I was skeptical. How can so few ingredients be so impressive? Then I believe I blacked out and didn't return until I had eaten the entire plate of pasta and also the plate. It's magical to think about how often the best recipes, and the greatest flavors, come from simple, good ingredients.

Because mac and cheese is an easy way to make a large quantity of pasta for a crowd, I wanted to bring these two friends together and I'm pretty pleased with the result. This hybrid features a basic white sauce (béchamel) loaded with fresh cracked pepper, lots of pecorino, and toasty bread crumbs to finish!

Bread Crumbs

1 tablespoon unsalted butter

¼ teaspoon salt

1 cup panko bread crumbs

Mac and Cheese

4 teaspoons salt, divided

1½ tablespoons freshly ground black pepper, plus extra to finish

4 tablespoons (½ stick) unsalted butter

4 teaspoons salt, divided

¼ cup all-purpose flour

3½ cups whole milk

1 pound medium-shell pasta

2 cups grated pecorino romano cheese (½ pound), plus extra to finish

Preheat the oven to 425°F.

TO MAKE THE BREAD CRUMBS: In a large pot over medium heat, melt 1 tablespoon butter. Once melted, add in ¼ teaspoon salt and 1 cup panko bread crumbs. Cook, stirring occasionally, until about half the bread crumbs are toasted a nice golden brown color, about 4 minutes. Set the bread crumbs aside.

TO MAKE THE MAC AND CHEESE: Fill that same pot halfway full with water, add 3 teaspoons salt, and bring to a boil over high heat.

While the pasta water is boiling, make the sauce.

In a second pot over medium-low heat, add 1½ tablespoons black pepper and stir just until aromatic, about 1 minute. (Yes, the pepper will become super-aromatic really fast. Yes, this is basically DIY pepper spray.) Add in 4 tablespoons butter and heat until melted. Whisk in ¼ cup flour and 1 teaspoon salt. Slowly, while constantly whisking, add in 3½ cups milk to create a smooth, thin sauce. The sauce will get thicker before

it gets thinner; just keep whisking! Crank up the heat to medium and bring the sauce to a boil, stirring occasionally.

This is probably the best time to toss your pasta into the boiling, salty water. Cook the pasta per the instructions on the package.

Once the sauce is boiling, reduce the heat to medium-low and cook, whisking occasionally, until it thickens, about 6 minutes. The sauce should be thick enough to easily coat the back of a spoon. Remove the pot from the heat and whisk in 2 cups pecorino.

Once the pasta is cooked, use a slotted spoon to transfer it to the pot containing the sauce. DO NOT THROW AWAY THE PASTA WATER. Return the pasta/sauce pot to the cooktop and cook over medium-high heat, stirring constantly until all the pasta is well-coated in sauce. Season to taste with additional pasta water. (It's salty, remember? And starchy, which will help create a sauce that will coat the pasta well. Win-win.)

recipe continues

Pour the mac and cheese into an ungreased 9 x 13-inch baking dish and top with the bread crumbs and a generous sprinkling of black pepper. Bake until the sauce is bubbling and the bread crumbs are a deep golden brown, 15 to 20 minutes.

Finish with some extra pecorino for good measure.

Let rest for 5 to 10 minutes before serving—burnt mouths are a dinner-party bummer.

Tips + Timing

1. A cheesy pasta dish is always best fresh. In a pinch, you can make the sauce in advance and add pasta water to thin it out just before tossing the pasta in it. The bread crumbs can be made up to a day in advance and stored in an airtight container at room temp.
2. The less water you use for boiling the pasta, the starchier and more awesome your pasta water will be.
3. Can you use parmesan if you can't find pecorino? Yeah, your dish will be less salty and tangy and a little nuttier . . . but still super-tasty.
4. This has a lot of pepper in it, obviously, so if you have a coffee grinder, that's the most efficient way to get the quantity needed.

COZY WINTER NIGHT BORSCHT

Makes 6 giant servings

Total time: 4 hours (including 2 hours hands-off time to cook the meat)

Borscht is one of my absolute favorites—an Eastern European soup that's made of beets, often with tender cubes of meat, lots of hearty winter vegetables, and finished with a healthy dollop of sour cream and a sprinkling of dill. It's a perfect reflection of the old Ukrainian lady inside of me who just wants to keep feeding you until you burst.

Until recently, I didn't make it very often because, frankly, it can be a pain in the butt. Traditional recipes are made by first preparing beet water and then, after a long period of waiting, straining it to use as stock. After that there's lots of shredding, boiling, separating, stirring, etc. Are you tired? I am now tired.

This much less time-intensive version, adapted from *Cook's Illustrated*, is not traditional in its method but yields a soup with layers of flavor. The veggies and potatoes are soft but distinctive, the broth has a balance of sweet and sour, and the meat is rich and delicious.

Serving it to a bunch of friends in giant bowls with crusty bread is my absolute favorite casual winter dinner party.

And!! It's easy to make this vegetarian. Just forget the entire meat part, use veggie stock (homemade, page 132, or store-bought), and double the potatoes.

Meat (if using)

1½ pounds beef chuck steak, cut into ½-inch cubes

1½ teaspoons salt

4 tablespoons canola oil, divided

4 cups beef stock

1 cup water

TO MAKE THE MEAT, IF USING: Season the meat with 1½ teaspoons salt. Grab two large pots and heat them both over medium-high heat. Add 2 tablespoons oil into each and then divide the meat between the two. Brown the meat on all sides, stirring occasionally, about 5 minutes. Move all the meat into one pot (if your two pots are different sizes, put all the meat into the smaller pot, reserving the beef fat in the empty larger pot) and cover the meat with 4 cups beef stock and 1 cup water. Allow the liquid to come to a boil and then reduce the heat to a simmer. Cook, uncovered, until the meat is tender, 2 hours. (At the end, there will be almost no liquid left and the meat should be starting to crisp, just a little bit, in the rendered fat).

recipe and ingredients continue

TIPS + TIMING

1. Much like our friend the brisket (page 41), borscht gets better with age. Make up to 3 days before serving and store in an airtight container in the fridge. Reheat over the stove and garnish before serving.
2. Borscht can be served hot or cold. My preference is to serve a meaty borscht hot and its vegetarian counterpart cold.

Borscht

2 tablespoons canola oil (for veg option)

1 yellow onion, chopped

4 large carrots, cut into ½-inch pieces

1 teaspoon salt, plus more to taste

3 garlic cloves, minced

2 tablespoons tomato paste

¼ cup plus 1 teaspoon red wine vinegar, plus more to taste

4 teaspoons sugar

5 cups beef stock (or veggie stock), divided

3 cups water

3 large red beets (2 pounds), peeled and cut into thin strips

4 large Yukon Gold potatoes, peeled and cut into ½-inch cubes

1 cup full-fat sour cream, to finish

4 green onions, white and green parts, thinly sliced, to finish

¼ cup finely chopped dill, to finish

Dark Russian bread, marbled rye bread, or Olive Oil–Drenched Sourdough (page 125), for serving

TO MAKE THE BORSCHT: After the meat has been cooking for 1 hour, start the soup. Set the empty pot with the remaining beef fat over medium-high heat (or add 2 tablespoons canola oil to an empty pot if you are going vegetarian). Once the fat is warm, add the onions, carrots, and 1 teaspoon salt. Cook until the onions are translucent, about 5 minutes. Add the garlic and cook for 1 minute. Mix in 2 tablespoons tomato paste and stir until the mixture becomes a deep red hue, about 3 minutes. Add ¼ cup plus 1 teaspoon vinegar and 4 teaspoons sugar and cook down for a minute. Pour in ½ cup stock and stir to dissolve the sugar. Stir in the remaining 4½ cups stock and 3 cups water. Toss in your beets. Bring the soup to a boil and then reduce to a simmer. Cook for 25 minutes and then add the potatoes. Simmer for another 20 minutes, until the potatoes are tender.

Add the meat into the borscht and add extra salt and vinegar to taste. Divide among bowls, and finish each serving with sour cream, green onions, and dill, with bread of your choice alongside. This would be a great time to almost hand your least sensitive friend a bowl and then pull it away, yelling, "No soup for you!"

PAN-CRISPED SAUSAGE WITH LEMON HERB VEGGIES

Serves 6
Total time: 1 hour 10 minutes

If you're looking for a dinner that's easy to throw together, there's really nothing better than this guy. Toss all the veggies on a baking sheet, pan-sear some sausage (which looks fancy but is very easy) and voilà! You've got a delicious dinner in no time.

When Andy and I were traveling in Germany a few years back, we basically ate something like this every day because it was (1) cheap and (2) delightful. Since returning, it's more or less in our weekly rotation. (Please don't ask me how my cholesterol is doing.) Go as crazy, or as basic, as you want with the sides and enjoy with an ice-cold beer, or not, whatever you prefer.

Caramelized Veggies

7 tablespoons extra-virgin olive oil

2 teaspoons salt, plus more to taste

½ teaspoon black pepper, plus more to taste

2 teaspoons garlic powder

2 pounds (about 10) small Yukon Gold or red potatoes, quartered

1 large yellow onion, cut into ½-inch wedges

2 red or orange bell peppers, cut into ¾-inch strips

1 bunch of broccolini, with any large pieces split in half through the stem

12 cornichons, coarsely chopped

½ teaspoon cornichon brine

2 tablespoons coarsely chopped parsley leaves

1 tablespoon coarsely chopped dill

2 teaspoons fresh lemon juice, plus more to taste

Sausages

2 tablespoons olive oil

12 sausages of your choice, scored diagonally every ½ inch on 2 sides

Sides for Serving

Store-bought sauerkraut or homemade Garlicky Cabbage with Whole-Grain Mustard (page 110)

Mustard(s)—I like offering both a spicy stone-ground and a whole-grain

Olive Oil–Drenched Sourdough (page 125)

Lots of beer!

HOW TO AVOID THE SEEDS IN A PEPPER

Preheat the oven to 450°F.

TO MAKE THE CARAMELIZED VEGGIES:
In a small bowl, whisk together 7 tablespoons olive oil, 2 teaspoons salt, ½ teaspoon pepper, and 2 teaspoons garlic powder.

In a large bowl, combine the potatoes with ¼ cup of the flavored oil and toss to evenly coat. Divide the potatoes between two large baking sheets (first line them with parchment if your pans are getting old) and roast for 10 minutes.

Place the onions and peppers in the same large bowl with 2 more tablespoons of flavored oil and toss to coat. Add the peppers and onions to the potatoes. Roast until the potatoes are golden and crispy, the peppers have charred spots, and the onions are lightly caramelized, about 30 more minutes, flipping halfway through.

In the same large bowl, toss the broccolini around with the remaining tablespoon of flavored oil; add it to

recipe continues

the baking sheets when you flip the other vegetables.

Start the sausages while the vegetables finish cooking.

TO MAKE THE SAUSAGES: Place 1 tablespoon of olive oil in two large skillets and heat over medium. Once the oil is warm, add the sausages. The sausages should sizzle when they hit the pan—if they don't, wait another minute. Be careful not to crowd them. If you need to do another round, that's okay! Cook the sausages, undisturbed, for 4 minutes. Flip, and repeat until all the sausages have fully crisped exteriors, about 8 minutes total. They should be golden brown and crispy with juicy centers and liquid that runs clear.

Put all the roasted veggies onto one baking sheet and toss with the cornichons, ½ teaspoon cornichon brine, parsley, dill, and 2 teaspoons lemon juice. Add extra salt, pepper, and lemon juice to taste.

Serve on a platter, or right on the baking sheet (!), with the crispy sausages, bring out your condiments/sides of choice, and feast!

TIPS + TIMING

1. Potatoes, onions and peppers, and broccolini can be cut and stored in 3 separate airtight containers in the fridge up to a day in advance. Everything should be cooked just before serving.
2. This meal will only be as tasty as the sausage itself (see page 230 for sausage recs). Look for a sausage that has a fun variety of spices and is plump and juicy. Because the name of the game is crispy, regardless of whether the sausage is precooked or raw, the timing is essentially the same. Just pick the best-looking sausage available to you.
3. Don't overcrowd the pan. If you don't give veggies space, they won't crisp, and a roasted uncrisped potato is an unwelcomed potato.
4. On that note, want the crispiest tates? Make sure the cut side of the potato is facing down.
5. Those of you bell pepper haters out there can swap out the peppers for fennel!

DINER-STYLE SMASH BURGERS

Makes 6 juicy burgers
Total time: 35 minutes

In Oregon, Tillamook dairy reigns supreme. So, obviously, the Tillamook Ice Creamery and Restaurant in Lake Oswego is the place to be if you're nine and you can get a parent to take you there. I would always get a burger and a peppermint milkshake, an order I will always stand behind. The flattened-out, crispy patty came on a soft, squishy bun with a mountain of cold, crunchy iceberg, a few pickles, a thin layer of melted sharp cheddar (Tillamook, of course), and was drowned in special sauce. All I ever want is to re-create this burger of my childhood dreams. In summer months, I add a big, juicy slice of tomato, and because I have a pickle addiction, I always add about five times more pickles than any sane human would deem acceptable. Other than that, I wouldn't change a thing!

Because these burgers are fatty and cook at a high heat, they'll create a tremendous amount of smoke in your kitchen and will almost certainly set off your smoke detector; it's part of the charm. Open any doors, windows, vents, yada yada yada, that you have around you. I also recently purchased a griddle top that sits across two burners so I can make many burgers at once, short-order-cook style, and it has changed the game. If you love a good sear and cooking for a crowd, I highly recommend it!

Special Sauce

½ cup mayo
2½ tablespoons ketchup
1 tablespoon yellow mustard
2 tablespoons minced dill pickle
¼ teaspoon smoked paprika
¼ teaspoon garlic powder

TO MAKE THE SPECIAL SAUCE: In a medium bowl, whisk together ½ cup mayo, 2½ tablespoons ketchup, 1 tablespoon yellow mustard, the pickles, ¼ teaspoon smoked paprika, and ¼ teaspoon garlic powder. Special sauce is easily tailored for your preferences; if you'd like anything to be different, follow the graph below. Set aside.

recipe and ingredients continue

SPECIAL SAUCE CHEAT SHEET

SWEETER — More Ketchup

TANGIER — More Mustard

SALTIER — More pickles

SMOKIER — More paprika

Burgers

½ head of iceberg lettuce, thinly shredded (about 3 cups)

1 cup dill pickle rounds

6 slices sharp cheddar cheese

6 squishy potato buns

3 tablespoons salted butter, divided, plus more as needed

2 pounds 80/20 ground beef, kept in fridge until ready to form patties

2 teaspoons salt

2 teaspoons black pepper

TO MAKE THE BURGERS: Before cooking up the burgers, you want to get everything else ready to go. Have the lettuce, pickles, and sauce out off to the side. Put the cheese by the stove and grab the buns and butter.

In two large, heavy-bottomed skillets, melt 1½ tablespoons of butter each over medium heat. Once the butter is melted, add in as many buns as you can fit, cut side down. Once the bottoms are nicely toasted and a light golden brown, about 3 minutes, remove them from the heat. Repeat until all the buns are toasty. If you want to keep the buns warm, put them on a baking sheet in a 300°F oven until the burgers are done. Wipe the butter and crumbs out of the pans with a paper towel and increase the heat to medium-high.

Take the meat out of the fridge and divide it into 6 roughly even-size balls. Place a piece of parchment paper on the counter. Press each ball into a patty about ½ inch thick, and place the patty on the parchment. Use your fingertips to press the meat down and out, until each patty is 5 to 6 inches in diameter and about ¼ inch thick.

After all the patties are formed, evenly distribute a total of 2 teaspoons salt and 2 teaspoons pepper over both sides of each burger.

Lay as many patties as you can in each skillet without letting any of the patties touch. Apply a lot of pressure with a flat metal spatula (or really anything that's flat) on top of each patty to get it as big, flat, and as stuck to the skillet as possible—this is key for crisping! Cook until there is obvious searing around the edges of each burger, about 2 minutes. Use downward force on a metal spatula to scrape up and flip the patties, and top each patty with a slice of cheese. Once the cheese is melted, remove the patties from the heat. If you are working in multiple batches, you can add the cooked patties to the baking sheet with the buns that is in the warm oven.

TO ASSEMBLE: Put special sauce on the bottom bun, followed by a patty, a few pickles, and *lots* of shredded lettuce (shredduce). Spread more special sauce over the top bun and give that burger a hat!

TIPS + TIMING

1. Special sauce can be made up to 3 days in advance and kept in an airtight container in the fridge. Feel free to chop the lettuce earlier in the day and store in a bowl in the fridge covered with a damp paper towel.

2. For the best texture, look for meat that has been freshly ground rather than vacuum sealed. You can find freshly ground meat at a butcher counter, or packaged. If it's packaged it will look fluffy and loosely packed rather than dense and tight.

3. The higher the fat, the bigger the flavor, so go for the fattiest meat you can find. Usually that's around 80/20, meaning 80 percent lean and 20 percent fat.

4. In professional kitchens, most smash burgers are fully smashed in the pan. But I find that it's much easier for home cooks (without griddle tops and special tools) to form flat patties first and then smash them more once they hit the heat of the pan.

5. Keep the meat in the fridge until you're ready to build your burger. It keeps the fat cold so you can smash the burger without losing moisture.

PEEL 'N' EAT SHRIMP WITH "I'D EAT THIS ON A SHOE" BASIL DIPPING MAGIC

Serves 6; about 7 shrimp per serving
Total time: 40 minutes

I have always, always loved shrimp. When I used to visit my grandma in New York, I would gorge myself on amazing shrimp-laden Cantonese takeout until I would get physically ill. If anyone here is a fan of the show *The Good Place*, I'm Eleanor Shellstrop. I would gladly shove shrimp cocktail down my bra for later enjoyment.

These Peel 'n' Eat Shrimp are easy easy easy and inspired by/adapted from my absolute favorite shrimp in all of the land, the shrimp on the menu at Son of a Gun (cue drooling).

I also need to give a special shout-out to my father-in-law, Aaron, who taught me the wonders of cooking seafood in beer, which makes the shrimp sweeter and, though I can't prove it, more tender too.

Now, go on and get messy with your people. It's one of the most fun and delicious ways to bond. Oh, and put out lots of extra paper napkins or cloth napkins or paper towels! Bibs encouraged.

Basil Dipping Magic

4 teaspoons lime juice, plus more to taste

1 cup mayonnaise

¼ cup spicy mustard

2 teaspoons brown sugar

¼ cup finely chopped basil

1½ teaspoons hot sauce (I like Frank's RedHot), plus more to taste

Salt to taste

Shrimp!

2 (12 ounce) cans of a lager, wheat ale, pilsner, or pale ale

4 cups water

4 tablespoons Old Bay seasoning, divided

1 teaspoon salt

1 lemon, cut into quarters

1 bay leaf

2 pounds shell-on jumbo shrimp, rinsed

2 tablespoons coarsely chopped parsley leaves

2 tablespoons lime juice

2 cups ice

3 limes, cut into wedges, for serving

TO MAKE THE BASIL DIPPING MAGIC: In a medium bowl, whisk together 4 teaspoons lime juice, 1 cup mayo, ¼ cup spicy mustard, 2 teaspoons brown sugar, the basil, and 1½ teaspoons hot sauce. Add extra lime and hot sauce and salt to taste. Refrigerate the dip until you're ready to serve.

TO MAKE THE SHRIMP: In a large stockpot, bring 2 cans of beer, 4 cups water, 2 tablespoons Old Bay seasoning, 1 teaspoon salt, the lemon, and 1 bay leaf to a boil over high heat.

While the liquid is becoming flavorful, prep your shrimp. For ideal peel 'n' eat shrimp, devein the shrimp without removing the shell. To do this, take a clean pair of scissors and cut a slit along the top of the shrimp to

recipe continues

1. Take scissors and cut a slit along the top of the shrimp to fully expose the vein

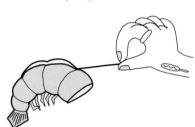

2. Gently remove the vein

3 Leave the rest of the shell intact

fully expose the vein and pull it out, leaving the rest of the shell intact. Look at you go! You're practically a fisherman now.

In a large bowl, whisk together the remaining 2 tablespoons Old Bay, the parsley, and 2 tablespoons lime juice. Set aside.

When all the shrimp are deveined, drop them into the stockpot and reduce the heat to a simmer. Cook until the shrimp are pink and opaque, 3 to 4 minutes.

While the shrimp are cooking, fill another large bowl with 2 cups of ice and add some water. When the shrimp are done, drain and add them to the ice water to stop them from cooking any further. Once they're cool to the touch, after about 1 minute, remove them from the water, transfer them to a bed of paper towels, and pat them dry.

Toss the shrimp in the bowl containing your Old Bay–parsley mixture. Serve with lime wedges and the basil dipping magic.

TIPS + TIMING

1. Feel free to make the shrimp and sauce a day ahead of time and store in separate airtight containers in the fridge. Take the shrimp out of the fridge an hour before dinner, and toss in the lime juice–herb mixture just before serving.
2. Each pound of jumbo shrimp (one of my favorite oxymorons) serves about 3 people at 7 shrimp each.
3. Cooking the shrimp with the shell on helps prevent overcooking and enhances the flavor. If you can't find those with the shell on, you can use peeled and deveined shrimp.
4. If you have frozen shrimp, thaw them in the fridge overnight or, if you need them ASAP, put them all in a colander and run cold water over them until thawed.
5. Take a sip of the beer before you drown your shrimp in it. If you don't like the way it tastes, you won't like it on your shrimp either!

FOOLPROOF LEMON AND FENNEL BRANZINO

Serves 6; each branzino serves 2 people

Total time: 45 minutes

I know the thought of cooking a whole fish can be intimidating, but it's the easiest way to prepare the most tender and delicious fish in town. You can look a fish right in the face and instantly tell how fresh it is. It should have bright, clear eyes and shiny, firm scales. When it's whole, the skin will add flavor and help prevent overcooking, without you having to put in any extra work. Yes, you do have to watch out for bones, but we're all adults here. If you are feeling concerned about deboning before serving, don't worry; we will cover that part on the next page.

Flavored Oil

1½ teaspoons fennel seeds

2 teaspoons salt

1 teaspoon red pepper flakes

10 chives

10 parsley sprigs, firm stems removed

Zest from 1 lemon

8 garlic cloves, peeled

4 green onions, white and green parts, cut in quarters

½ cup extra-virgin olive oil

Branzino

3 (1 to 1½ pounds) branzino, scaled, gutted, and cleaned (ask the fishmonger to do this)

2 teaspoons salt

2 lemons, 1 sliced into thin rounds and 1 cut into wedges

Red pepper flakes, to finish

1 tablespoon thinly sliced chives, to finish

1 teaspoon flaky sea salt, to finish

Make sure there is a rack in the upper middle of the oven. Preheat the broiler to high.

TO MAKE THE FLAVORED OIL: Heat a small skillet over low heat and toast 1½ teaspoons fennel seeds until aromatic, about 2½ minutes. Meanwhile, in a food processor or blender, combine 2 teaspoons salt, 1 teaspoon red pepper flakes, the chives, parsley, zest of 1 lemon, garlic, green onions, and, when they're ready, the fennel seeds. Pulse, scraping the sides down as needed, until the herbs are well-chopped. If the food processor or blender needs liquid to break down the herbs add the oil 1 tablespoon at a time until chopped. Transfer the herb mixture into a bowl and whisk in the remaining olive oil.

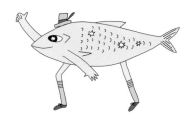

TO MAKE THE BRANZINO: Take the fish out of the fridge 30 minutes before preparing. Grab a large baking sheet. Wash the inside and outside of each fish and pat dry. Drop the fish on the baking sheet. Sprinkle the fish, inside and outside, with 2 teaspoons of salt. Set aside.

Evenly distribute three-quarters of the flavored oil among the fish, coating the outsides and cavities.

Stuff the cavities of the fish with the lemon rounds.

Broil for 5 minutes, until the top side is lightly charred. Reduce the oven heat to 425°F and cook until the meat is opaque and flaky, 15 to 20 minutes. If it's not, you can pop it back in for another minute. If you have a meat thermometer, you're looking for an internal temp of 140°F.

Serve whole, or debone (see page 62), and drizzle with the rest of the flavored oil, extra red pepper flakes, the chopped chives, and flaky sea salt. Serve with the lemon wedges.

recipe continues

TO DEBONE THE FISH: Remove the pin bones from the dorsal and bottom part of the fish by using a spoon to pull the bones away from the fish and a knife to assist.

Use the knife to break the skin where the head and tail meet the meat (heh). Use the spoon and knife to loosen the flesh till you get to the spine of the fish.

Run the knife along the spine of the fish to separate the fillet in half. Slide the top half of the fillet off the top and the bottom half off the bottom.

Place the knife underneath the spine at the tail end to loosen it, lift up carefully, and the entire spine should come loose. The head will also come off—whee! Get rid of any extra visible bones and remove the cooked lemon slices before serving.

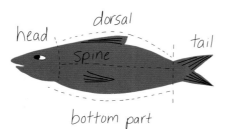

TIPS + TIMING

1. You can prep the fish and leave them in the fridge, uncovered, on the baking sheet for up to 4 hours; let them sit out on the counter for 30 minutes before cooking. The flavored oil can be made a day in advance and stored in an airtight container in the fridge; remove from the fridge an hour before using.
2. Once you get the technique down, you can mix up the flavors as you like. For example, try lime, ginger, and turmeric. Or olives, smoked paprika, and thinly sliced onion.
3. Can't find branzino? Striped bass, red snapper, and rainbow trout are all great substitutes!

GLORIOUS SPICY SAUSAGE PASTA

Serves 6
Total time: 45 minutes

This is a dish that I've been slowly tweaking over time whenever I feel like I have the most random odds and ends in the fridge. It seems like a ragtag group of ingredients, but the sausage, garlic, and blistered tomatoes come together to build an enormously rich and flavorful sauce. It's "pretty, pretty, pretty good," as Larry David (or my dad) would say—which I can assure you is actually very high praise.

Whenever I make pasta, I finish the dish by turning up the heat under the sauce and vigorously stirring in the pasta, with some reserved pasta water, for a few minutes to make sure the noodles and sauce become one. It's a small thing, but it makes a world of difference.

½ cup plus 2 tablespoons extra-virgin olive oil, divided

3 precooked hot Italian sausage links, sliced in half lengthwise, and then cut into ¼-inch half-moons

4 garlic cloves, thinly sliced

1 tablespoon plus ¾ teaspoon salt, divided

2 pints cherry tomatoes (about 50)

1½ pounds spaghetti

2 thick slices of sourdough bread, chopped into pea-size bits

1 tablespoon unsalted butter

6 ounces full-fat fresh mozzarella cheese, cut into ½-inch pieces

⅔ cup coarsely chopped basil leaves

Zest of 1 lemon, to finish

1 teaspoon red pepper flakes, to finish

½ cup grated parmesan cheese, to finish

½ teaspoon black pepper, to finish

In a large, high-sided pan, warm ½ cup olive oil over medium heat. Add the sausages and cook, stirring occasionally, until golden brown and crispy, about 8 minutes. Remove the sausages with a slotted spoon and set aside.

Reduce the heat to low and add the garlic, ½ teaspoon salt, and the 2 pints of tomatoes. Increase the heat to medium and cook, stirring occasionally, until the tomatoes separate from their skins, break open, and start to caramelize, about 20 minutes. Return the sausages to the pan and reduce the heat to a simmer until ready to add the cooked pasta.

Bring a pot of water to a boil and add enough salt to make the water taste like you gulped the ocean, at least 1 tablespoon. (Yes, you should taste it, but don't burn your mouth.) Once boiling, add the pasta and cook to

al dente per the instructions on the box.

Meanwhile, pour 2 tablespoons olive oil into another skillet over medium heat and, once the oil is hot, add the sourdough bread crumbs and ¼ teaspoon salt. Toast until golden, around 4 minutes. Set aside.

Once the pasta is cooked al dente, use tongs to move it from the water right into the sauce. DO NOT THROW OUT THE PASTA WATER. Turn the heat up to medium and stir to help the pasta absorb the sauce. If the pasta is looking dry, add pasta water 2 tablespoons at a time until the pasta is shiny and luxuriously coated with sauce. It. Should. Be. Saucy. Add 1 tablespoon butter, the mozzarella, and chopped basil. Toss to combine and taste. Add extra pasta water if you want it saltier.

recipe continues

To Serve

Family-Style: Serve out of the pan or move to a serving bowl and top with the zest of 1 lemon, 1 teaspoon red pepper flakes, ½ cup parmesan, ½ teaspoon pepper, and the reserved bread crumbs.

Plated: Divide the pasta among bowls, and then divide the toppings upon each serving. If anyone is spice averse, leave the red pepper flakes on the side. You can also leave off the parm and bring a block of it and a cheese grater to the table. Grating cheese and grinding pepper onto everyone's individual portions is a great way to pretend you're at an old-school Italian restaurant and make everyone uncomfortable. Be sure to say, "Say when."

TIPS + TIMING

1. The sauce and bread crumbs can be made up to 2 days in advance. Store the sauce in an airtight container in the fridge and the bread crumbs in an airtight container on the counter. Cook and toss the pasta in the reheated sauce just before serving.
2. Never, ever, for any reason, put your beautiful, perky tomatoes in the fridge. It causes tomato depression, which manifests in loss of flavor, a mealy texture, and general lackluster. Ask your doctor if room temperature tomatoes are right for you.
3. No sourdough? No problem! You can make bread crumbs out of whatever bread you have around—even pitas or bagels!

JUICY KOFTA WITH LEMON CORIANDER YOGURT

Serves 6; makes 12 kofta
Total time: 45 minutes

Kofta is a Middle Eastern and North African staple. In its most basic form, it's ground meat (usually lamb or beef) mixed with spices and onion, though the variations/names for the dish are practically endless. In my adventures abroad, I've had versions cooked slowly in a tagine, fried and stuffed in a pita, grilled and served with rice, and simmered in tomato sauce. So far, I haven't experienced one that I haven't loved.

I find myself making this version of kofta all the time because it's amazingly juicy and tender, easy to prepare, and has a really deep, well-rounded flavor that's so satisfying.

You'll notice that this recipe includes ras el hanout, a Moroccan spice blend. Often, kofta recipes will include a long list of spices, but I prefer using ras el hanout because its spices are already perfectly balanced. Less work, more flavor!

Lemony Coriander Yogurt

1½ cups plain, full-fat (5%) Greek yogurt

¾ cup finely chopped fresh cilantro

¼ cup fresh lemon juice, plus more to taste

1 small garlic clove, minced

2 tablespoons coarsely chopped mint leaves

½ teaspoon salt, plus more to taste

½ teaspoon black pepper

¼ teaspoon ground coriander

Kofta

3 pounds ground meat (80/20 beef and/or lamb)

1 small yellow onion, finely minced

6 garlic cloves, finely minced

6 tablespoons ras el hanout

1½ teaspoons red pepper flakes (optional)

⅓ cup finely chopped dill, plus extra to finish

⅓ cup finely chopped parsley leaves, plus extra to finish

⅓ cup finely chopped mint leaves, plus extra to finish

2 teaspoons salt

Canola oil, for the pans

Flaky sea salt, to finish

1 lemon, cut into wedges, to finish

TO MAKE THE YOGURT SAUCE: In a medium bowl, mix together 1½ cups Greek yogurt, the cilantro, ¼ cup lemon juice, the garlic, mint, ½ teaspoon each of salt and pepper, and ¼ teaspoon coriander. Add extra salt and lemon juice to taste. Pour into a serving bowl and chill in the fridge until the kofta is ready.

TO MAKE THE KOFTA: Make sure that all the herbs, onions, and garlic are chopped really, really fine so that the kofta hold together well. Put the meat in the bottom of a large bowl and add the onion, garlic, 6 tablespoons ras el hanout, 1½ teaspoons red pepper flakes (unless you made your own spice blend that already includes it), herbs (⅓ cup each of dill, parsley, and mint), and 2 teaspoons salt. Use your hands to fully incorporate all the goodness into the meat, but be careful not to squeeze too hard. You want to keep

recipe continues

the mixture loose so the kofta aren't too dense.

Heat two large skillets over medium-high heat.

 These are great cooked on a grill in the summer!

While the skillets are heating, form your kofta by grabbing about ⅓ cup of meat and creating a loosely packed log that's about 1 inch wide and 4 inches long. Repeat until you form all the kofta; you should end up with 12.

Add just enough canola oil into each skillet to lightly coat the bottom. Open all the doors and windows around you and turn on your oven's vent hood! (Unless you're in the mood to set off the smoke detector.) Add the kofta to the skillets, making sure not to crowd them—that's why you have two skillets! (If you have only one skillet and need to cook the kofta in batches, that's fine.)

Cook the kofta until the bottom sides are golden brown and nicely seared, about 2 minutes. Give the meat a quarter turn and sear again, about 2 minutes, then repeat on one more side so most of the kofta has a nice crispy exterior. Transfer to a serving dish, top with flaky sea salt and extra herbs, and serve with lemon wedges on the side.

Tips + Timing

1. Kofta is best hot off the pan (or grill), but the meat mixture can be tightly wrapped in plastic and stored in the fridge up to a day in advance.
2. Ras el hanout, a very popular Moroccan spice mix, translates to "head of the shop." Each storekeeper has their own special blend, so the recipe isn't consistent. It's easy to buy online, or you can make your own by combining 2 teaspoons ground cumin, 2 teaspoons ground coriander, 2 teaspoons paprika, 1 teaspoon ground ginger, 1 teaspoon ground turmeric, 1 teaspoon black pepper, ½ teaspoon red pepper flakes, ½ teaspoon ground cinnamon, ½ teaspoon cayenne, ½ teaspoon ground allspice, ½ teaspoon ground nutmeg, ½ teaspoon ground cardamom, and ½ teaspoon ground cloves.
3. Herbs are much easier to chop when they're dry. So wash and dry them after purchasing, wrap them in a paper towel, and store in a resealable plastic bag in the fridge.

PAN-SEARED SALMON FOR ANY MOOD

Serves 6 to 8
Total time: 30 minutes

Skin-on salmon fillets are my go-to because (1) they're easy to cook without drying out; (2) they're both flaky and buttery; (3) they're easy to find at various price points; and (4) they're packed with built-in flavor, so it takes little effort to throw together a salmon-centered meal. Seriously, this recipe is so straightforward that it's almost embarrassing to write it down.

Depending on your mood, there are three sauces to choose from. If you want simple, choose the lemon and dill. If you're feeling spicy, go pistachio-date salsa verde. And, if you're trying to class up the joint, pick the beurre blanc.

Salmon

2⅔ pounds skin-on salmon, cut into ⅓-pound portions (this makes 8 portions, to account for those who want seconds)

2 teaspoons salt

1 teaspoon pepper

4 tablespoons canola oil or other neutral high-heat oil

Option 1: Lemon-Dill Sauce

1 lemon, cut into wedges

¼ cup finely chopped dill

1 teaspoon flaky sea salt

Option 2: Pistachio-Date Salsa Verde Sauce

½ cup finely chopped parsley leaves

2 teaspoons dried oregano (chopped if the leaves are large)

4 garlic cloves, minced

3 green onions, white and green parts, finely chopped

1 Fresno chile, finely chopped

1 date, pitted and chopped

¼ cup chopped roasted and salted pistachios

2 tablespoons red wine vinegar

1½ tablespoons fresh lemon juice, plus extra to finish

1 teaspoon lemon zest (optional)

½ teaspoon salt, plus extra to finish

½ cup extra-virgin olive oil, plus more to taste

TO COOK THE FISH: Leave the fish out for 30 minutes so that it comes close to room temp. Generously season both sides of all the pieces using 2 teaspoons salt and 1 teaspoon pepper.

Heat a large nonstick or cast-iron skillet over medium-high heat. Once hot, add enough oil to barely coat the bottom of the skillet.

Pat both sides of the fish dry with paper towels and lay the fish, skin side down, in the pan. Do not crowd the skillet—add only as many pieces as you can with a half inch in between on all sides. It's okay to cook the fish in a few rounds or in multiple pans.

When there is visible uniform crisping and browning around the edges of the skin, and the sides of the fish are becoming a lighter color about halfway up after 4 to 5 minutes, give the fish a flip.

Cook for another 2 to 4 minutes to crisp the other side of the fish. If you like a medium-rare fish, opt for 2 minutes. If you like it more well-done, go for 4. If you're an extra-crispy person, go ahead and crisp up the sides too.

If you're concerned about the doneness of your fish, hit the thickest, most central part with a meat thermometer: 120°F is medium-rare, 130°F is medium, and 145°F is well-done. If you don't have a thermometer, you can always use a fork to peek into the middle to see if the fish flakes apart easily and is semiopaque in the middle; if it's still quite firm and raw-looking, continue cooking.

Remove the fish from the skillet and let rest for 5 minutes before serving. Finish with your sauce of choice.

TO MAKE THE SAUCE: Which will you choose?

LEMON-DILL SAUCE (a sensible, quick option, like throwing on sweatpants): Once the salmon is cooked, squeeze 2 lemon wedges all over the fish. Top with the dill and 1 teaspoon flaky sea salt and serve with the rest of the lemon wedges.

PISTACHIO-DATE SALSA VERDE SAUCE (a zesty option, like your favorite colorful, snazzy shirt): In a medium bowl, mix together the parsley, oregano, garlic, green onions, Fresno chile (start with half if you're worried

recipe and ingredients continue

Option 3: Beurre Blanc

½ cup (1 stick) unsalted butter, cold and cut into 1-tablespoon chunks

1 shallot, finely chopped (⅓ cup)

½ teaspoon salt, plus more to finish

⅓ cup dry white wine

1 tablespoon white wine vinegar

2 teaspoons lemon juice

about heat), date, pistachios, 2 tablespoons red wine vinegar, 1½ tablespoons lemon juice, the lemon zest (if using), and ½ teaspoon salt. Whisk in the ½ cup of olive oil. Add extra salt and lemon juice to taste. Serve on top of the salmon or alongside. Feel free to add more oil if you like a thinner sauce.

BEURRE BLANC (a fancy and sophisticated option, like a well-tailored suit): In a small pot over medium-low heat, melt 2 tablespoons butter. Add the shallot and ½ teaspoon salt and cook until soft and translucent, about 6 minutes. Add ⅓ cup wine (into the pot, not into your mouth, but also probably into your mouth) and 1 tablespoon vinegar and bring the heat up to medium. Allow the wine to reduce until there's about 3 tablespoons of thick sauce left, around 10 minutes. Turn off the heat and whisk in the remaining 6 tablespoons butter, 1 tablespoon at a time, whisking until each is fully incorporated before adding the next tablespoon. This technique prevents the sauce from separating. Finish with salt and up to 2 teaspoons of lemon juice, to taste. Serve on top of the salmon or alongside.

TIPS + TIMING

1. The salsa verde can be made up to 3 days in advance. Other sauces and the fish should be made just before serving.

2. Anytime you're cooking at a high heat over a cooktop, make sure you have the fan over your stove on and that any doors and windows close by are open. No one wants a lingering fish smell!

3. The easiest and most cost-effective salmon is Atlantic salmon, known for its low "fishiness" and high fat content. If you're looking for the crème de la crème, keep an eye out for Copper River king salmon when it's in season (May and June).

4. Truth is, pan-frying does cause splattering. To protect your clothes, you may want to wear an apron. If you have a splatter screen (I don't, but lots of smart people do), this is a great opportunity to pull it out of the depths of your junk drawer.

CRISPY-CRISPY TURKEY THIGHS WITH CARAMELIZED ONION JAM

Serves 6

Total time: 1¼ hours +
OVERNIGHT RESTING

This dish is pretty simple—garlicky, roasted turkey thighs crisped to perfection, topped with the sweetest caramelized-onion medley. There are a few tricks to take this humble and comforting dish to the next level.

TRICK 1: Whenever I can, I always salt the turkey and let it sit in the fridge, uncovered, overnight to dry out the skin. Drying the skin helps it crisp in the oven, and the prolonged salting makes it more flavorful.

TRICK 2: You can't rush the onions. The sweetness of the slow-cooked alliums almost mimics what cranberry sauce does for a T-Day turkey, but the process of coaxing out the sugar takes patience. I recommend making the onion mixture a day in advance so you can really take your time. Do it when you know you are home for a couple of hours. It's not labor-intensive, but every few minutes you just want to give the onions a lil' stir. It's simple but the flavor that it brings out in the onions is unreal.

Turkey

1 tablespoon salt

1½ teaspoons garlic powder

1½ teaspoons paprika (not smoked)

5 teaspoons baking powder

6 bone-in, skin-on turkey thighs (5 pounds) or 12 bone-in, skin-on chicken thighs

6 tablespoons (¾ stick) unsalted butter, room temp

1 tablespoon roughly chopped parsley leaves

½ teaspoon red pepper flakes

Caramelized Onion Jam

½ cup olive oil

5 large yellow onions, sliced into thin half-moons

1 large leek, white and greens, sliced into thin half-moons

4 shallots, sliced into thin half-moons

½ teaspoon salt

½ to 1 cup chicken stock

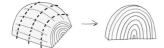

TO PREP THE TURKEY: In a small bowl, combine 1 tablespoon salt, 1½ teaspoons garlic powder, 1½ teaspoons paprika, and 5 teaspoons baking powder. Rub this mixture all over the turkey and set in the fridge on a rimmed baking sheet *overnight* to dry out the skin.

TO MAKE THE CARAMELIZED ONION JAM: In a large, heavy-bottomed pot, heat ½ cup olive oil over medium-low heat. Add in the sliced onions, leeks, shallots, and ½ teaspoon salt and stir to combine. First, the onions will sweat (lose water). Then the liquid will evaporate and they'll slowly start to shrink and caramelize into magical flavor nuggets. Stir regularly until the

onions are jammy and deeply, deeply golden and soft. This process takes much longer than you think, 1 to 1½ hours. Once the onions are fully jammified, add ½ cup chicken stock and cook until the liquid thickens and fully mixes with the onions, leaving you with a gravylike texture, 1 to 3 minutes. If your onions are still very thick, add up to another ½ cup stock.

TO MAKE THE TURKEY: Take the turkey out of the fridge 45 minutes before cooking and preheat the oven to 250°F.

In a small bowl, mix together the 6 tablespoons softened butter with the parsley and ½ teaspoon red

recipe continues

Warning: If your eyes are super-sensitive to onions, grab some tissues and get ready to weep. I made this dish once with my mom and she had to go upstairs for 20 minutes. It was funny but also sad.

Tips + Timing

1. The onions can be made up to 3 days in advance and stored in an airtight container in the fridge. Omit the stock from the first cook of the onions and before serving reheat in a small pot or pan with the stock over low heat, uncovered, stirring occasionally, until warm and jammy, about 5 minutes.

2. If the onions burn at all at the bottom of the pot, just turn off the heat and let them sit for 10 minutes. The steam should help release the burnt parts, then you can proceed!

3. How to wash a leek: Cut the leek in half lengthwise and run each half under cold water. Open the layers with your fingers so the water can get in the hard-to-reach spots.

pepper flakes. Divide the butter evenly among the thighs and tuck it under the skin. To do so, poke a hole under the skin with your finger and slide the butter between the skin and the meat. Apply even pressure with your fingers over the skin to spread the butter.

Put the baking sheet on the middle rack of the oven and roast the turkey for 30 minutes. Then increase the heat to 425°F and roast for another

25 to 30 minutes, or until the skin is crispy and the internal temp is 165°F (great temp for still-tender but fully cooked turkey—if you don't have a meat thermometer, you can pierce a knife into the center of the turkey thigh; the juices that run out should be clear). Let the turkey rest for 10 minutes before serving.

Spread the onion jam on the bottom of a serving platter and top with the turkey thighs.

RIGATONI WITH CONFIT TOMATOES AND BURRATA

Serves 6
Total time: 1½ hours

I am a person who likes to make things easy on myself. If something store-bought tastes just as good as homemade, I buy it. However, there are some things money can't buy . . . like the amped-up flavor of sweet, caramelized tomatoes slowly roasting in a warm bath of olive oil, garlic, and lots of basil. Mmmmmm.

Toss these confit tomato bad boys on some rigatoni and you have got yourself a ding-dang party! While the pasta choice is technically up to you, I strongly suggest a shape that allows for nooks and crannies to get coated in delicious roasty tomatoes.

Confit Tomatoes

6 cups cherry tomatoes

1 cup extra-virgin olive oil

1 teaspoon salt

½ teaspoon black pepper

1 cup loosely packed basil leaves

6 garlic cloves, skin on

Pasta

1 tablespoon salt

1 pound rigatoni or pasta of your choice

½ cup basil leaves

3 balls (12 ounces) of burrata cheese, patted dry with a paper towel

Freshly cracked black pepper

½ cup pesto, homemade (page 127) or store-bought

A small block of parmesan cheese, for grating over the pasta

Flaky sea salt, for the table

Red pepper flakes, for the table

TO MAKE THE CONFIT TOMATOES:
Preheat the oven to 300°F. In a high-sided, 8 x 8-inch baking vessel (it can be anything around this size), mix together the tomatoes, 1 cup olive oil, 1 teaspoon salt, and ½ teaspoon pepper. Tuck the basil and garlic under the tomatoes to make sure they don't get too crispy. For easier transport to and from the oven, set the baking vessel on a rimmed baking sheet. Place the baking vessel in the oven and roast until the oil is bubbling, most of the tomatoes have split or separated from their skins, and they smell fantastic, about 1 hour. (Can anyone out there make me a candle in this scent?) Use tongs to remove the garlic cloves and set aside until cool.

TO MAKE THE PASTA: Fill a stockpot halfway up with water and add 1 tablespoon of salt. Bring to a boil over high heat. Once the water is boiling, add the pasta. Stir it a few times, and cook for the lowest recommended time on the package.

Meanwhile, heat a large, high-sided pan over medium heat. (If you don't have a very large pan, you can also do this in a stockpot.) Transfer the roasted tomato-basil-oil mixture to the pan, and squeeze the garlic cloves out of their skin, mooshing them up a bit in the pan.

Once the pasta is cooked, use a large slotted spoon to lift it directly from the pot, giving it a quick shake to drain the bulk of the water, and add it right into the tomatoes. Stir vigorously until the pasta is evenly coated, and many of the tomatoes are broken open. Cook over medium-high heat for 5 minutes or until the sauce thickens and adheres to the pasta. (If your sauce isn't coating the noodles the way you want, just cook it for a few more minutes. Sometimes it takes a little time to work its magic.) Give the pasta a taste. To make the pasta saltier, add pasta water 2 tablespoons at a time until it's just right.

Tear the ½ cup fresh basil into the pasta just before serving. Top with the burrata, then add a healthy amount of freshly cracked black pepper and a scoop of pesto. Dust the pasta generously with parm, and serve with some flaky salt and red pepper flakes on the table in case anyone wants them.

Tips + Timing

1. You can make the confit tomatoes up to a week in advance and store in an airtight container in the fridge. Boil and prepare the pasta just before serving.
2. Roasting the garlic in its skin helps prevent it from burning.

PERFECT SEARED RIB EYE

Serves 6

Total time: 2 hours (includes an hour of resting for the steak before cooking)

This steak recipe has been traveling through my friend group for years, probably because it's low-stress and tastes professional. I love a rib eye because it's an easy cut of meat to get right; the extra fat ensures lots of flavor, and the thickness makes it harder to overcook and turn into shoe leather. Yes, I know some people like it that way (hi, Mom).

Because I like you a lot, I've given you two sauce options (soptions): Pistachio-Date Salsa Verde Sauce (if you want to live that spicy/herby life) and Bistro Compound Butter (if you want to transport yourself to France).

Just two things to keep in mind . . .

<u>Don't forget to turn on your vent hood</u> and open any available windows and doors before you start searing!

<u>Get yourself a good digital meat thermometer.</u> It's the only way to make sure you get exactly what you want out of a steak. You'll never look back.

Option 1: Pistachio-Date Salsa Verde Sauce (page 71)

Option 2: Bistro Compound Butter

6 tablespoons (¾ stick) European-style salted butter, room temp

1 tablespoon black pepper (freshly ground, if possible)

1 tablespoon finely chopped shallot

2 tablespoons cognac or brandy

1 tablespoon heavy cream

½ teaspoon salt, plus more to taste

Steak

3 pounds (1½-inch-thick) rib eye steaks (see Tip #2)

3 teaspoons salt

1 teaspoon black pepper

½ teaspoon flaky sea salt, to finish

TO MAKE THE PISTACHIO-DATE SALSA VERDE SAUCE: See page 71.

TO MAKE THE BISTRO COMPOUND BUTTER: In a medium bowl, combine 6 tablespoons room temp salted butter, 1 tablespoon black pepper, the shallot, 2 tablespoons cognac (or brandy), 1 tablespoon heavy cream, and ½ teaspoon salt. Whisk vigorously until fully combined (you can also whiz the ingredients together in a food processor). Add extra salt to taste. Lay out a piece of plastic wrap and plop the butter onto the center of it. Use the plastic wrap to roll the butter into a log. Refrigerate for at least 2 hours to harden. If you don't have time to refrigerate it, just serve it whipped at room temp.

TO MAKE THE STEAK: Pull the steaks out of the fridge one hour before cooking. Pat dry with paper towels and rub in the 3 teaspoons salt evenly on all sides (if you didn't already salt them to age in the fridge as recommended in the tip). On one side of each steak evenly distribute the teaspoon of black pepper.

Heat a large cast-iron skillet or a large stainless-steel pan over medium-high heat until it's screaming hot, about 5 minutes.

Pat the steaks dry again and lay them in the skillet, making sure none are touching. (You may need to do this in two rounds depending on the size of your skillet.)

recipe continues

Cook, pepper side down, undisturbed, until you can see each steak is forming a nice golden brown crust all around the edges, 3 to 5 minutes. Flip with tongs and repeat. The steaks should lift off the pan to flip easily; if not, give them another minute. Use tongs to hold the steaks up on their sides to sear all the edges until golden, about 30 seconds per side. Use a meat thermometer to check for doneness. Ideally, you want 120°F for a delicious, juicy, medium-rare steak. For a more well-done steak look for 135°F.

Rest the steaks on a cutting board for 10 minutes before slicing. Cut against the grain at a 45-degree angle in ½-inch slices. Top with the sauce of your choice and ½ teaspoon of flaky sea salt.

TIPS + TIMING

1. The sauces can both be made a day in advance and stored in airtight containers in the fridge; in fact, they're better that way! Cook the steaks just before serving.
2. If you happen to buy your meat 24 hours in advance, pat the steaks dry, generously sprinkle them with the 3 teaspoons salt, and set on a cooling rack over a rimmed baking sheet. Refrigerate uncovered, overnight, then cook as described. This is the most foolproof method for a flavorful steak with an excellent sear.
3. When selecting rib eye, you want nice, thick steaks with even marbling. I prefer them without a bone to make life easier as well.

VEGGIE POT PIE WITH PARM AND BLACK PEPPER PHYLLO

Serves 6 to 8; makes one 9 x 13-inch pie

Total time: 2 hours + OVERNIGHT THAWING for the phyllo

So, I have a confession. I'm allergic to chicken. You may have noticed that there are no chicken recipes in this book—well, now you know why. Weird, right? I always crave chicken pot pie, though, and for years I thought the days of a creamy, savory, satisfying pot pie were ancient history . . . until I started playing with this recipe.

I love serving this style of food at a dinner party, something that you can just place in the middle of the table and let everyone scoop out what they want. ☺ It's my favorite vibe, fresh and modern but also nostalgic. Using phyllo dough makes putting it together a breeze.

Filling

4 tablespoons (½ stick) unsalted butter

1 small onion, diced into ½-inch pieces (about 1 cup)

2 teaspoons salt, divided, plus more to taste

8 ounces button mushrooms, dirt brushed off and diced into ½-inch-thick chunks (3 cups)

2 tablespoons extra-virgin olive oil

3 garlic cloves, minced

1 celery stalk, cut into ½-inch pieces

3 large carrots, diced into ½-inch pieces (about 2 cups)

1 medium russet potato, peeled and diced into ½-inch cubes (about 2 cups)

½ teaspoon black pepper, plus more to taste

½ cup dry white wine

¼ cup all-purpose flour

2 cups whole milk

1 cup vegetable stock, homemade (page 132) or store-bought

1 teaspoon Dijon mustard

1 bay leaf

1 teaspoon coarsely chopped thyme leaves

¼ cup coarsely chopped parsley leaves

½ cup grated parmesan cheese

1 tablespoon fresh lemon juice

1 cup frozen peas, thawed

Phyllo

10 sheets of phyllo dough (about ½ pound), thawed

½ cup (1 stick) salted butter, melted

3 tablespoons grated parmesan cheese

2 teaspoons freshly cracked black pepper

¼ teaspoon flaky sea salt

TO MAKE THE FILLING: In a large pot over medium heat, melt 4 tablespoons butter. Add the onion and ½ teaspoon salt. Cook, stirring occasionally, until translucent, about 5 minutes. Add the chopped mushrooms and another ½ teaspoon salt and cook until the mushroom liquid has evaporated and the mushrooms have shrunk down, about 15 minutes. They should have a really delicious, buttery, nutty smell. Add

2 tablespoons oil and then toss in the garlic, celery, carrots, potato, 1 teaspoon salt, and ½ teaspoon pepper. Cook until the carrots begin to soften, about 5 minutes. Add ½ cup wine and simmer until reduced by at least half, 5 to 10 minutes.

Mix in ¼ cup flour and cook, stirring regularly, for 2 minutes. (This will eliminate any floury flavor.) Add the 2 cups milk ¼ cup at a time, fully incorporating each addition into the vegetables before adding the next to make a smooth, creamy sauce. Don't panic; the sauce will thicken before it thins out. Add 1 cup vegetable stock, 1 teaspoon Dijon mustard, the bay leaf, thyme, parsley, ½ cup parmesan, 1 tablespoon lemon juice, and 1 cup peas.

Preheat the oven to 375°F.

Reduce the heat to medium-low and allow the filling to simmer, uncovered, for 20 minutes. Season to taste.

TO MAKE THE PHYLLO: While the filling is simmering and the oven is

recipe continues

preheating, start working on the phyllo crust. Begin with a clean, dry work surface. Unroll the thawed phyllo and lay one piece flat on the counter. Using a pastry brush, brush the phyllo dough with a thin layer of melted butter and sprinkle with a little grated parmesan. Cover with another sheet of phyllo, rotating the sheet slightly clockwise so that the corners don't overlap. Brush it with more butter and a sprinkling of pepper. Repeat the process, alternating the parm and pepper, turning each sheet counterclockwise or clockwise to build up the layers until you've layered all ten sheets.

To assemble the pot pie, remove the filling from the heat and carefully pour it into a 9 x 13-inch baking dish (discarding the bay leaf). Gently lift the stack of phyllo dough and lay it over the filling, folding and tucking the excess around the edges. If you have any extra melted butter, brush it along the edges. Cut a few slits in the middle of the phyllo and sprinkle flaky salt on top. Bake until the top is golden brown, 18 to 20 minutes. Let the pot pie cool for 10 minutes before serving.

TIPS + TIMING

1. You can make the filling a day in advance. Put it in the baking dish and cover tightly with plastic wrap and refrigerate. When you're ready to assemble the pie the following day, remove the filling from the fridge and set out for an hour, then cover it with phyllo and bake.
2. Be sure to follow thawing instructions on the phyllo dough box. It's usually suggested that you thaw overnight in the refrigerator and then rest at room temperature for 2 hours before using.
3. Using homemade stock in this recipe really takes it to the next level, but you only need a small amount. So maybe you should also make a soup, like Tart Apple Butternut Squash Soup (page 30) or Hot Dog Soup (but Really Sausage) (page 14), in the same week to use up the rest of the stock, or you can freeze it for future use.
4. All the veggies should be chopped roughly the same size so they cook uniformly and look snazzy.

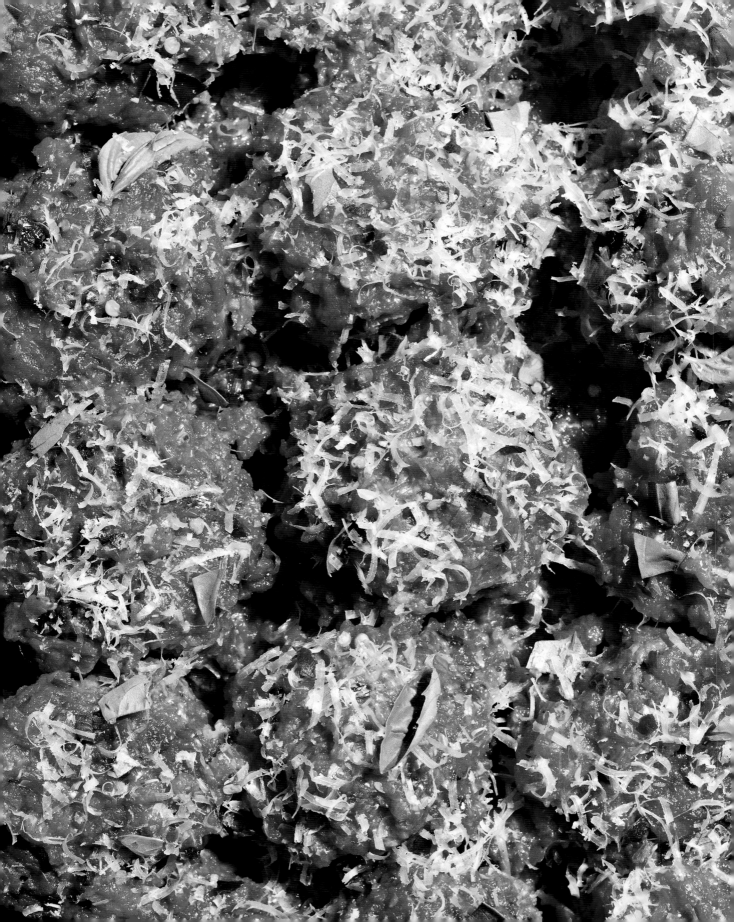

YOUR NEW FAVORITE HERBY MEATBALLS

Serves 6; makes 18 to 20 meatballs

Total time: 1 hour 30 minutes

These are insanely moist (can I use that word?), easy to master, and completely and totally jam-packed with deliciously aromatic herbs. Every year someone asks me to make these for them on their birthday, they're that scrumptious. You'll never go back to your old meatball recipe again. I like to enjoy these over pasta of some sort, but they're also great with brown rice and lots of veggies, spaghetti squash, or as an epic meatball sub.

½ cup extra-virgin olive oil, divided, plus more as needed

½ large yellow onion, roughly chopped (1¼ cups)

1¾ teaspoons salt, divided, plus more to taste

6 large garlic cloves, chopped

3 medium carrots, chopped into ½-inch chunks (1¼ cups)

½ teaspoon black pepper

½ cup basil leaves, packed, plus extra to finish

½ cup parsley leaves, packed

½ cup grated parmesan cheese, plus extra to finish

5 cups cubed sourdough bread (cut into 1-inch pieces)

2 pounds ground beef (80/20 fat or fattier)*

½ pound ground pork*

2 (24 ounce) jars of store-bought arrabiata sauce; marinara also works (I like Rao's)

Red pepper flakes, to finish

*For Turkey Meatballs: Swap out the beef and pork for 2½ pounds of ground turkey and add 3 eggs.

Preheat the oven to 400°F.

Warm ¼ cup olive oil in a large Dutch oven over medium heat. Once the oil is warm, toss in the onion and ½ teaspoon salt. Cook for 3 to 4 minutes, stirring regularly, until the onion is translucent and aromatic.

Add in the garlic, carrots, another ½ teaspoon salt, and ½ teaspoon pepper. Sauté for 5 minutes, until the onion is soft.

Transfer the onion mixture into a food processor and pulse until it forms a coarse paste. Add ½ cup basil and ½ cup parsley and pulse a few more times. Throw in ½ cup parmesan and 5 cups bread cubes and process again until the mixture is dense and uniform in texture.

Transfer the bread/onion deliciousness to a large bowl and add 2 pounds beef, ½ pound pork, and ¾ teaspoon salt; mix with your hands but please beware of overmixing, as it'll ruin the texture. You'll know it's well-mixed once the bread/herb mixture is evenly dispersed into the meat. As soon as it looks evenly distributed, stop mixing! Before forming all the meatballs, you may want to take a little bit of the meat and sear it in a pan until cooked to

make sure you're happy with the seasoning. Add more salt if needed.

Use your hands to gently form the meatballs, sized somewhere between a golf ball and a tennis ball (around 2.5 ounces per meatball). As each meatball is formed, set it on a baking sheet or a plate.

Once all the meatballs are formed, heat the largest nonstick pan (or pans) you have over medium; add the remaining ¼ cup olive oil.

When the oil is warm, add in the meatballs. Don't overcrowd them—leave at least 1 inch between each one. This will require doing the meatballs in a few batches and adding more oil as needed.

Cook for 5 to 6 minutes, until the bottom of each meatball is lightly seared and golden brown. Rotate and repeat with 2 more sides of each meatball (it'll look more triangular than circular). Use a metal spatula to release them from the bottom of the pan. Once the meatballs are seared, move them into the Dutch oven and continue until all are browned.

Pour both jars of sauce over the meatballs in the Dutch oven.

recipe continues

(If you want to serve the meatballs with pasta, now is a good time to start boiling heavily salted water for the pasta and cooking per the instructions on the box.)

Transfer the pot to the oven and bake, uncovered, for 20 to 30 minutes, until the internal temp of the meatballs is 155°F. If you don't have a meat thermometer, you can take a meatball out and cut it open. If it still has a reddish hue in the center, continue cooking them for a few more minutes.

TO SERVE WITH PASTA: Remove all the meatballs from the sauce with tongs. Set the Dutch oven over medium-high heat and, once the sauce is simmering, use a slotted spoon to move the cooked pasta from the pasta water into the Dutch oven. Cook for 5 minutes to fully coat the pasta, adding more pasta water to increase saltiness or to make more sauce. To serve, either plate each portion with pasta and add the meatballs on top (finished with red pepper flakes, basil, and grated parm) or serve family-style by adding the meatballs back into the Dutch oven and finishing the entire pot with red pepper flakes, basil, and grated parm.

TO SERVE WITH SIDES: Sprinkle the meatballs in the Dutch oven with red pepper flakes, basil, and lots of grated parm and serve family-style.

TIMING

Meatballs can be fully made up to 2 days in advance. Reheat them in the sauce in a large baking dish covered loosely with tinfoil at 425°F until hot, about 20 minutes. Alt: you can prep the meatball mixture up to 6 hours in advance, cover in plastic wrap, and refrigerate before forming and cooking.

These dishes are meant to be delicious served at just about any temp, so if you're new to dinner partying and worried about timing, lean into the sides and forget about a main. More sides = more variety. And everyone loves variety!

A SIMPLE BISTRO SALAD

Serves 6
Total time: 10 minutes

Sometimes a simple salad is the best salad. The trick here is to dress the lettuce first, put it in the serving bowl, and then dress the vegetables (with a little extra pepper) and place them on top of the lettuce. This ensures that each bite is coated in the correct amount of dressing, *and* you don't have to go fish through the salad for non-leafy items. Although this recipe iteration is all about super-peppery cucumbers, shallots, and radishes, you can select your own vegetables. (Just don't pick more than two or three. Keep it simple.)

One quick general salad note: Dressing is always a great thing to prep first because it gets better as it sits, and then you won't be scrambling right before dinner.

Dressing

1 small shallot, minced

¼ cup red wine vinegar

½ teaspoon salt, plus more to taste

1½ teaspoons honey, plus more to taste

½ cup extra-virgin olive oil

Salad

2 heads of romaine, green leaf, or butter lettuce, washed and cut into 2-inch strips

¼ cup coarsely chopped parsley leaves

¼ teaspoon salt

¼ teaspoon black pepper, plus extra freshly cracked pepper to finish

1 English cucumber, cut into ½-inch cubes

5 radishes, thinly sliced

TO MAKE THE DRESSING: Combine the shallot, ¼ cup red wine vinegar, ½ teaspoon salt, 1½ teaspoons honey, and ½ cup olive oil in a jar with a tight-fitting lid and shake it like crazy to emulsify.

Add extra salt and honey to taste.

TO MAKE THE SALAD: Add the lettuce, parsley, ¼ teaspoon salt, and ¼ teaspoon pepper into a large mixing bowl. Just before serving add 3 tablespoons dressing and mix to coat. Taste and add more dressing until you're happy with the flavor. Transfer the greens to a serving bowl.

Toss the cucumber and radishes in the mixing bowl with a tablespoon of dressing and a LOT of extra freshly cracked pepper. Place the dressed cucumbers and radishes on top of your greens. Voilà! Salad!

TIPS

1. Really mince those shallots—it improves the texture and flavor of the dressing!
2. If your lettuce is wet, the dressing won't adhere, creating a pool of excess water and dressing at the bottom of your bowl (yuck) rather than crispy, evenly coated leaves. So grab a salad spinner, or kitchen towels, and dry that lettuce.
3. **WHAT ON EARTH IS EMULSIFIED?** Often, liquids that are water-based and liquids that are fat-based don't get along. If they had their way, they wouldn't hang out at all. When making a dressing, you really want the two to combine so that you end up with a thick dressing that doesn't separate when left alone. In order to do this, you can vigorously shake the two together to combine.

TIMING

The dressing can be made up to 3 days in advance and stored in a
jar in the fridge; shake vigorously before using. Wash, prepare,
and store all the salad ingredients up to a day in advance.
Store the cut lettuce in dry kitchen towels in resealable
plastic bags in the fridge. Put the cut cucumbers and radishes
in an airtight container with a wet paper towel on top to keep
them from drying out. Chop the parsley and assemble and dress
the salad just before serving.

THAT SALAD WITH THE HERBY DRESSING
(a.k.a. A CHOPPED SALAD)

Serves 6
Total time: 20 minutes

When asking friends what recipes they thought I should add to this book, an embarrassingly large number of them said, "OH, THAT SALAD WITH THE HERBY DRESSING." It made me chuckle because (1) it begged the question "Do I make this salad way too often?!?" and (2) I always thought people were into it for all the crunchy fun treats buried within, not the dressing. But the crowd has spoken!

So here it is: "That salad with the herby dressing." I hope you'll love it as much as my friends and I do. And, if you feel like getting brownie points, double up the dressing so someone can take the extra home.

Dressing

¼ cup red wine vinegar

2 tablespoons fresh lemon juice, plus more to taste

1 garlic clove, minced

1 teaspoon mayo

½ teaspoon dried oregano

½ teaspoon salt, plus more to taste

¼ teaspoon black pepper, plus more to taste

½ cup extra-virgin olive oil

¼ cup finely chopped fresh herbs (I like parsley, chives, and basil)

Salad

2 heads of iceberg lettuce, chopped into ¼-inch slices

½ teaspoon salt

½ teaspoon black pepper

1 teaspoon dried oregano, divided

¼ cup olives of your choosing, halved and pitted

2 Persian cucumbers, cut into ½-inch cubes

1 pint cherry tomatoes (about 20), quartered

1 (15.5 ounce) can of chickpeas, drained and rinsed

1 (8 ounce) tub of ciliegine mozzarella cheese, strained and quartered

¼ red onion, thinly sliced, soaked in cold water for 10 minutes

½ cup shaved parmesan cheese

TO MAKE THE DRESSING: Combine ¼ cup red wine vinegar, 2 tablespoons lemon juice, the minced garlic, 1 teaspoon mayo, ½ teaspoon dried oregano, ½ teaspoon salt, ¼ teaspoon pepper, and ½ cup olive oil in a jar with a tight-fitting lid and shake it like crazy to emulsify.

Add extra salt, pepper, and lemon juice to taste. (Dressing always tastes better after it's settled for a bit so, if you can, make it at least 30 minutes before serving.)

TO MAKE THE SALAD: Be sure all the vegetables are chopped. Just before serving, put the cut-up lettuce in a large mixing bowl and toss with

recipe continues

TIMING

Dressing can be made up to 3 days in advance and stored in a jar in the fridge. Wash, prepare, and store all the salad ingredients (except the tomatoes) up to a day in advance. Store the chopped lettuce in dry kitchen towels in resealable plastic bags in the fridge. Put the cut veggies in an airtight container with a wet paper towel inside to keep them from drying out. Cut the tomatoes and assemble and dress the salad just before serving.

½ teaspoon salt, ½ teaspoon pepper, and ½ teaspoon oregano. Add 3 tablespoons dressing and toss to coat. Taste and add more dressing as you like. Transfer the lettuce into a serving bowl.

In the same mixing bowl, toss the olives, cucumbers, tomatoes, and chickpeas with another ½ teaspoon oregano and 1 tablespoon dressing. Put the dressed veggies over the lettuce, then top the salad with the mozzarella, thinly sliced red onion, and ½ cup shaved parmesan.

TIPS

1. The onions are soaked in cold water before serving. Why? Soaking helps disperse the sulfur compounds in the onion, leaving you with a perfectly crisp, not-too-biting onion slice.
2. The mayo helps bind the dressing and keep it emulsified. You can omit it or use Vegenaise if you prefer.
3. If you can't find Persian cucumbers, you can use any cucumber! I prefer the smaller cucumbers as they usually have a crisper flesh and fewer seeds.

CAROLE KING SALAD

Serves 6
Total time: 15 minutes

I LOVE SALAD. It's good to have a salad that can be tailored to work for the entire year—one dressing, four different salads to suit whatever season it is.

When I was working on this recipe, I could not focus because all I could hear in my head was Carole King singing, "Winter, spring, summer, or fallllll . . ." Iconic. [I know someone out there is going to get all angry that I attribute the song to Carole and not James Taylor, but (1) she wrote the song, and (2) *Tapestry* is one of the best albums ever written. If you wanna fight about it, you can find me on the internet.]

Dressing

3 tablespoons fresh lemon juice, plus more to taste

1 tablespoon Dijon mustard

2 garlic cloves, minced

1 teaspoon salt, plus more to taste

¼ teaspoon black pepper

1 tablespoon honey

2 tablespoons white wine vinegar

½ cup extra-virgin olive oil

Salad (choose one)

Winter:

10 ounces baby arugula (about 10 cups)

½ teaspoon salt, plus more to taste

¼ teaspoon black pepper, plus more to taste

2 crisp pears, thinly sliced

1 cup chopped candied pecans, homemade (page 135) or store-bought

½ cup shaved aged Gouda cheese

2 tablespoons finely chopped chives

Spring:

2 large heads of green leaf lettuce, roughly chopped (about 10 cups)

½ teaspoon salt, plus more to taste

¼ teaspoon black pepper, plus more to taste

2 ripe Hass avocados, skins and pits removed, chopped

2 cups snap peas, strings removed, thinly sliced

1 bunch of radishes, halved and thinly sliced

½ cup crumbled chèvre (or serve with a crusty bread and lots of soft salted butter)

¼ cup coarsely chopped dill

Summer:

2 large heads of butter lettuce, roughly chopped (about 10 cups)

½ teaspoon salt, plus more to taste

¼ teaspoon black pepper, plus more to taste

2 ripe, juicy peaches or nectarines, pits removed and thinly sliced

2 large ripe tomatoes, chopped into ½-inch pieces

½ cup shaved aged parmesan cheese

¼ cup coarsely chopped basil

Fall:

2 large heads of green leaf lettuce, roughly chopped (about 10 cups)

½ teaspoon salt, plus more to taste

¼ teaspoon black pepper, plus more to taste

1 fennel bulb, sliced paper-thin

2 carrots, peeled into strips

¼ red onion, thinly sliced, soaked in cold water for 10 minutes

⅔ cup chopped roasted and salted almonds

1 (4 ounce) ball of burrata cheese or fresh mozzarella cheese

½ cup coarsely chopped parsley leaves

← Make a small slit at the top of the snap pea and pull; flip the pea and repeat to remove the string from side two

recipe continues

"You just call out my name..."

TO MAKE THE DRESSING: Combine the 3 tablespoons lemon juice, 1 tablespoon Dijon mustard, the garlic, 1 teaspoon salt, ¼ teaspoon pepper, 1 tablespoon honey, 2 tablespoons white wine vinegar, and ½ cup olive oil in a jar with a tight-fitting lid and shake it like crazy to emulsify.

Add extra salt and lemon juice to taste.

TO MAKE EACH SALAD: In a large serving bowl, toss the greens with ½ teaspoon salt and ¼ teaspoon pepper. Add all of the additional salad ingredients except the nuts, cheese, and herbs (when applicable) and toss with 3 tablespoons of the dressing. Taste a leaf and add extra dressing and salt and pepper to taste. Once you're happy, top the greens with the nuts, cheese, and herbs (again, when applicable).

TIPS + TIMING

1. The dressing can be made up to 3 days in advance and stored in a jar in the fridge; shake vigorously before using. Wash, prepare, and store all refrigerated salad ingredients up to a day in advance. Store the lettuce in dry kitchen towels in resealable plastic bags in the fridge. Put cut veggies in an airtight container with a wet paper towel on top to keep them from drying out. Chop countertop produce (tomatoes, pears, avocados, peaches, etc.) and assemble and dress the salad just before serving.
2. When tasting the salad dressing before adding more seasoning, make sure to try it on the green that is going to be in the salad, since the greens will impart their own flavor.
3. Be sure your herbs are super-dry before cutting them for the salad. They'll stay fresh and flavorful much longer!

ROASTED CARROT BABIES

Serves 6
Total time: 45 minutes

I like a cooked carrot that's cut nice and small, hence, "carrot babies." Often at restaurants, I find I'm irrationally irritated when I'm presented with carrot chunks so large I have to either shove a 3-inch piece into my mouth or cut it with a knife. A knife and a carrot should never have to meet again once the carrot has been cooked. Don't be fooled by prepackaged "baby" carrots. They're old, misshapen carrots cut into small pieces parading as something special. (Why do I have so many feelings about carrots? It must be misplaced anger. Anyway . . .)

These carrots have a nice balsamic glaze to bring out the natural sweetness, and the leftovers are great thrown on a salad the next day.

2½ pounds carrots, peeled and cut on the bias in ½-inch pieces (7 cups)

3 tablespoons extra-virgin olive oil

1 tablespoon plus 1 teaspoon balsamic vinegar, divided

1½ teaspoons garlic powder

1 teaspoon salt, plus more to taste

½ teaspoon black pepper

¾ teaspoon finely chopped rosemary leaves, to finish

2½ tablespoons coarsely chopped parsley leaves, to finish

1 tablespoon unsalted butter, to finish

Preheat the oven to 375°F.

In a large bowl, toss the carrots with 3 tablespoons olive oil, 1 tablespoon balsamic vinegar, 1½ teaspoons garlic powder, 1 teaspoon salt, and ½ teaspoon pepper to evenly coat. Spread the carrots onto a large baking sheet. If they are at all crowded, divide them onto two baking sheets.

Roast until slightly blistered and you can poke a knife through one without too much effort, usually 25 to 30 minutes, turning once after 15 minutes. While still hot, toss the carrots with the rosemary, parsley, 1 teaspoon balsamic, and 1 tablespoon butter to gloss them up. Add extra salt to taste.

Tips + Timing

1. You can roast the carrots a day or two in advance, without adding the herbs, balsamic, and butter at the end, and store in an airtight container in the fridge. Rewarm them in a large pan over medium-high heat with a tablespoon of butter. Add the rosemary, parsley, and balsamic just before serving.
2. Your roasted carrots will only taste as good as the carrots you start with. Firm, plump carrots that are smooth and vibrant orange are a good start. If they have tops, make sure that the leaves are bright green.

SOUR CREAM MASHED POTATOES

Serves 6 to 8
Total time: 45 minutes

A classic mashed potato is hard to beat. In the past, I've added a zillion ingredients/potato varieties to mix it up, but I always come back to a basic smooshed russet potato with the essentials: cream (for liquid and substance), butter (for its luxurious texture), sour cream (for a little bit of tang), and garlic powder (for a very-well-distributed hint of garlic flavor). Sometimes, things are classic for a reason.

5 pounds russet potatoes (about 5 large potatoes), peeled and cut into 1-inch chunks

1 tablespoon salt, plus more to taste

1¼ cups heavy cream

5 tablespoons unsalted butter

1 cup full-fat sour cream

1 teaspoon garlic powder

½ teaspoon black pepper

¼ cup finely chopped chives, for serving

Put the cubed potatoes into a large stockpot and cover with cold water. Add 1 tablespoon salt and bring the water to a boil. Boil until the potatoes are fork tender, 15 to 20 minutes. Strain the potatoes in a colander over the sink.

In the (now-empty) stockpot, place 1¼ cups heavy cream and 5 tablespoons butter. Cook over low heat until the butter is melted and the cream is warm. Return the potatoes to the pot along with 1 cup sour cream, 1 teaspoon garlic powder, and ½ teaspoon pepper. Mash (using a potato masher, or a sturdy whisk, or a large fork) until *mostly* smooth and creamy (I like a few potato nuggets left for texture). Add extra salt to taste. Serve topped with the chives.

TIPS + TIMING

1. Make up to 3 days in advance and store in an airtight container in the fridge. To reheat, put the potatoes in a large stockpot over medium heat and cook, covered, until warm, about 15 minutes, stirring every minute or so to avoid burning/sticking. If the potatoes feel too stiff once reheated, add a dollop of sour cream and another few tablespoons of cream.
2. I tend to like a mashed potato that still has a ton of texture, but if you're a really creamy, puréed kinda person, you'll want to double up on the butter and add more cream until you reach the mashed potato creaminess of your dreams.

SUPER-CRUNCHY GREEN SALAD

Serves 6
Total time: 10 minutes

I like this salad a lot because it's incredibly bright and can really round out a meal, but it's also easy to throw together and fun to riff on. If you want to add other crunchy vegetables, or swap out the herbs, go for it.

If you're looking for a really simple meal, just add a grilled protein and call it a day!

Dressing

½ teaspoon lemon zest

1 tablespoon fresh lemon juice, plus more to taste

1 tablespoon red wine vinegar

¼ teaspoon salt, plus more to taste

¼ teaspoon black pepper

2 tablespoons extra-virgin olive oil

2 tablespoons coarsely chopped dill

2 tablespoons coarsely chopped parsley leaves

Salad

4 Persian cucumbers, peeled, halved lengthwise, and cut into ½-inch pieces (about 2 cups)

2 ripe Hass avocados, skins and pits removed, cut into 1-inch chunks

2 cups thinly sliced green cabbage

1 head of butter lettuce, cut into ½-inch strips

½ teaspoon salt, plus more to taste

¼ teaspoon black pepper

Whatever is left over from the herbs above, coarsely chopped, to finish

TO MAKE THE DRESSING: Combine ½ teaspoon lemon zest, 1 tablespoon lemon juice, 1 tablespoon red wine vinegar, ¼ teaspoon salt, ¼ teaspoon pepper, and 2 tablespoons olive oil in a jar with a tight-fitting lid and shake it like crazy to emulsify. Add the dill and parsley and shake again.

TO MAKE THE SALAD: In a large serving bowl, combine the cucumbers, avocados, cabbage, and lettuce and toss with ½ teaspoon salt and ¼ teaspoon pepper.

Pour the dressing over the veggies and mix just to combine. Add salt to taste. Serve with extra herbs on top.

TIPS + TIMING

1. The dressing can be made up to 3 days in advance. Wash, prepare, and store all salad ingredients (except for the avocados) up to a day in advance. Store the lettuce in dry kitchen towels in resealable plastic bags in the fridge. Put the cut veggies in an airtight container with a wet paper towel on top to keep them from drying out. Assemble the salad with the cut avocados just before serving.
2. See avocado tip on page 165.
3. If you can't find Persian cucumbers, you can use any cucumber! I prefer smaller cucumbers as they usually have a crisper flesh and fewer seeds.

ANDY-APPROVED KALE SALAD

Serves 6
Total time: 20 minutes

Though I'm a lover of just about any vegetable, my husband/roommate has a strong aversion to kale. When I asked Andy to test a bunch of kale salads side by side, he was VERY disgruntled. But when he tried this kale salad, he actually made an audible "yum" sound. It was almost disturbing—I thought perhaps he had been body-snatched. But, it turned out, I had just cracked the code on a kale salad.

Kale salads are great for entertaining a large group because they can sit dressed much longer than any other salad, and often get better as the dressing is really absorbed by the kale.

Love this salad and want to mix it up? Swap out the pecorino and avocado for chopped roasted almonds, a thinly sliced crisp apple, and small cubes of aged cheddar.

Dressing

2 garlic cloves, minced

2 tablespoons fresh lemon juice, plus more to taste

½ cup Veganaise (or mayo)

1 teaspoon salt

½ teaspoon black pepper

2 tablespoons extra-virgin olive oil

Salad

2 bunches (about 2 pounds) of curly kale, ribs removed, cut into ¼ inch strips

¼ teaspoon salt

¼ teaspoon black pepper, plus extra to finish

1 ripe Hass avocado, skin and pit removed, cut into chunks

½ cup grated pecorino romano cheese

TO MAKE THE DRESSING: In a small bowl, whisk together the garlic, 2 tablespoons lemon juice, ½ cup Vegenaise (or regular mayo), 1 teaspoon salt, ½ teaspoon black pepper, and 2 tablespoons olive oil. Taste the dressing on a piece of kale and add extra lemon juice, if desired.

TO MAKE THE SALAD: Dump the kale into a large serving bowl, sprinkle with ¼ teaspoon each salt and pepper, and toss. Deep tissue massage *half* the dressing into the kale with your hands for a full minute to really break down the kale and make it tasty. Taste a leaf and keep adding dressing until you're happy with the flavor. Add the avocado and gently toss to evenly distribute. Top with ½ cup grated pecorino and extra black pepper.

Tips + Timing

1. Make the dressing up to 2 days in advance and store in a jar in the fridge. Wash, dry, and store chopped kale wrapped in a dry kitchen towel in a resealable bag up to a day in advance. Assemble the salad just before serving.
2. The easiest way to remove the rib of the kale is to tear slits at the bottom of the leaf and hold the base of the stem with one hand and tightly grab the bottom of the leafy part with the other. Push the leaf up-stem to separate.
3. There are many types of kale to choose from. I recommend curly kale because I like how it holds on to the dressing, and the flavor is mild. However, if you can't find it, opt for dinosaur (lacinato) kale.
4. Make sure you buy fresh kale. Before putting it in your cart, look around real fast and, when no one is looking, sniff that kale. If it has a fresh, earthy smell, you're good to go. If it smells at all like a hard-boiled egg, don't buy it. If you get caught sniffing kale, you can blame it on me.

1 Tear slit in bottom of leaf by stem   2 Push up against leaf to separate

FLUFFY EVERYTHING PITA CLOUDS

Makes 10 pitas

Total time: 3 hours (including 2 hours 20 minutes hands-off rising time for the dough)

Pita is my favorite bread object to make at home. It's not complicated and it's just 100,000,000 times better than anything you'll buy at any store. This combination of mainly bread flour with the addition of a second, less-glutinous flour is my favorite, but feel free to use all bread flour if that's what you've got! The recipe does also work with regular all-purpose flour, but the texture will be less like dancing on a pillowy cloud.

This pita recipe gets a little flair with the addition of some EBS (everything bagel seasoning) sprinkled on at the end, but if you want to go classic that's A-OK! If you'd like to serve it with a comforting coconut butter, this recipe's got you covered. Chef's choice!

Pitas

1 package (2¼ teaspoons) of instant yeast

1 tablespoon sugar

1 tablespoon honey

2 cups warm water, divided

3½ cups (420 grams) bread flour, plus ¾ cup extra for the work surface and for shaping

½ cup (113 grams) whole wheat flour

2 tablespoons extra-virgin olive oil

1 tablespoon salt

Everything Bagel Seasoning (optional)

2 teaspoons sesame seeds

2 teaspoons dehydrated onion

1 teaspoon poppy seeds

1 teaspoon flaky sea salt

Coconut Butter (optional)

2 cups unsweetened coconut flakes

2 tablespoons unrefined coconut oil, or more as needed

⅛ teaspoon salt

2 teaspoons honey (optional)

TO MAKE THE PITAS: Cut ten 6½-inch squares of parchment and set them aside.

In a large bowl, combine 2¼ teaspoons yeast, 1 tablespoon each sugar and honey, and 1 cup warm water. Let sit until the yeast starts bubbling, 5 minutes. Stir with a wooden spoon. If the yeast doesn't bubble, it's dead—you'll need new yeast.

Add 3½ cups bread flour and ½ cup whole wheat flour to the bowl with the yeast. Mix with a wooden spoon just to combine. Whisk together the final cup water with 2 tablespoons olive oil and add to the bowl. Stir just to incorporate. Sprinkle in 1 tablespoon salt and mix and fold vigorously for a full minute with the spoon until the mixture forms a wet, shaggy dough. (It will seem really dry at first, but keep mixing and it'll look thick and wet like porridge.) Scrape down the edges of the bowl. Wrap the bowl tightly in plastic wrap, and let the dough rest in a warm spot (think: where would a cat want to take a nap?), until it has doubled in size, about 2 hours.

Coat your work surface with ¼ cup flour. Carefully remove the dough from the bowl (this is easiest with damp hands) onto the floured surface. Cover the dough with another ¼ cup flour. Divide in half and then dust the cut sides with flour. Shape the first half of the dough into a log and cut into 5 pieces, dusting all cut sides with flour. Repeat with the second half. You should have 10 pieces. Grab each blob individually and pull the sides of the dough up and then pinch them all together tightly, like you're tying up lunch in a cloth. Turn each ball seam side down on a less floured part of the counter, and use both hands, with pinkies touching the counter behind the ball of dough, to drag it toward you. The ball should still have the same side facing the top; it should just be much more taut at the bottom. Turn counterclockwise and repeat three more times until the dough is taut all around. If it's too sticky, add more flour. Flour each ball after it's fully formed.

Use a rolling pin to flatten each pita into a circle that's between ⅛ and ¼ inch thick. The easiest way to roll

recipe continues

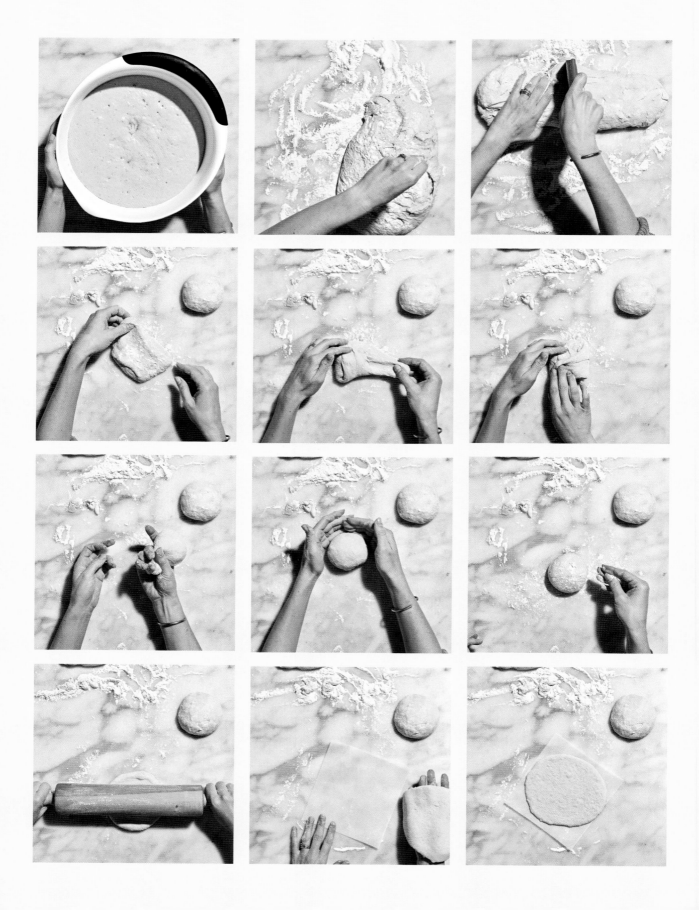

the balls out is to start in the middle and roll to the edges, flipping the dough over, and turning it a few turns to make sure it doesn't stick to the counter and rolls out evenly. It's important to make sure the pitas are rolled consistently thick or they won't puff up as well.

After each pita is rolled, set it on a piece of parchment. Cover with a clean dish towel and let rest for another 20 minutes.

Preheat the oven to 500°F. Put a baking sheet on both the top and middle racks in the oven. Preheating the pans is important, as the hot surface makes the pitas start to puff right away.

TO MAKE THE EVERYTHING BAGEL SEASONING MIXTURE (OPTIONAL):
In a small bowl, combine 2 teaspoons sesame seeds, 2 teaspoons dehydrated onion, 1 teaspoon poppy seeds, and 1 teaspoon flaky sea salt. Just before baking the pitas, brush, or spray, each one with a bit of water and sprinkle with a generous amount of the everything bagel seasoning.

TO MAKE THE COCONUT BUTTER (OPTIONAL): Toast 2 cups coconut flakes in a pan over medium heat for 2 to 4 minutes, until golden and fragrant. Transfer to a food processor and add 2 tablespoons of coconut oil and ⅛ teaspoon salt. Blend until smooth and creamy, 4 to 10 minutes. If you need a little more oil to loosen the butter, add it 1 tablespoon at a time. Add 2 teaspoons honey, if desired. Chill until ready to serve.

Pick up each pita by the parchment paper and place on either preheated baking sheet with enough space so none of them touch (about 3 per baking sheet). Cook on the top and middle racks of your oven for 3 to 5 minutes. The pitas should be fully puffed but still relatively pale. (If some of them only partially inflate, that's totally normal! Give them another minute, and if they're still flatties, just pull them out. Sometimes the pita pocket might not be entirely open, and that's okay—they'll still taste great.) Repeat until all the pitas are cooked. Let the pitas rest on a cooling rack until serving. Remove the parchment, and serve warm wrapped in a dry dish towel.

TIPS + TIMING

1. You can shape the pitas up to 24 hours in advance and store them in the fridge, in a single layer spaced at least an inch apart on a parchment-lined large baking sheet, covered in plastic wrap. Take them out an hour before baking. If using the everything bagel seasoning, add it just before baking. If you make the pitas in advance, to reheat them wrap a stack in tinfoil and bake for 6 minutes at 350°F.
2. If your pita dough is feeling sticky and hard to work with, just keep dusting it with a thin layer of flour and be sure your hands are clean and dry.
3. If you don't feel like making your own everything bagel seasoning, you can also buy a premade version. Jacobsen Salt Co. has a great one. Or keep your pitas plain.

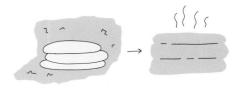

Wrap pita in foil and heat in oven at 350° for 6 minutes

GARLICKY CABBAGE WITH WHOLE-GRAIN MUSTARD

Serves 6
Total time: 25 minutes

Cabbage gets a bad rap, and I get why. You buy a head, you use a quarter of it, and the rest of it sits there begging for your attention every time you open the fridge. You say, "Don't worry, cabbage, I'll eat you tomorrow!" But then . . . tomorrow never comes, and one day you open the fridge and it's RIP cabbage. This recipe alleviates that issue.

I love this dish for dinner parties because it's great hot off the pan or served at room temp—very low-maintenance. You could also add it into a green salad, enjoy it as a side with any simple protein, or throw it onto a crispy pork sandwich.

2 tablespoons extra-virgin olive oil

2 large garlic cloves, minced

¾ teaspoon salt, divided, plus more to taste

1 small purple cabbage, halved and cut into ⅛-inch ribbons (about 8 cups)

2 teaspoons apple cider vinegar

1 tablespoon unsalted butter

2 teaspoons whole-grain mustard

1 tablespoon coarsely chopped parsley leaves

In a large skillet, heat 2 tablespoons olive oil over medium heat. Once the oil is warm, add the minced garlic and ¼ teaspoon salt. Cook, stirring occasionally, until it's aromatic with tiny, happy bubbles, about 2½ minutes. Add the cabbage and another ½ teaspoon salt. Cook, stirring occasionally, until the cabbage is about half the size it was at the beginning, approximately 6 minutes.

Throw in 2 teaspoons apple cider vinegar and cook until most of the cabbage is soft and deep purple, around 10 minutes. Mix in 1 tablespoon butter, 2 teaspoons whole-grain mustard, and 1 tablespoon chopped parsley until the butter is fully melted. Add more salt to taste.

TIPS + TIMING

1. This stores well in the fridge for up to 3 days in an airtight container. Remove 1 hour before serving.
2. Looking for a nice pop of color and tang like I have in the photo? Add a few extra spoonfuls of whole-grain mustard on top of the dish once you put it in the serving bowl!

GOLDEN COCONUT AND APRICOT RICE

Serves 6
Total time: 40 minutes

When my mom was growing up in Bayside, Queens, one of her closest friends had a mother who was one of those cooks you dream about. From the moment the family first emigrated to the United States from Iran in 1971, Mrs. Nadiri transformed their cramped apartment into a magical, fragrant, welcoming space. From her small galley kitchen she served a spectacle of mounded jewel-toned rice and delicious stews. Guests were always welcome to join her long and ornate dinner parties, and the warmth that emanated from the family matriarch was unlike anything my mom had experienced before.

Although my mom had bopped around the country since leaving New York, luckily for me, my grandma did not. So we got to visit Mrs. Nadiri's apartment of wonders on the way to Long Island every year. Learning about her culture, and experiencing the richness of flavor, will always and forever be one of my fondest memories, and this rice is an homage to that.

1 tablespoon unsalted butter

2 cups white basmati rice, rinsed

1 cup plus 1 teaspoon water, divided

1 (13.5 ounce) can of unsweetened, full-fat coconut milk

1 teaspoon salt, plus more to taste

Large pinch of saffron (about 20 threads) or ½ teaspoon ground turmeric

⅓ cup chopped sulfured dried Turkish apricots, cut in ½-inch cubes

Flaky sea salt, to finish

In a medium pot with a lid, bring 1 tablespoon butter, 2 cups rice, 1 cup water, 1 can of coconut milk, and 1 teaspoon salt to a boil over medium-high heat. Once the water comes to a rolling boil, reduce the heat to a simmer and cook the rice, covered, for 20 minutes.

Turn off the heat and let the rice rest, with the lid still on, for 5 minutes.

In a medium bowl, combine 1 teaspoon hot water with a large pinch of saffron (or ½ teaspoon turmeric) and let it sit.

Remove the lid from the rice and transfer 1 cup of the cooked rice to the bowl with the saffron (or turmeric), stir, and let it soak up all the color and glorious flavor. From now on we will call this the "golden rice."

Add the chopped apricots into the pot of rice and fluff the mixture with a fork. Add flaky sea salt to taste.

Pour the apricot rice from the pot into a serving bowl and top with the golden rice.

Timing

Make up to a day in advance and store in an airtight container in the fridge. Reheat in a microwave (to maintain fluffiness) or in a pan with butter (to give it a crispy texture).

BROWN RICE THAT DOESN'T SUCK

Serves 6
Total time: 1 hour

For the longest time I thought brown rice was gross: mushy, long-grained, and flavorless. But it turns out, brown rice cooked with a few tricks is actually quite delicious. Apparently, I am not alone in my thinking, because this is the most popular recipe that I've ever posted on my website.

This rice is layered with flavor, simple to throw together, and excellent cold the next day. The trick is to cook the rice with something nice and flavorful (in this case, a caramelized onion) and then finish it with a boatload of herbs and a little lemon zest for a delightful burst of flavor!

3 tablespoons extra-virgin olive oil

1 small yellow onion, sliced into thin half-moons

¾ teaspoon salt, divided, plus more to taste

2 cups brown rice

3 to 4 cups (depending on your rice) stock

⅓ cup finely chopped dill, plus more to taste

⅓ cup finely chopped parsley leaves, plus more to taste

⅓ cup thinly sliced chives or green onions, white and green parts

1 teaspoon lemon zest, plus more to taste

1 lemon, cut into wedges

In a medium pot with a lid, heat 3 tablespoons olive oil over medium-low heat. Add the sliced onion and ½ teaspoon salt and cook, stirring occasionally, until all the excess liquid is gone and the onions are lightly caramelized, about 12 minutes.

Rinse 2 cups rice until the water runs clear, and then add the rice to the onions. Stir to evenly combine. Add the amount of stock specified on the package of rice, but subtract ¼ cup to account for the liquid in the onions. Bring to a boil, then reduce the heat to low. Cook, covered, for the duration of time specified on the rice package, typically 30 to 45 minutes. Turn off the heat and let the rice sit for 10 minutes before removing the lid. Do. Not. Open. That. Lid! After 10 minutes, open it up, add the final ¼ teaspoon salt, the dill, parsley, chives (or green onions), and 1 teaspoon lemon zest, and fluff with a fork. Add extra salt, zest, and herbs to taste. Serve with lemon wedges in case anyone would like some extra acid thrown in.

TIPS + TIMING

1. Make up to a day in advance and store in an airtight container in the fridge. Reheat in a microwave (to maintain fluffiness) or in a pan with butter (to give it a crispy texture).
2. When it comes to brown rice, I find standard long-grain rice to be mushy. Stick to basmati (classic), short-grain (chewier), or jasmine (buttery).
3. You can use any stock you like for this recipe. If you want a veggie one, try the homemade Veg Stock (page 132). Some store-bought brands are better than others, so give a few a try and see what works for you. I like the bone broths from Fire & Kettle, though they're a bit pricey.
4. Change up the flavor by switching the herbs:
   - To give this a Mexican vibe, swap out the dill for cilantro and the lemon for lime.
   - To complement Italian dishes, swap out the dill for basil.
   - To serve with Indian food, swap out the dill for mint.
   You just need a full cup of whatever herb combo you want. You get the picture.

LATKE-STYLE SMASHED POTATOES WITH DILLY CRÈME FRAÎCHE

Serves 6
Total time: 1 hour

I LOVE A SMASHED POTATO. I mean, really, you can sign me up for any potato. But I am especially enamored with this fun twist on latkes. In my family, we make latkes only once a year for two very good reasons . . . (1) Hanukkah, the fried food holiday, happens only once a year, and (2) they're a messy nuisance to make.

This recipe gets you crispy, crackly potatoes, sweet and tender apples, AND tangy dairy all in a package that takes way less time and effort. Will it replace the latke? No. Should it become a regular staple in your rotation? Yes.

Smashed Potatoes

2 pounds peewee or fingerling potatoes (see illustration for ideal size)

1¾ teaspoons salt, divided

½ cup plus 3 tablespoons extra-virgin olive oil, divided

1½ teaspoons distilled white vinegar

⅓ cup water

1 teaspoon black pepper

1½ teaspoons onion powder

3 crisp, sweet apples, cut into 1-inch slices (I like Fuji or Pink Lady apples)

Chopped dill, for serving (optional)

Dilly Horseradish Crème Fraîche

1½ cups crème fraîche (or full-fat sour cream)

1½ tablespoons coarsely chopped dill

1½ tablespoons finely chopped chives

¾ teaspoon salt, plus more to taste

¾ teaspoon black pepper, plus more to taste

2 tablespoons prepared horseradish, plus more to taste

Preheat the oven to 425°F.

TO MAKE THE SMASHED POTATOES: Grab a large baking sheet and put the potatoes on it. Season with 1 teaspoon salt, 3 tablespoons olive oil, 1½ teaspoons vinegar, and ⅓ cup water. Cover the baking sheet tightly with aluminum foil and roast until fork tender, about 35 minutes.

While the potatoes are roasting, make the crème fraîche.

TO MAKE THE DILLY HORSERADISH CRÈME FRAÎCHE: In a medium bowl, whisk together 1½ cups crème fraîche (or sour cream), the dill, chives, ¾ teaspoon each salt and pepper, and 2 tablespoons prepared horseradish. Season with extra salt, pepper, and horseradish to taste. Refrigerate until ready to serve.

When the potatoes are tender, remove the foil and let them rest until they're cool enough to handle. In a large bowl, toss the potatoes with ¾ teaspoon salt, 1½ teaspoons onion powder, 1 teaspoon pepper, and ½ cup olive oil. Divide the potatoes and sliced apples between two baking sheets. Using anything flat (a spatula,

the bottom of a mug, your palm, a cup measurer), smash the potatoes so they're all no taller than a half inch. Rip any larger potatoes in half to create extra texture. The craggier the potato, the crisper the potato. Make sure there is enough room for everything to lay flat without any overlapping. Pour any extra olive oil from the bowl over the potatoes.

Bake the potatoes and apples until the bottom edges of the potatoes are mega-crispy and the apples are caramelized, about 15 minutes. Flip and continue cooking until the second side is crispy, 10 to 20 more minutes. If any of the apples begin to burn, remove them and add them back in before serving.

I like to serve these on a big platter with the crème fraîche on the bottom and the potatoes lounging in the sauce with extra dill on top!

POTATO TO SCALE

2 to 2-½"

TIPS + TIMING

1. The first roast on the potatoes can happen anytime up to 3 days before serving; smash and crisp just before serving.

2. If the potatoes are sticking to whatever you're smashing with, put a piece of parchment paper between the potato and the smasher.

3. My genius cousin Sascha suggests serving this with caviar for New Year's Eve. Brilliant.

4. Got extra dilly horseradish crème fraîche? Use it as a dip or dressing!

CHARRED LEMON BROCCOLINI

Serves 6
Total time: 20 minutes

Broccolini is my standard fallback vegetable when I really don't know what to make and want to keep it simple. It's like broccoli, but better, cause the stems are tender and the florets crisp up quicky. This basic technique of roasting the broccolini with lemon adds a really lovely dimension of warmth and sweetness. It's like a pat on the head from Grandpa in roasted vegetable form. But don't worry; it's not all saccharin—it also has enough heat from the red pepper flakes to keep it balanced and varied.

6 garlic cloves, skins removed and smashed

¼ cup extra-virgin olive oil

1 teaspoon salt, plus more to taste

¼ teaspoon red pepper flakes, plus more to taste

½ lemon, sliced into ¼-inch rounds

2 bunches of broccolini (6 to 8 ounces), with the very ends of the stems removed

Preheat the oven to 425°F.

In a large bowl, combine the garlic, ¼ cup olive oil, 1 teaspoon salt, and ¼ teaspoon red pepper flakes. Whisk really well and smash up the garlic a bit to infuse the oil.

Divide the lemon slices onto 2 large baking sheets (you need two to ensure the broccolini isn't crowded) and set both sheets next to the bowl.

Add the broccolini into the bowl and mix with your hands to coat in oil.

Evenly distribute the broccolini over the lemons (making sure to take all the garlic nuggets with you). Roast for about 13 minutes or until the tops are lightly crisped and the stalks are just cooked through.

Transfer the broccolini and lemons to a serving bowl. Toss to distribute the juice from the charred lemon rounds and add more salt or red pepper flakes to taste. Serve away!

Tips + Timing

1. The broccolini can be washed and trimmed up to a day in advance and stored in a resealable plastic bag with a dry paper towel. Roast just before serving.
2. Pick bright green broccolini with nice firm stalks that aren't flowering.
3. If any of the broccolini stems are super-thick, slice the whole thing in half lengthwise.
4. If you love lemon, go ahead and slice up and use the whole lemon.

To smash the garlic, place the flat side of a knife on each clove and press firmly on the blade.

ROASTED SQUASH WITH SAGE YOGURT

Serves 6
Total time: 1 hour 15 minutes

The autumnal flavors of this dish take me back to my fondest memories of childhood in Oregon—Halloween time, when we would visit at least three pumpkin patches for the hay mazes and apple cider doughnuts.

The sweetness from the caramelized squash, the earthiness from the sage, the tang from the yogurt, and the freshness from the gremolata really sell cozy for me.

All the comfort of a PNW fall without getting drenched in the rain like a wet rat!

Squash

3 medium butternut squash (about 5 pounds), peeled and seeded, sliced into 1-inch half-moons

2 tablespoons extra-virgin olive oil

1 teaspoon salt

½ teaspoon black pepper

Cayenne pepper or red pepper flakes (optional), to finish

Sage Yogurt

½ cup plain, full-fat (5%) Greek yogurt

1 teaspoon honey, plus extra to finish

1 teaspoon extra-virgin olive oil

1½ teaspoons finely chopped sage

¼ teaspoon black pepper

Salt, to taste

Gremolata

¼ cup coarsely chopped parsley leaves

2 tablespoons lemon zest

2 teaspoons fresh lemon juice, plus more to taste

2 garlic cloves, minced

3 tablespoons extra-virgin olive oil

½ teaspoon salt, plus more to taste

¼ teaspoon black pepper

Preheat the oven to 425°F.

TO ROAST THE SQUASH: Grab 2 large baking sheets and pile all of the sliced squash onto one pan. Sprinkle with 2 tablespoons olive oil, 1 teaspoon salt, and ½ teaspoon black pepper. Mix well with your hands and, once the squash is evenly seasoned, divide between both baking sheets. Roast until the tops are equally bronzed, about 30 minutes. Flip the squash and roast until both sides are nicely golden with a few little crispy bits, another 15 minutes or so.

While the squash is cooking, whip up the yogurt sauce and gremolata.

TO MAKE THE SAGE YOGURT: In a small bowl, combine ½ cup yogurt, 1 teaspoon honey, 1 teaspoon olive oil, 1½ teaspoons chopped sage, and ¼ teaspoon black pepper and whisk

to incorporate. Give it a taste and add salt as needed; the amount you use will depend on the yogurt you purchase.

TO MAKE THE GREMOLATA: In a small bowl, combine the parsley, 2 tablespoons lemon zest, 2 teaspoons lemon juice, the garlic, 3 tablespoons olive oil, ½ teaspoon salt, and ¼ teaspoon pepper. Whisk to incorporate and add extra lemon juice and salt to taste.

When the squash pieces are done cooking, add half of the gremolata onto them and toss to haphazardly coat.

To serve, spread the yogurt on the bottom of a serving dish, cover with the squash, and drizzle with the rest of the gremolata. Finish with cayenne or red pepper flakes, if desired.

TIPS + TIMING

1. The yogurt and the gremolata can be made a day in advance and stored separately in airtight containers in the fridge. Roast the squash just before serving.
2. See page 31 for how to peel and cut butternut squash.

OLIVE OIL-DRENCHED SOURDOUGH

Serves 6 to 8
Total time: 10 minutes

Look, I've seen all of you take a beautiful, thick slice of delicious sourdough and put it in a toaster, converting its supple, moist interior into a dry wasteland of carbohydrates. I'm not mad. *eye twitch* But, I am here to set this travesty right once and for all. A toaster is for an old bagel or a piece of emergency toast that you're eating as you run out the door. That's it. Everything else gets toasted. In. A. Pan. Or. On. A. Grill. Period. It's the only way to get that perfect, crispy, shattery exterior while keeping the center all warm and soft. Okay? Good. Now . . . let's get toasting.

1 loaf of sourdough, cut into 1-inch-thick slices

½ cup extra-virgin olive oil, or as needed

Serving Options

Flaky sea salt

½ cup (1 stick) salted European-style butter, room temp

2 cups roasted tomatoes (page 34)

2 raw garlic cloves

TO MAKE THE TOAST

IN A PAN: Heat a large skillet over medium heat. Once the pan is hot, add in enough oil to coat the bottom in a ⅛-inch layer. Wait until the oil is nice and warm and then add in as many slices of bread as can fit. Toast until the bottom edges are visibly golden, about 4 minutes. Flip and cook the other side until lightly crisped, another 2 minutes, adding more oil as needed. Set the toast on a plate and cover it with a kitchen towel while you finish toasting the rest of the bread.

ON THE GRILL: Preheat the grill to high. Generously brush both sides of the slices of bread with olive oil. Brush the grill with olive oil. Set the bread on the grill and cook until there are visible grill marks all across the slices, about 2 minutes. Flip and repeat.

TO SERVE

Choose one of the following:

1. Sprinkle with flaky sea salt.
2. Serve with flaky sea salt and the warm roasted tomatoes (page 34) on the side.
3. Serve with room temp salty butter on the side.
4. Rub raw garlic cloves on the slices for a punchy, garlicky surprise and finish with flaky sea salt.

TIPS + TIMING

1. You can slice the bread up to a few hours in advance and keep it in a resealable plastic bag. Crisp the slices just before serving.
2. It's always best to buy an uncut loaf of bread and cut it to your desired thickness. The bread stays fresher longer, and everyone knows a thick slice of bread is better than a flimsy one.
3. When selecting a loaf of sourdough, look for one with a nice, crusty exterior that is relatively firm but gives a little when you squeeze it. Too hard and it could be dry on the inside; too soft and the crust is probably not great.

PARTY PESTO

Makes 1 cup
Total time: 10 minutes

In my house, pesto is a thing we fight about. Andy thinks all pesto is good pesto and will put it on anything. I think pesto with too many pine nuts is insulting to basil. I also think I might be a little allergic to pine nuts? They make my tongue go crazy. But that is not the point. The point is that pesto is a delicate balancing act, and for me this version is just right . . . and Andy also loves it! I will say pesto is way better on day two, so have this be something you make in advance or, heck, make some weekly and put it on everything. Andy will come live with you!

The cheese is folded into the pesto at the end because adding it before blending the pesto can create a bit of a gritty texture. It's also nice because if someone at your party doesn't eat dairy, you can easily leave it off for them.

¼ cup pine nuts

3 cups loosely packed basil leaves

4 garlic cloves

1 teaspoon salt, plus more to taste

½ cup extra-virgin olive oil

¼ cup grated parmesan cheese (optional)

TO TOAST THE PINE NUTS: In a small skillet, heat ¼ cup pine nuts over medium-low heat and shake until lightly toasted and fragrant, about 3 minutes. Don't step away; they toast quickly.

TO MAKE THE PESTO: In a food processor, combine 3 cups basil, the toasted pine nuts, 4 garlic cloves, and 1 teaspoon salt. Pulse 5 to 10 times until the basil is roughly chopped.

Slowly pour ½ cup olive oil through the top of the food processor and pulse until the basil is finely chopped and the goodies are evenly distributed in the oil.

TO SERVE: Fold ¼ cup parm into the finished pesto, if desired, and add extra salt to taste.

Tips + Timing

1. Make up to two days in advance and store in an airtight container in the fridge. Mix well before serving.
2. Ingredients matter. A fragrant, bright green basil will make a better pesto than defeated fridge basil that is wilted and partially black. A good olive oil will also make a big difference. Pesto prefers a clean, buttery olive oil, not a bright, peppery one. So pick something mild and round! No idea what that means? Check out page 230 for some suggestions.
3. To preserve your basil, dry it well, wrap it in a dry paper towel, place the wrapped basil in a resealable plastic bag, and store it in the fridge.
4. If you like a punchier pesto, add a strip of lemon peel before pulsing or add lemon zest into the finished pesto.
5. Don't feel like spending the $$ on pine nuts? Substitute walnuts, almonds, pumpkin seeds, sunflower seeds, macadamia nuts, or hazelnuts.

ROASTED VEG PARADE

Serves 6
Total time: 40 minutes

A well-roasted vegetable is a glorious thing. It brings out all the best the veg has to offer: its natural sweetness, an idyllic texture, and a mellowed sharpness. I suppose it's sort of like when you give a human the right SSRI. I love this version, brightened with fresh cilantro at the end for serving with Mexican food, but as you can imagine, this technique works with just about any veggie combination (see suggestions below). When I'm looking to make a quick, satisfying meal, I serve it with a grilled protein and herby rice, like Brown Rice That Doesn't Suck (page 114).

¼ cup extra-virgin olive oil, plus more as needed

1 teaspoon chipotle powder

½ teaspoon salt, plus more to taste

½ teaspoon ground cumin

½ teaspoon dried oregano

½ teaspoon dried coriander

½ teaspoon cayenne pepper or red pepper flakes

½ teaspoon black pepper, plus more to taste

1 large cauliflower, cut into bite-size florets (5 to 6 cups)

2 red or orange bell peppers, cut into ½-inch strips

1 red onion, cut into ¼-inch half-moons

1 tablespoon finely chopped fresh cilantro

Preheat the oven to 425°F and line 2 baking sheets with parchment paper (it makes cleanup faster, but it's not necessary).

In a large bowl, whisk together ¼ cup olive oil, 1 teaspoon chipotle powder, ½ teaspoon salt, ½ teaspoon cumin, ½ teaspoon oregano, ½ teaspoon coriander, ½ teaspoon cayenne (or red pepper flakes), and ½ teaspoon black pepper. Add the cauliflower florets, bell pepper strips, and onion slices and toss well to coat. If any of the vegetables feel dry, add another glug of olive oil.

Distribute the vegetables evenly onto both pans, leaving a bit of space (school dance–style) between each piece. If you run out of room, grab another pan or roast the veggies in batches. Without space, they won't caramelize.

Roast until the peppers and onions begin to char and the cauliflower is fully cooked, 25 to 30 minutes total, flipping the vegetables midway through cooking.

Once the veggies are done, transfer them to a serving bowl, add the cilantro, and toss. Serve with extra salt and pepper to taste.

TIPS + TIMING

1. Roasted vegetables are always best on the day they are made, but you can precut the vegetables a day in advance and store them in a resealable plastic bag in the fridge.
2. Don't crowd your veggies in the pan. Mosh-pit vegetables will remain sweaty, while the vegetables in the spaced-out seats have the room to become golden and crisp.
3. Like this technique and want to try other flavor combos? Try:
   - onions, fennel, and carrots with fennel seeds, salt, and pepper
   - mushrooms, turnips, and parsnips with rosemary, salt, and pepper
   - onions, broccoli, and asparagus with lemon zest, salt, and red pepper flakes
   - potatoes, green beans, and leeks, with mustard seeds, salt, and pepper

HOW TO CUT A PEPPER

SHALLOT COMPOTE GREEN BEANS

Serves 6
Total time: 30 minutes

What's the deal with green beans? They're one of the only veggies that are available fresh year-round and yet they are consumed "on average" 1.54 times a year. Green beans are delicious, people—let's show them some love! This tender, crispy, shallot-laden, easy-to-munch version will have you eating GBs at least 23.83 times per year. These are great for a gathering because they're simple to throw together but they have a little bit of an unexpected vinegar twist. #gbsarenotjustforthanksgiving

¼ cup red wine vinegar

1 tablespoon sugar

½ cup plus 2 teaspoons salt, divided, plus more to taste

¼ cup extra-virgin olive oil

3 large shallots, sliced into ⅛-inch rounds

½ teaspoon baking soda

1 pound green beans, stems removed, cut into 2-inch pieces

In a small bowl, whisk together ¼ cup vinegar, 1 tablespoon sugar, and 2 teaspoons salt.

In a large skillet, heat ¼ cup olive oil over low heat. Once the oil is warm, add the sliced shallots and *half* of the vinegar solution. Cook, stirring occasionally, until the shallots are translucent and super-soft, 8 to 10 minutes. If you notice any browning while they're cooking, reduce the heat to medium-low.

Meanwhile, fill a large bowl with ice water and set aside. Fill a large pot about halfway with water, add ½ cup salt and ½ teaspoon baking soda, and bring to a rolling boil. Add the cut green beans and cook for 1 minute. Strain, rinse, and place them in the bowl of ice water.

Once the beans are no longer warm, lift them out of the ice bath and shake them dry before adding them to the pan with the shallots. Increase the heat to medium-high, add the rest of the vinegar mixture, and cook until most of the liquid has evaporated, 2 to 3 minutes. Add extra salt to taste.

TIPS + TIMING

1. Green beans are best cooked just before serving, but you can make the shallot compote and blanch the beans up to 2 days in advance, then store in the fridge in separate airtight containers. Simply rewarm the shallots and add the chilled green beans as described at the end of the recipe.
2. Pick good beans! They should be firm without wrinkles or mushy spots. A dilapidated GB will never reach its full glorious potential.
3. If you like a tender, thin bean, opt for haricots verts (a.k.a. French green beans—I like to imagine they have a thin mustache and a striped shirt on).

VEG STOCK

Makes 6 cups

Total time: 1 hour 40 minutes
(1 hour 30 minutes hands-off
simmering)

Homemade stock is just one of those things that makes everything taste better. I pretty much always have some on hand in the freezer for using in soups, adding to braises, or preparing sauces. I try to freeze it in airtight containers that hold around 4 cups so there's never a huge excess of stock after I finish whatever I'm making. (Oh, and label any food you put in the freezer. I sometimes forget to and then have no idea what's what. It's like freezer roulette!)

2½ quarts (10 cups) water

5 large carrots, cut into 2-inch pieces

3 celery stalks, cut into 2-inch pieces

1 large tomato, quartered

8 button mushrooms, wiped clean of any dirt, quartered

1 garlic head, halved, with skin still on

1 yellow onion, quartered, with skin still on

1 tablespoon black peppercorns

2 bay leaves

In a large stockpot, combine 2½ quarts water, the carrots, celery, tomato, mushrooms, garlic, onion, 1 tablespoon black peppercorns, and 2 bay leaves. Bring to a rolling boil over high heat and then reduce the heat to medium-low. Simmer for 1½ hours.

Strain and use right away or allow the stock to cool for an hour before straining and storing in heatproof airtight containers.

Tips + Timing

1. To make your life easy, always make stock in advance and store in an airtight container in the fridge for up to a week or in the freezer for up to 3 months. (Leave a little empty space in the container if you're freezing, as frozen liquids expand.)

2. Where's the salt? Salt gets added once you turn that stock into soup. Keep it unsalted so you can salt each dish to taste.

3. The onion skins will make the stock a little darker, but they'll also give it a bit of a richer flavor. Plus, leaving them on makes your life easier since you won't need to peel the onion.

A VERY ADULT SALAD
(a.k.a. GRAPIES AND GREENIES)

Serves 6
Total time: 45 minutes

Sometimes you just want a salad that seems fancy, and *this* salad seems *fancy*. The roasted grapes give it a silky sweetness that you almost can't put your finger on, the candied nuts supply a satisfying crunch, the dressing—laden with mustard and apple cider vinegar—makes it intriguing, and the cheese . . . well, it's cheese—everybody loves cheese. Annnd, I think that's the longest run-on sentence in this book. Basically, this is a good salad. You will like it.

Feel free to buy the candied pecans—no need to make them if you don't want to!

Roasty Grapes (makes 1 cup)

2 cups large seedless red grapes, stems removed

2 tablespoons extra-virgin olive oil

1 tablespoon aged balsamic vinegar

½ teaspoon salt

½ teaspoon coarsely chopped rosemary leaves

Candied Pecans (makes 2 cups)

½ cup powdered sugar

½ teaspoon salt

1 tablespoon finely chopped rosemary leaves

4 teaspoons water

2 cups raw unsalted pecans

1 teaspoon granulated sugar

½ teaspoon flaky sea salt

Dressing (makes ½ cup)

1 small shallot, finely chopped (about 1½ tablespoons)

½ teaspoon finely chopped thyme

1½ tablespoons apple cider vinegar, plus more to taste

2 tablespoons apple cider

2 teaspoons Dijon mustard

1 garlic clove, minced

Pinch of sugar

¼ teaspoon salt, plus more to taste

¼ teaspoon black pepper

¼ cup extra-virgin olive oil

Very Adult Salad

6 ounces baby arugula

½ teaspoon flaky sea salt, plus more to finish

¼ teaspoon black pepper, plus more to finish

1 cup roasty grapes

1½ cups chopped candied pecans

½ cup shaved pecorino romano

TO MAKE THE ROASTY GRAPES:
Preheat the oven to 425°F. Mix together 2 cups grapes, 2 tablespoons olive oil, 1 tablespoon balsamic, ½ teaspoon salt, and the chopped rosemary leaves in a 9 x 13-inch baking pan. Roast, stirring occasionally, until the grapes are extremely soft and deflated, about 20 minutes. Allow them to cool for 15 minutes before adding them to the salad.

TO MAKE THE CANDIED PECANS:
Preheat the oven or adjust the temperature to 350°F. In a large bowl, whisk together ½ cup powdered sugar, ½ teaspoon salt, the chopped rosemary leaves, and 4 teaspoons water. Add 2 cups pecans and toss to coat. Spread the nuts out on a baking sheet and bake, stirring occasionally, until lightly golden and shiny, about 16 minutes. As soon as the nuts come out of the oven, lay them on a piece of parchment and sprinkle with 1 teaspoon granulated sugar and ½ teaspoon flaky sea salt. Separate the nuts if needed. Allow them to cool for 10 minutes before using.

TO MAKE THE DRESSING: Combine the shallot, thyme, 1½ tablespoons apple cider vinegar, 2 tablespoons apple cider, 2 teaspoons Dijon mustard, the garlic, a pinch of sugar, ¼ teaspoon salt, ¼ teaspoon pepper, and ¼ cup olive oil in a jar with a tight-fitting lid and shake it like crazy to emulsify.

Add extra salt and vinegar to taste.

recipe continues

TO MAKE THE VERY ADULT SALAD: In a large serving bowl, toss 6 ounces arugula with ½ teaspoon flaky sea salt and ¼ teaspoon black pepper. Start by pouring in ¼ cup of the salad dressing. Toss and add more dressing to taste and pile the salad with 1 cup roasty grapes, 1½ cups chopped candied pecans, and ½ cup shaved pecorino romano. Finish with extra flaky sea salt and fresh cracked black pepper, if desired.

TIPS + TIMING

1. The grapes and dressing can be made up to 3 days in advance and stored in the fridge in separate airtight containers.
2. The nuts are best fresh, so make them within a few hours of dinner and leave out at room temp.
3. No time to make the candied pecans? Just buy 'em!

WORLD'S BEST OVEN FRIES WITH PARSLEY AND PARM

Serves 6
Total time: 1 hour 10 minutes

These are truly the crispiest, most delectable oven fries out there. They can be seasoned any which way you like and the technique can be used over and over again for world-class oven fries. Yeah, that's right: World. Class. The not-so-secret secret to getting them crispy-as-all-get-out (why is that a saying?) is . . . parmesan. I add a bit at the beginning to create more surface area and a little at the end to amp up the flavor and texture.

3 large russet potatoes, peeled
½ cup extra-virgin olive oil
1 tablespoon garlic powder
1 tablespoon onion powder
1½ teaspoons salt, plus more to taste
1½ teaspoons paprika
½ teaspoon black pepper, plus more to taste
½ cup plus 3 tablespoons grated parmesan cheese
3 tablespoons coarsely chopped parsley leaves
Aioli (page 29) or Special Sauce (page 53), for serving

Preheat the oven to 400°F.

Cut 3 large potatoes in half. Slice each half in half again, and then slice each half into 4 or 5 wedges.

Place the wedges in a large bowl and coat in ½ cup olive oil, 1 tablespoon garlic powder, 1 tablespoon onion powder, 1½ teaspoons salt, 1½ teaspoons paprika, ½ teaspoon black pepper, and ½ cup parm. Toss it all really well and make sure the seasoning is evenly distributed on all the potatoes. Divide the potatoes between 2 baking sheets, leaving a bit of space between each piece. (Two baking sheets are essential to ensure the potatoes crisp rather than steam.)

Roast for 40 to 50 minutes total, flipping every 15 minutes to reduce the risk of burning. The finished potatoes should look irresistibly golden. If they're not, continue cooking, checking every 5 minutes until you just can't wait another minute.

Sprinkle on the remaining 3 tablespoons parm and roast until the parm is melted, 4 to 5 minutes. Add extra salt and pepper to taste.

Toss in the parsley just before serving with aioli or special sauce.

TIPS+TIMING

1. These fries reheat surprisingly well. They're still best fresh from the oven, but in a pinch, you can definitely make them a day in advance and reheat in a 400°F oven until crispy again.
2. How to pick a stellar potato (yes, the potato matters): it should feel firm, smooth, uniform in color, and NOT have any eyes. Your potato should never be able to look back at you.
3. You may use any type of potato you like in this recipe, but as far as I'm concerned, the russet is king. It yields the fluffiest interior.

HONEY-DRIZZLED ZUCCHINI FRITTERS

Serves 6 as a side; double the recipe for a main

Total time: 30 minutes

Most of the time, I find zucchini fritters to be a sad relative of the latke—soggy, flavorless, and a lot of work. (How am I doing at selling this recipe?) Well, these fritters changed my mind. The combination of fresh green vegetables with generous amounts of lemon zest and pockets of feta make this a dish I keep going back to. Fritters are a bit of work, but are great as a side for a meaty main, or served as a main with other vegetable sides for a full veg feast!

Lemony Herby Yogurt

1½ cups plain, full-fat (5%) Greek yogurt (or labneh)

1 garlic clove, minced

1 tablespoon finely chopped chives

½ teaspoon salt, plus more to taste

½ teaspoon black pepper

1 tablespoon fresh lemon juice, plus more to taste

1 teaspoon lemon zest

Za'atar, to finish (optional)

Fritters

15 thin asparagus spears, hard ends snapped or trimmed off

6 to 8 green onions, white and green parts

1 large zucchini

1 teaspoon salt

¼ teaspoon red pepper flakes

Zest of 1 lemon

1 egg

½ cup all-purpose flour

1 tablespoon coarsely chopped mint

¼ cup feta cheese, very finely crumbled, plus extra to finish

2 tablespoons cold sparkling water

Vegetable oil

Honey (plain or spicy, see page 151), to finish

1 teaspoon flaky sea salt, to finish

TO MAKE THE LEMONY HERBY YOGURT: In a medium bowl, whisk together 1½ cups Greek yogurt (or labneh), the garlic, chives, ½ teaspoon each of salt and pepper, 1 tablespoon lemon juice, and 1 teaspoon lemon zest. Add extra salt and lemon juice to taste. Finish with a generous sprinkling of za'atar, if desired. Refrigerate until ready to serve.

TO MAKE THE FRITTERS: Using the large shredding blade on a food processor (or the large holes on a box grater), shred the asparagus, green onions, and zucchini. (If you're using a grater, feel free to finely chop any of the vegetables that are too difficult to grate.)

Put all the grated veggies into a large colander over the sink—discarding any large pieces—and add 1 teaspoon salt. Mix well and let sit for 10 minutes. After 10 minutes, press down firmly to remove any excess liquid.

In a large bowl, combine all the grated vegetables, lemon zest, egg, ½ cup flour, the mint, and ¼ cup feta. Mix thoroughly to combine. Add 2 tablespoons cold sparkling water and mix again.

Heat a large skillet over medium-high heat and add enough oil to cover the bottom of the pan with a thin layer. Once the oil is warm, add quarter-cup scoops of the batter, leaving 2 inches between each scoop. Use a spatula to gently flatten each fritter into a ¼-inch-thick patty. Fry until the bottom side is crispy and golden, about 2 minutes. Flip the fritter and firmly flatten with the spatula. Cook the second side until golden, about 2 more minutes.

Transfer the fritters to a plate lined with a paper towel and repeat until all the batter is used, adding more oil as needed to keep the levels the same.

Serve the fritters with the lemony herby yogurt on the side to dip, and top with a drizzle of honey, crumbled feta, and flaky sea salt.

TIMING

The yogurt can be made a day in advance and stored in an airtight container in the fridge. Fritters should be made just before serving.

A pizza party is always a good idea. No one has ever been sad at a pizza party. It's customizable, it's interactive, it's ridiculous, and it lets you fling dough in the air. In this section you'll learn everything you need to nail pizzas at home, including my favorite same-day dough, techniques for shaping, how to not overtop your pizzas, and most important, how to make Pizza Sprinkles, the pizza topping you never knew you needed.

(You don't have to turn pizza night into a pajama party, but I certainly wouldn't be upset if you did.)

Pizza Basics

Make and shape your dough. To shape the dough, lightly dust a clean, dry countertop and the tops of each dough ball with flour. Using the middle three fingers on each hand, press gently on the dough, starting in the middle and working your way out to the edge of the dough to make a nice 6-inch pie. Flip it over and repeat the process.

Pick up the dough by the crust and rotate it as if you are steering a car in two full rotations. This should stretch the dough and help form a nice crust. To finish stretching the dough, make both of your hands into fists and rest the dough on top of them. Stretch carefully by separating your fists and turning in a few different positions. When you hold the dough up to the light, it should be evenly translucent. Once the pizza dough is the thickness you're looking for, it's time to top it.

Build your pizza. You want to be careful not to add too many heavy toppings or else your pizzas will be really floppy. I recommend starting with 3 tablespoons of sauce right in the middle of each pie and spreading it outward in a spiral with the back of a spoon until you get to the crust, followed by up to about 6 ounces (1½ cups) of cheese per pie.

Bake. You can cook your pizza on a baking stone or a baking sheet (or multiple baking sheets). For a baking stone or single baking sheet, position the rack in the middle of the oven. To use multiple baking sheets, place one rack just above the middle of the oven and one just below.

Serve. Pizza sprinkles are to be served on the table for everyone to use at their own discretion! You can slice up the pizzas or serve them on the table whole and provide a pizza wheel, a sharp knife, or, if you're that person, kitchen shears for cutting them up.

How to Use a Baking Stone and Peel

Set your baking stone on a rack in the middle of the oven. You'll cook your pizza directly on the stone.

You'll use a pizza peel (a wooden board with a long handle) like a giant spatula to transfer your pizza onto the stone. Dust the pizza peel with flour and put the shaped dough on top. Wiggle it to make sure it isn't sticking. Do this before you add your toppings.

When you're ready to cook your pizza, shimmy it to the back of the baking stone, using the peel, and release the pizza onto the stone. (If your pizza is stuck, you can lift up a corner and blow underneath the pizza to release it.)

When the pizza is done, grab an edge of the crust with tongs and ease the pie onto the peel.

SAME-DAY DOUGH

Makes three 9-ounce dough balls (1⅔ pounds dough)

Total time: 3½ hours (including 3 hours of resting the dough)

The thing about bread is that you can't really take shortcuts if you want it to be great. It's just one of those things that, if you want to do it right, you have to give it the time it needs.

When I was testing pizza dough, I tried about 18 different popular recipes. I wanted to find a dough with enough rising time to result in something special but not so long that you couldn't eat it the same day. Let me tell you . . . that's a tall order. Turns out there are a lot of really bad pizza dough recipes out there. This dough, however, is tender, malleable, and crisps up like a dream! If you have a great time making this and you want to get into pizza making, I highly recommend investing in a baking stone or a portable pizza oven! For my pizzas I use a portable Gozney oven.

1½ cups warm water

2 teaspoons sugar

2¼ teaspoons instant yeast

4 cups minus 2 tablespoons 00 flour, plus more for dusting

2¾ teaspoons salt

1 tablespoon extra-virgin olive oil

In a large glass or plastic bowl, whisk together 1½ cups warm water and 2 teaspoons sugar and then gently sprinkle 2¼ teaspoons yeast evenly over the top. Set a timer for 10 minutes. After 10 minutes, the yeast should be foamy. (If it's not, your yeast is dead and you need new yeast.)

Add in 4 cups minus 2 tablespoons flour and 2¾ teaspoons salt and mix with your hands to fully incorporate. The dough will seem pretty dry at this point. Once well-mixed, squish the dough through your fingers for a full minute—this will start to make the dough more hydrated. Scrape down the edges of your bowl with a plastic bowl scraper or spatula. Form the dough into a ball, as best you can, and scrape off any dough that may be sticking to your hands. Place the ball back into the bowl, and tightly cover the bowl with plastic wrap. Set aside for 20 minutes.

Lightly dust a countertop (and your hands) with flour, turn out your dough gently, and firmly knead the dough on the counter for a minute. Coat the bowl with 1 tablespoon olive oil and put the dough back in. Cover the

bowl tightly with plastic wrap and rest for 1 to 1½ hours, or until the dough has doubled in size.

Lightly dust the countertop with more flour and turn out the dough ball. Cut into three equal pieces, form three balls, and sprinkle each with flour. Grab your first dough ball

recipe continues

Fold the dough in half

Use the heels of your hands to rock forward and press flat

Turn the dough and repeat

and, while leaving the dough on the counter, pinch one side and pull it as far as you can, then fold it on top of itself. Rotate and repeat this all around the dough so it looks like a messed-up dumpling. Turn the dough ball over so the seam is face down and place both of your hands on the far side of the dough. With your pinkies touching the countertop, apply pressure and drag the dough toward you to tighten the surface tension. The dough should not be rolling; it should maintain contact with the counter at all times. Turn the dough a quarter turn clockwise and repeat three or four times until you have a nice-looking, tight dough ball. Repeat with the other two balls. Rest all the dough balls in a lightly floured high-sided baking dish (or two), leaving at least 6 inches between each ball for room to expand, and cover tightly in plastic wrap. Rest for 1 to 1½ hours, or until the balls have doubled in size, and then get to pizza making!

HOT TIP For an even better crust, refrigerate the dough overnight and remove from the fridge 1 hour before shaping the pizza crusts.

Tips + Timing

1. If you can find 00 flour (a very finely ground flour), that is ideal for an extra-tender, crispy, and flavorful crust. But this recipe works very well with all-purpose flour too.

2. How to measure flour: Use a spoon to fluff the flour and fill the measuring cup, then level it off with a knife.

Fluff the flour   Fill the measuring cup   Level off with the knife

SPICY SOPPRESSATA PIZZA

Serves 6; makes 3 pies

Total time: 45 minutes plus cook time (10 minutes per pie)

This Spicy Soppressata Pizza shows off how hot honey can really take a pizza over the edge into uncharted territory. If you've been to Roberta's then you know that this is basically their Bee Sting pizza; if you haven't been, you can pretend I invented hot honey on pizza. :) Don't skimp on the honey: the stickier, spicier, and sweeter the pizza, the better.

00 flour, for dusting

1⅔ to 2 pounds pizza dough, homemade (page 147) or store-bought

Extra-virgin olive oil, if using baking sheets

1 (13 ounce) jar of pizza sauce

1 pound shredded low-moisture, full-fat mozzarella cheese

6 ounces soppressata or pepperoni or other cured dry salami

¼ cup honey (or use store-bought hot honey)

1½ tablespoons hot sauce (if making your own spicy honey)

Pizza Sprinkles (page 153)

Serve with ranch dressing (optional, but is it?)

Take pizza dough out of the fridge one hour in advance of preparing.

Position your oven racks (see page 144) and preheat the oven to 500°F, or as high as it will go. If you have a convection fan, turn that on as well. Set out all of your pizza toppings and, if you haven't already done so, make the Pizza Sprinkles (page 153).

Once the oven is hot, turn on the broiler to get the oven hotter while shaping the dough.

Shape the dough as described on page 144.

IF USING A BAKING STONE: Dust the pizza peel with flour and put the shaped dough on top. Wiggle it to make sure it isn't sticking.

IF USING BAKING SHEET(S): Brush the baking sheet with a tiny bit of olive oil, to help the crust crisp, and lay down the shaped dough.

Spoon 3 tablespoons of sauce right in the middle of each pie and spread it outward in a spiral with the back of the spoon until you get to the crust. Top each pie with up to 1½ cups cheese and then add the soppressata.

IMPORTANT!! Remember, your oven is set to broil. Turn the oven back to 500°F (with the convection fan on, if you've got one) before putting the pizzas in the oven.

IF USING A BAKING STONE: Use the peel to transfer your pizza to the stone (see page 144).

IF USING THE BAKING SHEET(S): Place the baking sheets on the appropriate racks.

Cook until the cheese is bubbly and melted and the crust is golden and delicious-looking, 8 to 12 minutes, depending on how hot your oven is.

TO MAKE THE SPICY HONEY: While the pizza is cooking, in a small microwave-safe bowl, combine ¼ cup honey and 1½ tablespoons hot sauce. Microwave in 20-second intervals until the honey is thin and runny. Use right away.

Just as the pizzas come out of the oven, brush the crusts with olive oil and finish with a drizzle of spicy honey. Serve with Pizza Sprinkles and ranch dressing on the side, if desired.

WINE-DRUNK ONION AND FENNEL PIZZA

Serves 6; makes 3 pies

Total time: 45 minutes plus cook time (10 minutes per pie)

I always feel sad for vegetarian friends on pizza night. Their options are always so limited; it's either a margherita (delicious), a mushroom (delicious), or a thousand random vegetables thrown on top of a pizza. As a person who is openly distrustful of green bell peppers, the random vegetable pizza is a no for me, because you know it's going to have a thousand green bell peppers all over it. So I made this little number for all my veg friends out there! This pizza nails how earthy undertones and a little bit of smoke can make a pizza sultry. Sultry pizza is not pizza I had known before.

Wine-Drunk Onions

3 tablespoons extra-virgin olive oil

1 yellow onion, sliced into ¼-inch rings

½ teaspoon light brown sugar

½ teaspoon salt

1 cup red wine (cab sauv works well), plus more as needed

Pizza

00 flour, for dusting

1⅔ to 2 pounds pizza dough, homemade (page 147) or store-bought

Extra-virgin olive oil, if using baking sheets

1 (13 ounce) jar of pizza sauce

6 ounces shredded smoked mozzarella cheese

10 ounces shredded low-moisture, full-fat mozzarella cheese

1 fennel bulb, sliced paper-thin

1 tablespoon ground fennel seed

Pizza Sprinkles (page 153)

Take pizza dough out of the fridge one hour in advance of preparing.

Position your oven racks (see page 144) and preheat the oven to 500°F, or as high as it will go. If you have a convection fan, turn that on as well. Set out all of your pizza toppings and, if you haven't already done so, make the Pizza Sprinkles (page 153).

TO MAKE THE WINE-DRUNK ONIONS:
Heat a large skillet over medium heat. Add 3 tablespoons olive oil and, once the oil is warm, add the onion, ½ teaspoon light brown sugar, and ½ teaspoon salt. Cook, stirring occasionally, until the sugar is dissolved, and the onion is soft and translucent, about 6 minutes. Add 1 cup wine and bring the heat up to medium-high. Soft boil, stirring occasionally, until the wine has evaporated, and the onion is super tender, 15 to 20 minutes. If, at any point, there is browning or burning, reduce the heat right away and add a touch more wine.

Once the oven is hot, turn on the broiler to get the oven hotter while shaping the dough.

Shape the dough as described on page 144.

IF USING A BAKING STONE: Dust the pizza peel with flour and put the shaped dough on top. Wiggle it to make sure it isn't sticking.

IF USING BAKING SHEET(S): Brush the baking sheet with a tiny bit of olive oil, to help the crust crisp, and lay down the shaped dough.

Spoon 3 tablespoons of sauce right in the middle of each pie and spread it outward in a spiral with the back of the spoon until you get to the crust. Top each pie with up to 1½ cups cheese total. Generously layer on the fennel and then the onion.

 IMPORTANT!! Remember, your oven is set to broil. Turn the oven back to 500°F (with the convection fan on, if you've got one) before putting the pizzas in the oven.

TIMING

You can get all the ingredients ready and stored in bowls in the fridge up to a day in advance. Pizza Sprinkles can also be made a day in advance, but don't cut, or add, the basil until serving time. Wine-drunk onions can be made up to a week in advance and stored in an airtight container in the fridge. No need to reheat the onion before it goes on the pizza.

IF USING A BAKING STONE: Use the peel to transfer your pizza to the stone (see page 144).

IF USING BAKING SHEET(S): Place the baking sheets on the appropriate racks.

Cook until the cheese is bubbly and melted and the crust is golden and delicious-looking, 8 to 12 minutes, depending on how hot your oven is.

Just as the pizzas come out of the oven, brush the crusts with olive oil and finish with a generous sprinkling of ground fennel seed. Serve with Pizza Sprinkles.

PIZZA SPRINKLES

¾ teaspoon flaky sea salt
1 tablespoon finely chopped basil
2 tablespoons grated parmesan cheese
1 teaspoon red pepper flakes
1 tablespoon dried oregano

In a small bowl, combine ¾ teaspoon flaky sea salt and 1 tablespoon finely chopped basil. Use your fingers to massage the basil into the salt, helping to break it up and flavor the salt. Add 2 tablespoons grated parm, 1 teaspoon red pepper flakes, and 1 tablespoon oregano. Mix and serve alongside the pizza!

A collection of my go-to tacos—from my adventures in Mexico, a decade of taco trucks in LA, and weirdly enough, a trip to Alaska.

FISH-FRY TACOS WITH SMOKY MAYO

Serves 6; 3 tacos per person
Total time: 45 minutes

Believe it or not, these tacos are inspired by a taco I ate in Cordova, Alaska. (I currently live in a city basically bordering Mexico—the irony is not lost on me.) I was invited to Cordova to learn about Copper River salmon, and let me tell you, I learned a lot about salmon, and I am now a Copper River salmon mega-fan. But we are not here to sell salmon. We're here to talk tacos.

What I loved about those tacos was their very simple, humble toppings, highlighting how ridiculously fresh the fish was. The taco stand in Alaska had a daily fresh fish—not just "salmon," but, rather, the specific species of salmon that was swimming in the river at the moment. This is why these fish tacos are a Choose Your Own Adventure–style taco. Whatever seafood looks to be the best quality the day you pick it up, use it! If you're not sure what's great, ask the fishmonger at the market or grocery store—they'll tell you what's up.

Taco Fixins

½ small green cabbage, grated or shredded (4 cups)

1 small shallot, finely chopped

2 juicy limes, cut into wedges

¾ cup smoky chipotle mayo, homemade (page 164) or store-bought

1 cup salsa of your choosing

2 Hass avocados, skins and pits removed, sliced

18 small flour tortillas, warmed (see page 159)

Fried Fish

3 pounds Whatever-Sea-Creature-You-Want, skin removed, cut into 1½-inch cubes (or whole peeled, deveined shrimp with tails removed)

2 teaspoons salt, divided

2 large eggs

1 (12 ounce) can of Budweiser (or other crisp American lager)

¼ cup yellow mustard

½ teaspoon black pepper

1 cup all-purpose flour, plus more as desired

6 cups vegetable oil, or as needed

TO MAKE THE TACO FIXINS: In a medium bowl, place the shredded cabbage with the shallot and add a big squeeze of lime. Toss to combine and then transfer to a small serving bowl. While you're at it, set out the rest of the taco fixins so when the fish is hot and crispy, everything is ready for serving.

TO MAKE THE FRIED FISH: Pat the fish dry with paper towels and season with 1½ teaspoons salt.

In a large bowl, whisk the 2 eggs. To the eggs, add 12 ounces beer, ¼ cup mustard, ½ teaspoon salt, and ½ teaspoon pepper and whisk again. Add 1 cup flour, 2 tablespoons at a time, whisking well to make sure there are no lumps or clumps, until the texture resembles a thin pancake batter. (If you like a thicker coating, feel free to add up to another ¼ cup flour.)

In a large heavy-bottomed pot, add enough oil so it's about 4 inches deep. Heat over medium-high until the oil registers 350°F. (If you don't have a thermometer, you can drop a dime-size scoop of batter into the oil. If it starts to bubble and crisp right away, you're good to go. If not, give it another minute or two.) Using tongs, drop the fish into the batter and then pull it out, allowing any excess liquid to run back into the bowl. Carefully add the fish into the oil. DON'T OVERCROWD THE POT! Make sure to leave at least ½ inch of space on all sides of the fish. Fry the fish until the batter is a deep golden brown on all sides, 3 to 4 minutes. Scoop out the fish, using a large slotted spoon, spider, or tongs, letting any excess oil drip back into the pot, and lay the pieces on a plate covered with a paper towel while you fry the rest.

Transfer the fish to a serving bowl and serve with all the fixins and warm tortillas!

TIPS + TIMING

1. Get the salsa, limes, and cabbage ready up to a day in advance and leave them in small serving bowls covered in plastic wrap in the fridge. Make chipotle mayo up to 3 days in advance and store in the fridge in an airtight container or a squeeze bottle. Fry the fish, slice the avocados, and warm the tortillas just before serving.

2. Not sure what kind of seafood to use? Try:
   - Shrimp   - Halibut
   - Salmon   - Cod
   - Mahimahi   - Haddock

SMOKY SPICY SEARED FISH TACOS

Serves 6; 2 tacos per person
Total time: 20 minutes

This dish is suuuuuper easy. Take all the dry ingredients, put them in a resealable plastic bag, and give the bag a shake. Add in the fish and shake again. Crisp it up, serve with sides, and you've got yourself a light-cleanup, easy-as-pie dinner.

When you cook your fish, make sure to give enough room between the fillets so they can properly cook. This is a versatile cooking technique that works for lots of different fish and can lean into different cuisines, depending on the spices you select. The spices outlined below are perfect for serving the fish in a fresh tortilla with a big squeeze of lime.

Taco Fixins

½ cup coarsely chopped fresh cilantro

2 limes, cut into wedges

2 cups thinly sliced cabbage

12 (8 inch) corn tortillas, warmed (see illustration)

Green salsa of your choosing

Quickled Onions (page 166)

Avocado Crema (page 165)

Fish

3 tablespoons all-purpose flour

3 tablespoons panko bread crumbs or other unseasoned bread crumbs

1 teaspoon garlic powder

1 teaspoon onion powder

½ teaspoon cayenne pepper

½ teaspoon smoked paprika

1 teaspoon ground coriander

2 teaspoons chipotle powder

1½ pounds American or Canadian tilapia fillets

2 teaspoons salt

1 teaspoon black pepper

1 cup canola oil or other neutral high-heat oil

1 teaspoon flaky sea salt

TO MAKE THE TACO FIXINS: Gather all the ingredients and set them out in bowls for everyone to make their tacos.

TO MAKE THE FISH: In a gallon-size resealable plastic bag, combine 3 tablespoons flour, 3 tablespoons panko, 1 teaspoon garlic powder, 1 teaspoon onion powder, ½ teaspoon cayenne, ½ teaspoon smoked paprika, 1 teaspoon coriander, and 2 teaspoons chipotle powder. Shake well and set aside.

Pat the fish dry with a paper towel and generously season both sides of each piece with a total of 2 teaspoons salt and 1 teaspoon black pepper. Add the fish to the plastic bag. Make sure the bag is well-sealed and shake it vigorously to coat each piece of fish. Feel free to dance while completing this step.

Heat a large sauté pan over medium-high heat. Once warm, add just enough oil to cover the bottom of the pan.

Before adding the fish, make sure the oil is evenly hot across the pan by touching the corner of a piece of fish to the oil in a few spots. If the oil sizzles and is having a party when the fish touches it, it's good to go. If it sounds like a place you'd need a library card, wait another minute.

Shake each piece of fish over the plastic bag to allow any excess flour to fall off. Lay the fish down in the pan with ½ inch of space between each fillet. You will probably have to cook the fish in batches. Cook until the bottom side is golden brown, about 3 minutes, then carefully flip. Repeat until side two is equally crispy and golden, about 2 more minutes.

Transfer the cooked fish to a plate lined with paper towels and continue to fry the rest of the fish.

Serve sprinkled with a teaspoon of flaky sea salt and all the fixins on the side. Let everyone tear up pieces of the fish and assemble tacos to their own preference.

TIPS + TIMING

1. You can coat the fish in the flour/spice up to 4 hours in advance; refrigerate, uncovered, on a lightly floured baking sheet, and remove from the fridge 30 minutes before pan-frying. Avocados brown quickly, so I like to make the crema within 2 hours of serving and keep it in the fridge until go-time. All other sides can be prepped up to a day in advance and stored in small serving bowls covered in plastic wrap in the fridge.

2. To warm the tortillas, either heat each tortilla over a medium open flame on a gas cooktop for 15 seconds per side, or wrap stacks of 5 tortillas in tinfoil and bake for 15 minutes at 350°F.

REHEATING TORTILLAS

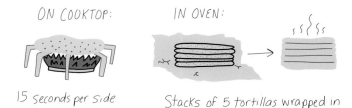

ON COOKTOP:

15 seconds per side

IN OVEN:

Stacks of 5 tortillas wrapped in foil, cooked for 15 minutes at 350°

SORT-OF-KIND-OF COCHINITA PIBIL

Serves 6; 3 tacos per person

Total time: 5 hours (4 of which are hands-off baking) + 4 TO 24 HOURS MARINATING TIME

I feel like the luckiest gal in the world to live in a city that is crawling with delicious food from every corner of the Earth. My partner-in-crime, Andy, is a true lover of tacos, so we've tried—I don't know—150 different tacos in LA? Who's counting!? One of my favorites is cochinita pibil, a slowly roasted pork dish from the Yucatán. Traditionally, it is either a whole suckling pig or pork shoulder marinated in a bath of citrus with achiote and other spices and then cooked in banana leaves until it's the tenderest.

To make a version that is easily re-creatable for those without access to banana leaves or achiote, I came up with this little number. It's a very satisfying facsimile that makes for some of the greatest leftovers known to humankind. I use a combination of turmeric and paprika to mimic the achiote, and a whole bunch of citrus to attempt to replicate the unique flavor of bitter oranges. It's a perfect bite of moist, lightly spicy, and incredibly flavorful, tender pork. Wrap it in a tortilla and life is good.

3 pounds bone-in pork shoulder, cut into 3 large chunks

2½ tablespoons salt, divided

2 teaspoons sugar

1 garlic head, cloves separated and peeled

1 tablespoon ground cumin

1 tablespoon black peppercorns

2 whole cloves

1 cinnamon stick

1 tablespoon dried oregano

2 teaspoons ground turmeric

2 teaspoons smoked paprika

⅓ cup fresh lime juice (about 3 limes)

⅓ cup fresh orange juice (about 1 orange)

⅓ cup fresh grapefruit juice (about 1 grapefruit)

¼ cup water

1 white onion, sliced into thin half-moons

Taco Fixins

1 cup coarsely chopped fresh cilantro

1 white onion, diced

1 cup pickled radish (see page 166)

Spicy red salsa, or salsa of your choosing

18 small corn tortillas, warmed (see illustration, page 159)

The night before cooking (or for a few hours before cooking, if you forget), rub the pork with 1 tablespoon salt and 2 teaspoons sugar. Store in the fridge and remove 1 hour before cooking.

Turn on the broiler. Once it's hot-hot-hot, put the garlic cloves on a baking sheet and toss into the oven as close to the broiler as possible. Watch them carefully. Pull them out once they begin to char and have a few blackened spots, about 2 minutes. Set aside.

Reduce the oven temperature to 300°F.

Heat a small, heavy-bottomed skillet over medium heat and toast 1 tablespoon cumin, 1 tablespoon peppercorns, 2 cloves, 1 cinnamon stick (don't worry, your blender will whiz it up no problem!), 1 tablespoon oregano, 2 teaspoons turmeric, and 2 teaspoons smoked paprika until aromatic, about 1 minute.

Add the spices to a blender with the garlic, 1½ tablespoons salt, ⅓ cup lime juice, ⅓ cup orange juice, ⅓ cup grapefruit juice, and ¼ cup water. Blend until smooth.

Place the pork shoulder in the bottom of a Dutch oven and pour the citrus marinade over the meat. Scatter the white onions on top of the meat and marinade.

recipe continues

Bake, covered, for 4 hours, until the meat is fork-tender.

Let the meat rest until it's cool enough to handle, 30 minutes or so, and then shred into bite-size pieces, removing any excess fat, if you like. Serve with all the fixins.

TIPS + TIMING

1. The longer this sits, the better. You can make this up to 3 days in advance. Shred and broil until hot and crispy a few minutes before serving. Sides can be prepped up to a day in advance and stored in small serving bowls covered in plastic wrap in the fridge.
2. I like to cook the meat with all the fat on and then remove the fat before tearing the meat apart. It is, however, more work, so feel free to trim the fat before tearing. If you refrigerate the cooked meat overnight before removing the fat and tearing it up, it's much easier.

Using bone-in meat helps flavor the meat and sauce as it cooks, but if you can't find it, you can use boneless.

SMOKY CHIPOTLE MAYO

Serves 6; makes 1 cup

Total time: 5 minutes

Chipotle mayo is one of those things where every time I see it I think "ehhh," and then when I eat it I think "mmmmmm." It really just hits all the pleasure sensors. And as you will see, it's insanely easy.

½ cup mayo

¼ cup Mexican crema or sour cream

3 tablespoons adobo sauce from a can of chipotle peppers in adobo sauce, to taste

2 tablespoons fresh lime juice, plus more to taste

⅛ teaspoon salt

In a small bowl, whisk together ½ cup mayo, ¼ cup crema (or sour cream), 2 tablespoons adobo sauce, 2 tablespoons lime juice, and ⅛ teaspoon salt. Add the remaining tablespoon of adobo sauce and lime juice to taste. Refrigerate until serving.

AVOCADO CREMA

Serves 6; makes 3½ cups
Total time: 10 minutes

2 ripe Hass avocados, skins and pits removed

¾ cup lightly packed fresh cilantro

1 (13.5 ounce) can of full-fat, unsweetened coconut milk

1 garlic clove, peeled

3 tablespoons fresh lime juice, plus more to taste

¾ teaspoon salt, plus more to taste

½ jalapeño pepper, plus more to taste

This crema is adapted from one in Yotam Ottolenghi's book *Flavor*. I was floored by how delicious the combination of coconut milk and avocado was. For the Smoked Spicy Seared Tacos (page 158), I wanted to amp the flavors up and create a zestier, spicier version that you would want to drizzle on everything!

In a food processor or blender, combine the avocados, cilantro, coconut milk, garlic clove, 3 tablespoons lime juice, ¾ teaspoon salt, and the jalapeño. Blend until velvety smooth, scraping down the sides as needed. If your crema is too thick for your liking, add water a tablespoon at a time and reblend until it's pourable and luxurious. Add extra lime juice, jalapeño, or salt to taste.

Tips + Timing

1. How to tell if your avo is ripe:
   - Apply gentle pressure. It should give, but not feel mushy, and it certainly shouldn't be easy to push your thumb through.
   - Did it pass the first test? Great! Now, flick off the stem. Is it green below? You're good to go. Is it brown? Put it down!
2. If you are a bit more sensitive to spiciness, remove the white pith and seeds from the jalapeño prior to adding it to the blender.
3. My favorite thing to do is to whip this up and put it in one of my reusable squeeze bottles (they're very cheap) and then put it on the table and let everyone go to town, putting it on roasted vegetables, in a taco, straight into their mouths . . . whatever.

QUICKLED ONIONS

Serves 6; makes 3½ cups
Total time: 10 minutes

Quickle (*n*.): an incredibly easy and quick-to-make slightly pickled food object.

It's like the red lipstick of food. Slap it on just about anything and it makes it look like you tried, even if you just rolled out of bed and still have a twig in your hair from a hike yesterday.

1 large red onion, thinly sliced
½ cup fresh orange juice (about 1 large, juicy orange)
¼ teaspoon peppercorns
½ teaspoon dried oregano
¾ cup apple cider vinegar
2 teaspoons sugar
1½ teaspoons salt

Pack the onion slices into a 16-ounce glass jar and cover with ½ cup orange juice, ¼ teaspoon peppercorns, and ½ teaspoon dried oregano.

In a small saucepan over medium heat, bring ¾ cup apple cider vinegar, 2 teaspoons sugar, and 1½ teaspoons salt to a simmer. Once all the solids have dissolved, after about 3 minutes, pour over the onions.

Cool on the counter for 30 minutes, put the lid on, give it a quick shake, remove the lid, and refrigerate until chilled, about 1 hour. (Leaving the lid off will help the onions cool more quickly in the fridge; once chilled, put the lid back on to store.) Shake again before serving.

HOT TIP **TO MAKE QUICKLED RADISHES:** Swap out the onion for a bunch of radishes (cut into ½-inch cubes), swap the oregano for coriander seeds, and add 2 sliced jalapeño peppers.

TIPS + TIMING

1. Make the Quickles up to 4 days before serving; store in an airtight jar in the fridge.
2. Instead of recycling glass jars from jam, peanut butter, or mustard, wash them and keep them around for future batches of Quickles (or for storing salad dressings).
3. There are two ways you can slice an onion to make a Quickle (see illustration): half-moon (tender) or root to stem (crisper).
4. Apple cider vinegar imparts an extra sugary taste to the onions, which I love, but feel free to use a different type of vinegar.

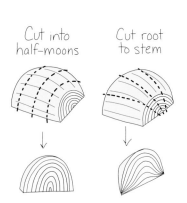
Cut into half-moons   Cut root to stem

HONEY-JALAPEÑO BLACK BEANS

Serves 6
Total time: 45 minutes

This is a recipe that I make almost every week. Honey and jalapeño are an unexpected match made in heaven. Trust me, this dish is a huge crowd-pleaser and everyone will go nuts for it, so you might want to double the recipe. While the beans aren't refried exactly, the low-and-slow temperature with lots of stirring brings out an incredibly creamy and alluring side of the black bean. You'll want to get to know her.

3 tablespoons extra-virgin olive oil

1 yellow onion, finely chopped

½ teaspoon salt, divided, plus more to taste

2 garlic cloves, minced

1 jalapeño pepper, seeds and ribs removed, minced

¼ teaspoon black pepper, plus more to taste

2 tablespoons honey

3 (15.5 ounce) cans of black beans, strained and rinsed

¼ cup coarsely chopped fresh cilantro

1 lime, juiced (plus an extra lime, just in case you need it)

Heat a medium pot over medium heat.

Add 3 tablespoons olive oil and, once the oil is warm, toss in the chopped onion and ¼ teaspoon salt. Stir regularly until the onions are translucent, about 3 minutes.

Add the garlic, jalapeño, and ¼ teaspoon each salt and black pepper. Stir until the onion is aromatic and soft, about 4 minutes.

Add 2 tablespoons honey and stir until fully incorporated.

Add the black beans and stir to evenly distribute the onion/garlic mixture.

Cover the beans with a tight-fitting lid, reduce the heat to low, and cook for 30 minutes, stirring vigorously every few minutes to ensure nothing burns or sticks to the bottom. If you find the beans aren't breaking down and getting soft, you may need a bit more time and a bit more oil. The beans should not look dry at all; they should be glossy, so if they're not, throw in another good glug of oil and let them cook.

Before serving, add in the cilantro and the juice of a lime. Add extra salt, pepper, and lime juice to taste.

TIPS + TIMING

1. These are great to make a day or two in advance; store in an airtight container in the fridge. Reheat in a covered pot over medium heat, stirring occasionally, until warm.
2. The more vigorously you stir the beans, the more of a starchy, refried-bean texture they will acquire.
3. If you're worried about the spiciness level for anyone, feel free to use just half the jalapeño; you can put the rest on the table for people to add into their beans.

Because sometimes
breakfast for breakfast
isn't enough.

BAGELS AND LOX WITH HOMEMADE CREAM CHEESE

Serves 6

Total time: 40 minutes + > 4 HOURS OF FRIDGE TIME FOR THE CREAM CHEESE

Once a year—to break the fast for Yom Kippur—Jews eat bagels for dinner. And, personally, I think that is an appallingly low percentage of the year to have your evenings end in bagels. If pancakes for dinner are a thing, then there is no good reason that bagels for dinner can't be one also. It's a super-fun, surprising, whimsical, and delicious way to entertain friends.

You may ask yourself, "What's up with making your own cream cheese?" Well, for one, having control over the quality of the milk, cream, and sour cream is what I'd call a good time. If that isn't doing it for you, it's also incredibly delightful to watch the childlike joy on people's faces when they discover that you made your own cream cheese.

P.S. Just so you know how much I love bagels and cream cheese, here's a Lego mosaic I forced Andy to make for me of the iconic New York deli Russ & Daughters. It hangs over our dining room table.

P.P.S. I always stop at Russ & Daughters before a JFK flight, even when it creates a logistical nightmare, because I'd do anything for the bagel, baby. Anything.

Cream Cheese

6 cups whole milk

2 cups heavy cream

½ cup sour cream

3½ teaspoons salt, plus more to taste

6 tablespoons white vinegar

Fixins

Choose what you want!

- Sliced tomatoes
- Sliced cucumbers
- Thinly sliced red onion or Quickled Onions (page 166)
- Lox or smoked salmon (3 ounces per person)
- Capers
- Sliced avocado
- Chopped dill
- Lemon wedges

- Cream cheese (⅓ cup per person), homemade or store-bought
- Peppercorns in a pepper mill so people can crack their own pepper on top
- Flaky sea salt
- Za'atar or everything bagel seasoning, homemade (page 106) or store-bought
- Salmon roe

BAGELS, OBVIOUSLY (1 to 2 per person)

recipe continues

Tips + Timing

1. Cream cheese can be made up to 4 days in advance and kept in an airtight container in the fridge. Veggies (except tomatoes and avocado) can be cut up to 10 hours in advance and stored on a platter covered in plastic wrap in the fridge.

2. Don't want to make cream cheese? Buy a block of Philadelphia, bring it to room temp, and whip it (whip it good). It tastes much better than the pre-whipped stuff, and you can add anything you like into it! Try:
   - chopped chives and green onions
   - small bits of lox
   - grated fresh horseradish
   - or even caviar (whhaaaaaaaaat?!?!)

TO MAKE THE CREAM CHEESE: In a medium pot over medium heat, whisk together 6 cups whole milk, 2 cups heavy cream, ½ cup sour cream, and 3½ teaspoons salt. Cook, stirring occasionally, until the mixture comes to a rapid simmer. (If you have a thermometer, you want the heat to hit 205°F.) Turn off the heat and add 6 tablespoons white vinegar. Stir and let sit for 5 minutes. Set a fine-mesh strainer covered with a layer of cheesecloth over a large bowl in the sink. Pour the mixture over the cheesecloth and strain for 30 minutes, dumping out the watery contents of the bowl twice to make sure it doesn't overflow. Grab the ends of the cheesecloth, pull them up, and tie with a rubber band so no cream cheese can fall out of the sides. Drain the liquid from the bowl one more time and place something heavy (and clean) on top of the

wrapped cream cheese to help remove any excess liquid. (I use a ceramic bowl with a can in it.)

Set in the fridge for at least 4 hours—the longer you let it rest, the thicker the cream cheese will be. Before serving, fluff the cream cheese either with a whisk (for a traditional dense texture) or in a food processor (to make it extra light and fluffy). Add extra salt to taste. Put it in a serving bowl and store it covered in plastic wrap in the fridge until dinnertime.

TO SERVE THE BAGELS: Make a platter with all the fixins you've selected. Stick some forks and butter knives around the platter so everyone can dig in. If your bagels are fresh, no need to toast! If they're yesterday's bagels, plug an extension cord into your toaster and plop it right on the table.

HOW TO SLICE AN AVOCADO

1. Cut 2. Peel back skin 3. Slice (or whatever)

ANYTHING GOES BUTTERMILK PANCAKES AND CRISPY OVEN BACON

Serves 6
Total time: 1 hour

You can serve whatever you ding-dang please at your dinner party! If you want to serve dino nuggets, fries, and ice cream, that's a dinner party. If you want to serve a variety of foods you can dip in ranch, that's a dinner party. And if you've had a long day or a stressful week and you want to eat pancakes with your friends, then you should have pancakes with your friends for dinner!!!

Andy likes—nay, LOVES—chocolate chip pancakes, so we make a lot of pancakes in our house. If you follow me on Instagram, you know we like pancakes so much that we do pancake recipe-offs. Our tastes occasionally change, favoring extra-tangy pancakes or super-fluffy pancakes, but this (slightly adapted) *America's Test Kitchen* recipe is one that all our friends agree on. It is a perfect proportion for delivering slightly-crispy-on-the-outside, fluffy-yet-diner-style-chewy-on-the-inside pancakes. It's also puffy enough that it can handle whatever toppings you want. Just plop 'em into each pancake as they're cooking. So if you want to have three kinds of pancakes, anything goes! (Anything, anything, anything, anything gooooooeees.)

Bacon

12 slices thick-cut applewood smoked bacon (or whatever bacon you prefer)

Pancakes

4 cups all-purpose flour

¼ cup sugar

2 teaspoons baking powder

1 teaspoon baking soda

1½ teaspoons salt

3 eggs, room temp

2 cups whole milk

2 cups buttermilk (or soured whole milk; see the tip on page 174)

6 tablespoons (¾ stick) unsalted butter, melted

1 tablespoon vanilla extract

Canola oil, for the pan

2 cups of Anything Goes toppings (chocolate chips, fresh blueberries, sliced bananas, nuts, bacon, whatever you want!)

For Serving

Salted butter, room temp

Maple syrup

TO MAKE THE BACON: Preheat the oven to 400°F.

Line a baking sheet with parchment paper and lay the strips of bacon on top, making sure none of the strips touch (use a second baking sheet if you need it). Bake until the tops are crispy and golden, about 15 minutes—no need to flip. Use tongs to transfer the bacon to a plate lined with paper towels. Turn the oven off.

TO MAKE THE PANCAKES: In a large bowl, stir together 4 cups flour, ¼ cup sugar, 2 teaspoons baking powder, 1 teaspoon baking soda, and 1½ teaspoons salt.

In a medium bowl, whisk together 3 eggs until frothy, about 1 minute. Add 2 cups whole milk, 2 cups buttermilk, 6 tablespoons melted butter, and 1 tablespoon vanilla. Whisk again to fully combine.

Make a well in the dry ingredients and pour in the wet ingredients; using a silicone spatula, fold just until combined—a few lumps and bumps are expected. The less you mix, the better the texture of the pancakes. Set aside for 10 minutes.

Heat a large nonstick skillet over medium heat and set your toppings off to the side of the stove.

Lightly grease the skillet with canola oil so it glistens—you need very little oil when making pancakes. Scoop about ⅓ cup of batter at a time onto the skillet, leaving an inch between each pancake. Scatter the topping of choice evenly on each pancake and use an implement (like a chopstick or a toothpick, or the back of a spoon) to gently push the topping ingredient into the pancake. (This will help prevent it from burning when the pancake is flipped.)

recipe continues

Cook on the first side until all of the edges have started to curve under and you see large bubbles forming and popping on the surface, about 3 minutes (this time can vary greatly depending on your stove and pan). When you think it's ready to flip, lift up a corner with a spatula first and make sure it's lightly golden brown. Flip and cook until the second side is set and begins to turn golden, about 2 minutes.

Move the pancakes onto a baking sheet as they're done and keep them warm in the oven (it's off, but should still be warm inside from cooking the bacon) until all the pancakes are cooked; regrease the pan as needed.

About 5 minutes before serving, remove the paper towel from the bacon and set the plate in the oven to warm the bacon up.

Serve the pancakes with the bacon, ample salted butter, and syrup.

TIPS + TIMING

1. You can make the batter the night before and store it in the fridge in an airtight container. Make the pancakes no more than 30 minutes before serving them. Keep them warm in a 325°F oven.
2. However tempting it may be to cook your pancakes in butter or lots of oil, don't. Butter leads to a less-crispy, quicker-to-burn exterior, and too much oil makes them dense and heavy. While your pan still needs to be slightly greased, less oil equals better pancakes!
3. No buttermilk? Take 2 cups of whole milk, replace 2 tablespoons of the milk with lemon juice or white vinegar, and let stand for 10 minutes.
4. If your syrup is cold, make sure the lid is fully closed and run hot water over the container until warm.
5. If you're making blueberry pancakes, add a teaspoon of lemon zest into the batter. Blueberry and lemon are best friends when it comes to pancakes.

A FRITTATA FOR ALL SEASONS

Serves 6
Total time: 40 minutes

Some people measure "a year in the life" in love. I measure mine in seasonal frittatas. A frittata is the very best egg dish to serve your buds. It's easy to make for lots of people, it's beautiful, and you don't have to eat it right away in order for it to be great.

There are a few things that are crucial to making an epic frittata . . .

1. Sauté your vegetables first (to help remove excess liquid and build flavor); the dryer the veg, the better the texture in the end.
2. Whisk your eggs before adding them into the pan (to aerate them, which helps keep the frittata fluffy).
3. Cook your eggs low and slow (because no one wants tough, bubblegum-textured eggs).
4. Slow the cooking process of the eggs by adding fat (milk, sour cream, or butter) in two stages.

The frittata you are about to make incorporates all four principles, resulting in what could be your favorite frittata of all time. And the great thing is, you don't need these particular veggies, herbs, or cheeses. You can use whatever you have lying around. For this size frittata, I like using about 4 cups of cooked vegetables.

Fall Vegetables

3 tablespoons extra-virgin olive oil

½ yellow onion, finely chopped

1 teaspoon salt, divided

2 cups diced peeled butternut squash (cut into ½-inch cubes)

3 garlic cloves, minced

½ teaspoon black pepper

1 bunch of chard, stems separated from leaves, leaves roughly chopped and stems thinly sliced (about 2 cups)

Frittata

10 large eggs

½ teaspoon salt

½ cup whole milk, divided

2 tablespoons extra-virgin olive oil

½ cup shredded low-moisture, full-fat mozzarella cheese

To Finish

1 cup ribbons of shaved Alpine cheese (a.k.a. "Super Melters"; think Alp Blossom, Gruyère, or Swiss)

1 tablespoon roughly chopped parsley leaves

Extra-virgin olive oil

½ teaspoon flaky sea salt

¼ teaspoon black pepper

Preheat the oven to 450°F.

TO MAKE THE VEGETABLES: In a 10-inch oven-safe pan, warm 3 tablespoons olive oil over medium heat. Add the onions and ½ teaspoon salt and cook until the onion is translucent, about 5 minutes. Add the butternut squash, garlic, ½ teaspoon pepper, and another ¼ teaspoon salt. Add the chard stems into the mix.

Once the butternut squash is soft around the exterior, about 8 minutes, stir in the chard leaves and another ¼ teaspoon salt. Cook, stirring occasionally, until the chard is wilted, about 2 more minutes. Remove all the veggies from the pan and set them aside in a medium bowl.

TO MAKE THE FRITTATA: In a large bowl, whisk 10 eggs with ½ teaspoon

recipe continues

salt and ¼ cup milk. Coat the pan with 2 tablespoons olive oil and reduce the heat to medium-low. Add the eggs and cook, stirring constantly with a spatula, until they begin to set, 6 to 8 minutes. The consistency will resemble loose cottage cheese. Add the final ¼ cup milk, all of your veggies, and ½ cup mozzarella. Mix well to evenly distribute the cheese and veggies among the eggs.

Use the spatula to smooth out the top, as if you were frosting a cake. Transfer the pan to the oven and cook until the center is set and there is some caramelization happening around the outside of the frittata, about 15 minutes. (If you like a crispy top to your frittata, drizzle it with a little more olive oil and broil for 2 minutes.)

Let the frittata sit on the countertop for 10 minutes. Use a knife to loosen the edges from the pan. Lay a plate upside down on top of the pan and while using oven mitts carefully invert the frittata onto the plate. Then lay a serving plate on top of the frittata and carefully flip it again.

TO FINISH: Top with 1 cup shaved cheese, 1 tablespoon chopped parsley, a drizzle of olive oil, ½ teaspoon flaky sea salt, and ¼ teaspoon black pepper.

TIPS + TIMING

1. Frittatas are great at room temp. So make it 3 to 4 hours in advance and leave it out, or make it the day before, refrigerate once cool, and let it sit out for at least an hour to come to room temp before serving.
2. My ideal pan for this operation is an oven-safe nonstick pan. If you don't have one, cast-iron works really well too. If using a stainless-steel pan, be sure to oil it really well.
3. Keep it simple and seasonal by following the recipe in the fall, but swap out the ingredients based on the time of year for the other seasons.
   - **WINTER:** Whisk the eggs with parsley, thyme, and garlic, and stir in 1 pound sautéed mushrooms and low-moisture, full-fat grated mozzarella; once cooked, finish with a pile of shaved pecorino on top.
   - **SPRING:** Stir in caramelized onion, a few roasted potatoes, fresh asparagus, and cubes of cheddar (try Beecher's flagship); once cooked, finish with heaps of grated hard sheep's milk cheese (try Ossau-Iraty) on top.
   - **SUMMER:** Stir in 1 cup completely strained and chopped confit tomatoes (page 76), ⅓ cup pesto (page 127), 10 ounces thawed and wrung-out frozen spinach, and cubes of Comté cheese; once cooked, finish with a soft goat cheese (try Piper's Pyramid for a super-fun hit of smoky) on top.
   - Or, go crazy and put in all the veggies you've got at home!

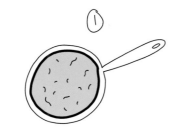

LOOSEN EDGES WITH A KNIFE

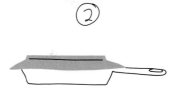

LAY A PLATE ON TOP

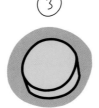

FLIP!

LAY A PLATE ON TOP

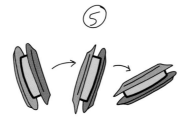

FLIP!!

FINISH WITH TOPPINGS

HOT TIP

If you're not feeling optimistic about flipping the frittata, you can also serve it right out of the pan!

I always want some sort of kitschy, childlike dessert to end a meal. No matter what has happened earlier in the day, or how serious a culinary endeavor the dinner was, a whimsical treat to finish makes everyone extremely happy. These sprinkle-filled, marshmallow-laced treats will end your evenings on a high note every time.

If you're exhausted by this point, don't panic. You don't have to make dessert! There are plenty of desserts that are easy to pick up and plop on the table. The only unacceptable dessert is no dessert at all. Let's begin with a few you don't have to make . . . and then on to the fun stuff.

DESSERTS YOU DON'T HAVE TO MAKE

IF YOU CAN'T SUMMON THE FLAMES DIRECTLY FROM HELL, STORE BOUGHT IS FINE

INA GARTEN

Angel food cake with whipped cream and fruit

Ice cream sandwiches

Soft, creamy cheese and fig jam

Corn flakes on vanilla ice cream

Frozen NY Cheesecake with warmed berry jam

Costco apple pie

Pocky sticks

Broiler s'mores (assemble and broil open faced until the marshmallow is just the tiniest bit burnt, top with the final graham cracker, and enjoy)

Everyone brings their favorite
ice cream and an unusual topping

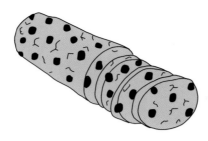

An assortment of frozen or
refrigerated cookie dough

Girl Scout cookies you've
hoarded over the years

Affogatos (with cold brew)

Watermelon or mangos
with Tajín and lime

Grocery store brownies

In-season fruit (or berries)
and whipped cream

Pepperidge Farm cookies

Fun Popsicles

Entenmann's cakes and donuts

Jell-O chocolate vanilla swirls

Tell your friend to
bring a surprise

BABKA-*ISH* MONKEY BREAD

Serves 6 to 8; makes 1 loaf
Total time: 1 hour 10 minutes

Monkey bread is the first recipe I ever made. In third grade, my homeroom teacher, Miss Larson, invited a bunch of students to her house for a cooking class (where I wore patterned leggings and an oversize Betty Boop T-shirt, my signature third-grade look), and I distinctly remember this being the most delicious thing I had ever tasted or smelled. It was impossibly sweet, sticky, and buttery. I looked high and low for the original recipe, but it got lost somewhere. So this is it (more or less) from a sense memory with an extra dollop of whimsy thrown in by way of babka-ish fillings. Yes, you can obviously make a fun dough from scratch, but for me, the joy of this dessert is how easy it is. You're just a few stirs and snips away from childhood nostalgia! You can set this out and have everyone pull from it family-style, or you can let it cool for 10 minutes and slice it up like a babka. Up to you!

Monkey Bread

4 tablespoons unsalted butter, melted and cooled

1 (16⅓ ounce) tube of refrigerated biscuit dough (I like Pillsbury Original Biscuits)

3 tablespoons sugar

1 teaspoon cinnamon

¼ teaspoon salt

½ cup (3 ounces) chopped semi-sweet chocolate

½ teaspoon flaky sea salt, divided

Sauce

6 tablespoons (¾ stick) unsalted butter

½ cup packed light brown sugar

¼ teaspoon salt

1½ tablespoons cocoa powder

1 teaspoon vanilla extract

Preheat the oven to 350°F. Lightly spray a 9 x 5-inch metal loaf pan lined with parchment paper.

TO MAKE THE MONKEY BREAD: Pour the 4 tablespoons melted and cooled butter into a large resealable plastic bag.

Pop the dough out of the tube and use a pair of kitchen shears to cut each biscuit into 6 wedges. As you cut, toss all the cut biscuit dough in the bag. Once you're done giving the biscuits a haircut, seal up the bag and shake it.

Add 3 tablespoons sugar, 1 teaspoon cinnamon, and ¼ teaspoon salt into the bag and shake again, vigorously.

Cover the bottom of the metal loaf pan with half of the sugar-covered biscuit pieces and evenly sprinkle

with ½ cup chopped chocolate and ¼ teaspoon flaky sea salt.

Add the rest of the biscuits and apply mild pressure to even out the top. (Too much pressure, and the sauce won't be able to get in all the nooks and crannies.) If you have extra sugar left in the bag, shake it on top. (Why the heck not?)

TO MAKE THE SAUCE: In a small skillet, melt 6 tablespoons butter over medium heat. Add ½ cup brown sugar and ¼ teaspoon salt, and whisk continuously, until the sugar dissolves and the mixture comes together, 3 to 4 minutes. Remove from the heat and whisk in 1½ tablespoons cocoa powder and 1 teaspoon vanilla.

Pooouuuurrrr the saucy deliciousness evenly over the monkey bread. Tilt the pan around to make sure the sauce is fully covering the top, as this is the glue that holds your bread together.

recipe continues

Bake until the top is golden brown and glassy and the inside is cooked through, roughly 30 to 40 minutes. If you're unsure if it's cooked, slide a cake tester or a toothpick into the center; if it comes out clean (aside from a smear of melted chocolate), it's done! Top right away with the remaining ¼ teaspoon flaky sea salt.

Your kitchen should now smell like an old-fashioned doughnut shop. You're welcome.

Let the monkey bread rest in the pan for 20 minutes. Slide a knife around the edges to make sure the bread isn't adhering to the pan and then use the wings of the parchment paper to lift it out onto a plate. Remove the parchment and serve warm.

TIMING

You want this friend warm from the oven, but you can still feel free to assemble up to a day in advance and store in the fridge. Take it out an hour before baking and then toss it in the oven while enjoying dinner.

CLARA'S COFFEE CAKE

Serves 6 to 8; makes 1 cake
Total time: 1 hour 45 minutes

When my mom recalls her favorite childhood food memories, she thinks of the smell of cinnamon and sugar and the old-world recipes handed down to her grandma Minnie from her great-grandma Clara, including this beloved sour cream coffee cake. Minnie always walked around the kitchen gripping a knife with a cigarette dangling from her lips. She never sat down to eat with the family but stalked around making sure everyone was eating enough. It's an image that makes me laugh and seems kind of charming, but it's something I'd say is typically not a good look to make your guests feel snuggly in your home.

Clara loved coffee cake with a cup of tea before bed, but if you are more of a morning coffee cake sort of person, you're in luck—morning happens every day and you can have the leftovers tomorrow!

Filling and Streusel

1 cup packed light brown sugar
¾ cup all-purpose flour
2½ teaspoons ground cinnamon
¼ teaspoon flaky sea salt
5 tablespoons unsalted butter, cubed
⅓ cup finely chopped walnuts
1 tablespoon turbinado sugar, to finish

Coffee Cake

1¾ cups all-purpose flour
1 cup sugar
1½ teaspoons baking powder
½ teaspoon baking soda
½ teaspoon ground nutmeg
½ teaspoon salt
1 cup full-fat sour cream
½ cup whole milk
¼ cup (½ stick) unsalted butter, melted and cooled to room temp
¼ cup canola oil
2 large eggs, room temp
1 teaspoon vanilla extract

Preheat the oven to 350°F. Lightly coat an 8 x 8-inch pan with cooking spray or butter and line it with parchment paper (see illustration on page 185).

TO MAKE THE FILLING: In a medium bowl, combine 1 cup brown sugar, ¾ cup flour, and 2½ teaspoons cinnamon. Move half into a small bowl for the streusel topping.

TO MAKE THE STREUSEL: To the small bowl add ¼ teaspoon flaky salt, 5 tablespoons cubed butter, and ⅓ cup chopped walnuts. Cut the butter into the sugar mixture by rubbing the sugar and butter cubes between your thumbs and fingers, breaking them up into irregular bits until the mixture resembles wet sand. Move it into the fridge, uncovered, until you're ready to put it on top of the cake.

TO MAKE THE COFFEE CAKE: In another medium bowl, whisk 1¾ cups flour, 1 cup sugar, 1½ teaspoons baking powder, ½ teaspoon baking soda, ½ teaspoon nutmeg, and ½ teaspoon salt together and set aside.

In a large bowl, whisk 1 cup sour cream, ½ cup milk, ¼ cup melted butter, ¼ cup canola oil, 2 eggs, and 1 teaspoon vanilla until well-combined. Add the flour mixture and fold in with a spatula or wooden spoon until just combined. It's okay to have a few lumps left; better that than overmixing, which will cause the cake to get slightly spongy.

Pour half of the batter into the pan and use a spatula to even it out. Sprinkle the filling evenly over the batter.

Pour the rest of the batter on top of the filling, smoothing the batter all the way to each end of the pan with a spatula.

recipe continues

Sprinkle the streusel topping over the batter, finish with 1 tablespoon turbinado sugar (to make the top extra-crunchy), and bake.

The cake is done when the top is golden brown and doesn't jiggle if you shake the pan, and a cake tester (or toothpick) stuck through the center comes out clean, 50 to 70 minutes. Start checking for doneness after 50 minutes. Let the cake cool for 10 minutes before devouring.

Tips + Timing

1. The raw batter, filling, and topping can be fully assembled in the pan and refrigerated for a few hours before dinner. Bake while enjoying dinner.
2. Room temp eggs will create a silkier batter that will bake more evenly. Leave them out on the counter for an hour before making the cake. Alternatively, you can give the eggs a nice warm water bath ("Egg Spa!") for 5 minutes.

BROWN BUTTER AND SAGE RKTs

Makes 18 squares of
deliciousness
Total time: 20 minutes

I have always been a huge fan of the Rice Krispie treat, but I am often left wishing they were ooey-er and gooey-er. I really cranked up the marshmallows in this recipe to get to what I think is the perfectly proportioned Rice Krispie treat. Your friends will not be able to put their finger on exactly what makes this RKT so special, but they'll know *something* is up, and you'll know that that something is brown butter and sage.

Cooking spray

8 tablespoons (1 stick) unsalted butter

8 sage leaves

1 (16 ounce) bag of mini marshmallows

¼ teaspoon salt

7 cups Rice Krispies from a 12-ounce box

¼ teaspoon flaky sea salt, to finish

Line a 9 x 13-inch baking dish with parchment paper and grease the heck out of it with cooking spray, or canola oil.

In a large pot, melt and brown 8 tablespoons butter over medium heat. To brown it, cook until the butter foam begins to disappear and there are little brown specks in the butter, about 3 minutes. It should smell like toasted heaven. Add 8 sage leaves and stir until aromatic, about 1 minute.

Remove and discard the sage leaves. Add in the bag of marshmallows and ¼ teaspoon salt. Cook, stirring regularly, until the marshmallows

are dissolved, and you're left with a deliciously gooey mess.

Stir in 7 cups Rice Krispies and use those forearms to make sure all of the marshmallow is evenly distributed.

Pour the marshmallow-cereal goodness into the baking dish. Cover your hands in cooking spray, or canola oil (so they don't stick), and pat the mixture flat with a light but consistent pressure across the top—too much pressure and you'll make 'em dense.

Sprinkle the top with ¼ teaspoon flaky sea salt and set aside for an hour to firm up. Cut into squares and enjoy the sugar high.

Tips + Timing

1. Make these up to 1 day in advance; cut into squares and store in an airtight container on the counter.
2. If you can't find/don't have Rice Krispies, these treats are delicious made with a variety of cereals like Corn Flakes, Cocoa Krispies, or Lucky Charms. If your cereal has more of a specific flavoring, omit the sage and proceed with brown butter treats.
3. If you want to get crazy you can fry up some sage in hot oil for about 15 seconds to dress the tops of the RKTs.

OOPS, I FORGOT DESSERT! CHOCO-DIPPED FRUIT

Serves 6
Total time: 40 minutes

I can't tell you how many times I've cooked a really nice big meal for friends and then, after dinner, realized I hadn't thought about dessert for even one second. But, because I am both a chocoholic and a fruit head (?), chocolate and fruit are two things I always happen to have around.

If you want to be all fancy, make the chocolate-dipped fruit in advance and present it on a plate à la mid-'90s Martha. OR you can drop the melted chocolate on the table with the fruit and lots of forks, à la fondue, and let people go to town. If you have random cookies, a slice or two of pound cake in the freezer, or anything else that sounds fun to dip in chocolate, you can put that out as well. One time I dipped a cucumber in chocolate just to see . . . It was not good. I'm a scientist.

1 cup (6 ounces) chopped semi-sweet chocolate

Pick Your Fruit! (choose one or a combo)
30 to 40 (2 pounds) ripe strawberries
6 ripe, juicy peaches
12 clementines
A bag of summer cherries
A few bananas
Whatever fruit you love!

Pick Your Toppings!
Toasted unsweetened coconut
Cacao nibs
Sprinkles
Flaky sea salt
Crushed cookies
Crushed candy bar
Chopped nuts

If applicable, wash, dry, peel, and cut all fruit. Line a baking sheet with a large sheet of parchment paper.

In a microwave-safe bowl, heat the chocolate in the microwave for 15-second intervals until mostly melted, stirring after each time. Stop before the chocolate is completely melted. The residual heat will melt the rest of it with a stir or two.

Dip each piece of fruit into the chocolate and twirl it around to cover all sides. Let it drip over the bowl for a few seconds before putting it onto the parchment.

Once all the fruit is dipped in chocolate, sprinkle the pieces with your toppings of choice. Set aside for 30 minutes to harden before serving or put in the fridge to serve later!

TIPS + TIMING

1. Prepare dipped fruit up to 6 hours in advance. Store in the fridge, uncovered, and remove 30 minutes before enjoying.
2. Get whatever fruit is in season and smells fragrant and delicious! A farmers' market is a great source if you have one in your area.

CHURRO HOT CHOCOLATE

Serves 6; makes 7 cups
Total time: 10 minutes

What's to explain? This is a really comforting and indulgent hot chocolate with a little cinnamon and an option to add cayenne to make your night just a bit more exciting. You can also omit the spices if you want a simple, perfect cup of drinking chocolate.

1 cup half-and-half

9 ounces bittersweet chocolate, chopped

6 tablespoons sugar, plus more to taste and finish

1 teaspoon ground cinnamon, plus extra to finish

1 teaspoon vanilla extract

¼ teaspoon cayenne pepper (optional)

¼ teaspoon salt, plus more to taste

5 cups whole milk

2 cups heavy whipping cream or 1 can store-bought whipped cream

1½ cups mini marshmallows (optional)

In a medium pot, bring 1 cup half-and-half to a simmer over low heat. Add the chocolate, 6 tablespoons sugar, 1 teaspoon cinnamon, 1 teaspoon vanilla, ¼ teaspoon cayenne (if using), and ¼ teaspoon salt. Whisk to melt the chocolate and dissolve the sugar. Yes, it's quite thick at this point. While whisking, slowly pour in 5 cups milk until all of it is used. Add extra sugar and salt to taste. Keep the hot chocolate at a simmer over low heat, stirring occasionally, while preparing the whipped cream.

Put 2 cups cream in a large bowl and place the bowl in the freezer for 5 minutes. Using a hand mixer, beat the cream on low speed for a minute, followed by the highest speed for 20 seconds. The cream should have medium-stiff peaks; if it's not quite there yet, keep whipping.

Ladle hot chocolate into mugs and finish with a generous dollop of whipped cream, a sprinkling of cinnamon and sugar, and some mini marshmallows, if you like. If the hot chocolate gets too thick from sitting on the cooktop too long, add extra whole milk or water to get your desired consistency.

TIPS + TIMING

1. Make the hot chocolate up to 2 days in advance: store in an airtight container in the fridge and warm on the cooktop before serving. Whip the cream up to 4 hours in advance and store in the fridge covered in plastic wrap.
2. Your chocolate matters! Chocolate chips tend to have stabilizers (soy lecithin) to help them keep their perky form. Using a chocolate bar will ensure a smoother and shinier finish.
3. Give that bar a taste before you use it. Does it taste good? Great! If it tastes bad, guess what? Your hot chocolate will also taste bad.
4. If you want a professional-looking sprinkle of cinnamon, put some cinnamon and sugar (50/50) in a fine-mesh strainer and shake over each cup of finished hot chocolate.

ORANGE DREAM GRANITA

Serves 6

Total time: 5 hours (includes 4¼ hours of mostly hands-off freezing time)

Granita (an Italian shaved ice) is a miraculous thing. It somehow strikes this perfect balance between rich and creamy and refreshing and icy. When I was testing this recipe at first, I made it with just oranges (using Orange Julius as my inspiration). But I found the recipe always remained a smidge too icy and not as exciting as I wanted. I then thought really hard about this nostalgic Orange Julius, Creamsicle flavor profile and I thought "AHA! Peaches!" and that was when the magic happened. The peaches add subtle sweetness and, more important, aid in creating a creamy texture—perfection.

Granita

¾ cup sugar

¾ cup fresh orange juice (from 3 to 4 oranges)

1 teaspoon vanilla extract

¼ teaspoon salt

2¼ cups chopped ripe juicy peaches (about 3 peaches)

1 large orange, peeled and seeds removed

1 tablespoon fresh lemon juice

Whipped Topping

1 cup heavy whipping cream

Fruit, like orange or peach slices, optional

TO MAKE THE GRANITA: Clear room in the freezer for a 9 x 9-inch baking dish. Leave it in there to get cold before using.

In a small pot, combine ¾ cup sugar, ¾ cup orange juice, 1 teaspoon vanilla, and ¼ teaspoon salt over medium heat. Stir until the sugar dissolves, about 3 minutes. Set aside.

In a blender or food processor, whiz up the peaches and orange with 1 tablespoon lemon juice until smooth, about a minute. Add the sugar mixture from the pot into the blender and blend again.

Pour the granita mixture into the frozen baking dish. Once every hour over the course of about 4 hours (or until the granita is firmly frozen),

stir/scrape the mixture with a fork, reaching all the way to the bottom of the dish, to create small shavings.

Optional (but heavenly): Before serving, scoop the granita into a blender or food processor and process it until really smooth and almost tacky, like sorbet.

Divide the granita among 6 cups and put the cups in the freezer for 5 to 30 minutes before serving.

TO MAKE THE WHIPPED TOPPING: Whip the cup of cream to medium peaks using a hand mixer—no sugar needed.

Divide the cream evenly over the granita. Top with fruit for flair as desired, and serve.

TIPS + TIMING

1. Make the granita up to a week in advance and store in an airtight container in the freezer. Make sure it is fully fluffed before tucking it into bed for the week. Whip the cream up to 4 hours before serving and store in the fridge in a bowl covered with plastic wrap.
2. If it's not peach season, use frozen peaches!

SISTERHOOD OF THE TRAVELING LEMON CAKE

Serves 6; makes 1 loaf cake
Total time: 1 hour 5 minutes

When it comes to cake, Ina Garten knows best. I adapted this cake from her lemon cake recipe to make it more of a tea cake rather than a dense pound cake, but the heart is still there. ☺ One time I made the cake, gave a nice chunk to my friend to take home to her husband, and it traveled to the other side of the city (which, in LA, is basically a road trip). He loved it. The next day, my cousin came over with her partner and I gave them some—they loved it. The day after, I gave the rest of the loaf to another friend, and she and her family (despite saying they weren't lemon fans) devoured the rest. This lemon syrup–soaked pound cake gets better the longer it sits, and it appears as though it fits everyone's basic dessert needs, whether or not they think they like lemon cake. Delicious with coffee or milky black tea.

Cake

Cooking spray (or butter), for the pan

4 tablespoons turbinado sugar, divided

1 lemon, seeds removed, sliced into thin rings

1½ cups all-purpose flour

1 teaspoon baking powder

½ teaspoon salt

½ cup sour cream

1½ tablespoons fresh lemon juice

1 tablespoon lemon zest

1 cup sugar

¾ cup (1½ sticks) unsalted butter, room temp

3 eggs, room temp

Lemon Syrup

2 tablespoons sugar

¼ cup water

1½ tablespoons fresh lemon juice

Preheat the oven to 350°F.

TO MAKE THE CAKE: Line a 9 x 5-inch metal loaf pan with parchment paper and grease with cooking spray (or butter). Add 2 tablespoons of turbinado sugar to the bottom. Shake the sugar around to make sure some sticks to the edges of the pan. Spread the lemon slices across the bottom and sprinkle the lemons with 1 more tablespoon of turbinado. Set aside.*

In a medium bowl, sift together 1½ cups flour, 1 teaspoon baking powder, and ½ teaspoon salt. Set aside.

In a small bowl, stir together ½ cup sour cream and 1½ tablespoons lemon juice; set aside.

In the bowl of a stand mixer (or in any large bowl), combine 1 tablespoon lemon zest and 1 cup sugar and mix with your hands to infuse the sugar with the lemon oil. It should smell really good. Add ¾ cup butter and cream it with the paddle attachment or with a hand mixer until the butter-sugar mixture is light and fluffy, about 5 minutes. Scrape down the sides and add the 3 eggs one at a time, mixing well between each addition. Add one third of the flour mixture and mix just to combine. Add half the sour cream mixture, mix to combine, then repeat with another third of the flour, the second half of the sour cream, and then the last bit of flour. The batter will be very thick, almost biscuitlike.

Scoop the batter into the loaf pan and spread it out evenly. Sprinkle the remaining 1 tablespoon of turbinado sugar over the top.

Bake for 50 minutes. When you stick a cake tester (or toothpick) into the center of the cake, it should come out clean; if not, give it a few more minutes in the oven. The cake should not have any significant color change when it's baked.

recipe continues

* If you want to turn this recipe into a drinking game, take a shot every time I ask you to put anything aside.

TO MAKE THE LEMON SYRUP: In a small pot, combine 2 tablespoons sugar, ¼ cup water, and 1½ tablespoons lemon juice and bring to a boil. Boil for a few minutes, until the mixture is reduced by half. SET ASIDE. (If you are making the syrup in advance, only boil it down by a quarter, as it will thicken as it cools).

Allow the cake to cool for 10 minutes and then poke a dozen small holes in the top with a toothpick and pour the lemon syrup over the cake.

Let the cake rest for at least 30 minutes before flipping it upside down onto a large plate, slicing, and serving.

TIPS + TIMING

1. This cake is BEST on day 2, which makes it a perfect dinner-party recipe. Just make it, remove it from the pan once it's cool, wrap it tightly in plastic, then set it aside on the counter until go-time.
2. If you forgot to bring your butter to room temperature, just microwave it for 5 to 10 seconds. Alternatively, you can pour hot, steamy water into a bowl, pour it out, and place that bowl upside down over the butter on the counter!
3. Turbinado sugar is also sold under the name raw sugar. It's just a large-grain, partially refined sugar that will help make the top of this cake sticky and glazed.

NOT YOUR GRANDMA'S PINWHEEL COOKIES

Makes 20 cookies

Total time: 1½ hours + 2 HOURS REFRIGERATION

This recipe is adapted from my great-great-grandmother Clara's version. Hers is more authentic to the OG Eastern European pinwheel cookie, as it has less sugar and a milder chocolatey flavor. But I've modernized it with some extra salt, fun textures, and, of course, sprinkles. It's sort of a mash-up of a few of my favorite childhood cookies rolled into salty, crunchy, sugary, slightly crispy, Jewish deli–style goodness. It's perfect for dunking into coffee. And it also doesn't hurt that when you stare at a cookie, it's like you're entering *The Twilight Zone*.

Vanilla Dough

1 cup (2 sticks) unsalted butter, room temp

1 cup sugar

½ cup heavy whipping cream

½ teaspoon salt

2 teaspoons vanilla extract

3¼ cups all-purpose flour

1 tablespoon baking powder

Chocolate Dough

3 tablespoons cocoa powder

2 tablespoons heavy whipping cream, plus more as needed

2 tablespoons Nutella

2 teaspoons instant coffee

1 teaspoon flaky sea salt, divided

Sprinkle Salt

½ cup rainbow sprinkles

1 teaspoon flaky sea salt

TO MAKE THE VANILLA DOUGH: Using a stand mixer fitted with the paddle attachment, or a hand mixer and a large bowl, cream together 1 cup butter and 1 cup sugar until light and fluffy, 1 minute on low and then 3 to 4 minutes on medium-high.

Add in ½ cup heavy whipping cream, ½ teaspoon salt, and 2 teaspoons vanilla, and mix on low for 1 minute, then turn the speed up to medium-high to fluff, 1 more minute. Add 3¼ cups flour and 1 tablespoon baking powder. Mix on medium until the crumbly mixture turns into a dough ball that can hold together and is tender to the touch, about 1 minute.

TO MAKE THE CHOCOLATE DOUGH: Divide the vanilla dough in half and transfer one half into another large bowl. Into the original bowl, add 3 tablespoons cocoa powder, 2 tablespoons heavy whipping cream, 2 tablespoons Nutella, and 2 teaspoons instant coffee. Mix until the texture resembles the vanilla dough. If the dough still looks crumbly, add an extra tablespoon of cream.

Divide the vanilla dough in half and, using a rolling pin or a wine bottle, roll each half into a 7 x 8-inch rectangle on a large sheet of parchment paper. Repeat this process with the chocolate dough.

Stack one vanilla dough rectangle over one chocolate dough rectangle and sprinkle with ½ teaspoon flaky sea salt. Make a second stack with the remaining dough and flaky sea salt. Roll each stack, starting with the longer end, tightly into a log.

Wrap both logs in plastic wrap and refrigerate for at least 2 hours or up to 2 days.

Preheat the oven to 350°F with a rack in the middle.

TO MAKE THE SPRINKLE SALT: In a small bowl, mix ½ cup rainbow sprinkles with 1 teaspoon flaky sea salt.

recipe continues

Slice each dough log into ¼-inch-thick rounds and roll the edges of each cookie in the sprinkle salt. Place the cookies on an ungreased cookie sheet, spacing them 2 inches apart.

Bake until the bottom is slightly golden and the cookie is firm to the touch, 10 to 14 minutes. These cookies aren't supposed to be soft and chewy. If they're feeling gooey at all, throw them back in the oven for 2 to 4 minutes. Let them cool on the baking sheet for 10 minutes before transferring them to a wire rack to cool completely.

TIPS + TIMING

1. Make the dough up to 2 days in advance and store in the fridge. Slice, sprinkle, and bake before dinner begins.
2. The texture of the dough should be stiff enough to roll out and not be tacky. If it's still tacky or too soft, you can add a touch more flour and roll it out on parchment paper.

JUICY FRUIT GREEK YOGURT PANNA COTTA

Serves 6

Total time: 4 hours 25 minutes
(includes 4 hours of refrigeration)

I made this for my friend, and after her seven-year-old-daughter took a bite, her eyes got all wide and she said, "WE NEED TO LIVE IN A WHOLE HOUSE FULL OF PANNA COTTA." That is all.

Panna Cotta

2 tablespoons water, room temp

1 (¼ ounce) package of gelatin (about 2½ teaspoons)

1½ cups heavy whipping cream

½ cup sugar

½ teaspoon salt

1 teaspoon vanilla extract (or seeds of one vanilla pod)

2 cups plain, full-fat (5%) Greek yogurt

Topping

3 cups halved or sliced ripe, juicy strawberries

2 tablespoons sugar

¼ teaspoon fresh lemon juice

2 teaspoons minced basil

TO MAKE THE PANNA COTTA: In a small bowl, combine 2 tablespoons water and 1 package gelatin. Whisk until dissolved and set aside.

In a small pot over medium heat, whisk together 1½ cups heavy whipping cream, ½ cup sugar, and ½ teaspoon salt until the sugar is dissolved and the cream is simmering with small bubbles forming at the surface, about 3 minutes. Add the gelatin blob to the cream and whisk until the gelatin is dissolved. Turn off the heat.

In a large bowl, whisk to combine 1 teaspoon vanilla and 2 cups yogurt. Add the contents from the pot and

whisk vigorously to fully incorporate. Divide the panna cotta into 6 cups. Tap each cup on the counter to break any bubbles trapped in the panna cotta and refrigerate, uncovered, for at least 4 hours to set before serving.

TO MAKE THE TOPPING: About an hour before serving, combine the strawberries, 2 tablespoons sugar, and ¼ teaspoon lemon juice in a jar and shake. (This step will break down the fruit and make it a little bit jammy.) Set aside.

Right before serving, toss the basil into the fruit and shake once more. Divide the fruit among the cups of panna cotta. Please invite me over.

TIPS + TIMING

1. Cover each panna cotta in plastic wrap once fully cooled and store in the fridge for up to 2 days before serving. The fruit topping can be prepared at the same time, but wait to fold in any herbs until just before serving.
2. Make sure the basil is really dry before chopping, otherwise it'll turn into mushy goo when you try to cut it.
3. Can't find strawberries? Here's a list of other great fruit combos!
   - Peaches and basil
   - Fresh figs and a touch of fresh rosemary
   - Mango and unsweetened coconut flakes
   - Pitted cherries and mint
   - Apples and cinnamon
   - Pomegranate seeds and honey

PINK LEMONADE BARS

Makes 9 nice-size bars

Total time: 30 minutes, plus cooling time

When playing with lemon bars, I discovered that it's a real Goldilocks situation. Lots are too tart, too sweet, or too light, and some are dense enough to be used as weapons. After trying about fifteen recipes for lemon bars, I came across a Key lime bar from blogger Marzia Aziz, which I've since adapted, that strikes the perfect balance of tartness, sweetness, and density. The inside is almost cheesecake-textured, and the ratio of crust to filling is appropriately portioned at 1:1. I added some unexpected flavor by way of grapefruit, and created some whimsy with a swirlllll!

13 full-size graham crackers

¼ cup pecans

2 tablespoons sugar

½ teaspoon salt, divided

½ cup (1 stick) unsalted butter, melted

Cooking spray (or butter), for the pan

3 egg yolks, room temp

1 (14 ounce) can of sweetened condensed milk

1 tablespoon lemon zest

2 teaspoons grapefruit zest

5 tablespoons fresh lemon juice (about 1 lemon)

6 tablespoons fresh red grapefruit juice (about 1 grapefruit)

3 drops yellow food coloring

2 drops red food coloring

½ cup unsweetened heavy whipping cream, whipped (optional), for serving

1 grapefruit, rind removed, cut into segments (optional), for serving

Preheat the oven to 350°F.

In a food processor, pulse together the 13 graham crackers, ¼ cup pecans, 2 tablespoons sugar, and ¼ teaspoon salt until the mixture becomes a fine powder. Add the ½ cup melted butter and pulse until all of the crumbs are saturated. (If you don't have a food processor, crush the graham crackers and pecans in a resealable plastic bag until fine and mix the crust together in a bowl.)

Lightly coat an 8-inch pie tin or tart pan with cooking spray or butter. Press the graham cracker mixture into the bottom and 1½ inches up the sides of the dish to make a uniform crust. Bake for 10 minutes.

In a large bowl, whisk the 3 egg yolks until frothy, about a minute. Slowly pour in the condensed milk, ¼ teaspoon salt, and the lemon and grapefruit zests and juices. Whisk for

2 minutes to create a light and fluffy batter. Add the yellow food coloring and pour into the crust, leaving about 3 tablespoons of batter in the bowl. Bang the baking dish on the counter a few times to get rid of any air bubbles.

Add the red food coloring to what's left of the batter and whisk to evenly distribute. Pour over the batter in the baking dish in a zigzag or spiral shape. Use a chopstick or other thin kitchen utensil to swirl the pink into the yellow.

Bake until set and slightly puffed up, about 15 minutes. Let cool on the counter and then refrigerate for at least 1 hour before serving. Cut into squares or triangles and serve. If you like, you can top each slice off with a touch of whipped cream and a sliver of grapefruit.

Tips + Timing

1. This dessert is good super-cold, so make it a day in advance and pull from the fridge just before serving.
2. If you've got a surplus of a different citrus you'd like to use, have at it!
3. If you overmix the graham crackers and pecans you may end up with a crust that is too loose, it's ok, just bake it until it firms up to the texture of a chocolate chip cookie, and let it cool completely before filling the shell.

FUDGY CHOCOLATE CAKE WITH SALTED CARAMEL FROSTING

Serves 12; makes 1 cake
Total time: 1½ hours

When I was growing up, my mom worked in advertising and I thought she had the coolest job ever. When I visited her office, I got to hear radio ads, snoop around the creative department, and watch people list off ideas while they drank coffee on beanbag chairs and ate copious snacks. But most important, if anyone was having a birthday, there was a generous lady named Jen who made THE MOST TENDER CHOCOLATE CAKE I HAD EVER HAD. Whenever they celebrated a staff birthday, my mom would bring me home a slice, and it would make my week. It was a cake so light and fluffy, yet rich and moist with little surprise chips laced throughout.

As an adult, I am now the one who brings this to dinner parties—and everyone asks for the recipe. One day, I'll figure out how to not be embarrassed when I say it's a box mix with Jell-O pudding and sour cream whirled inside of it.

It's my great honor to share this magnificent cake with you—just be careful, 'cause once you start making this cake, no one will ever let you stop; it's a delicious curse! So, to everyone who has asked me for this cake recipe, here ya go!

Cake

Cooking spray (or butter), for the pan

1 box (15.25 ounce) of devil's food cake mix

1 box (5.1 ounce) of instant chocolate pudding

4 large eggs, room temp

1 cup full-fat sour cream, room temp

½ cup canola oil

½ cup water

1½ cups semi-sweet chocolate chips

Frosting

½ cup (1 stick) unsalted butter, cut into chunks

1 cup packed light brown sugar

¼ cup heavy whipping cream, plus extra as needed

¼ teaspoon salt

¾ to 1½ cups powdered sugar

¼ teaspoon flaky sea salt, to finish

TO MAKE THE CAKE: Preheat the oven to 350°F. Lightly coat a 9 x 13-inch cake pan with cooking spray, butter, or high-heat oil, and line with parchment paper (see illustration on page 185).

Using a stand mixer with a whisk attachment, or a large bowl with a hand mixer, beat together the cake mix, instant pudding, 4 eggs, 1 cup sour cream, ½ cup canola oil, and ½ cup water, scraping down the sides if needed, for 5 minutes.

Fold in 1½ cups chocolate chips and pour the batter into the cake pan. Use a spatula to smooth the top and bang the pan a few times on the counter to get out any air bubbles.

Bake the cake until the batter doesn't do a major jiggle dance when you shake it, the edges of the cake peel away from the cake pan, and a cake tester (or toothpick) stuck through the center comes out clean, 30 to 35 minutes.

Cool the cake completely before making the frosting. Once cool, use the parchment wings to remove the cake from the pan. Transfer onto a platter and ditch the parchment paper.

TO MAKE THE FROSTING: In a small pot over medium heat, melt ½ cup butter with 1 cup brown sugar, ¼ cup heavy whipping cream, and ¼ teaspoon salt. Stir just to dissolve the sugar and then let it sit untouched (stirring causes clumping) until the mixture's bubbling and turns a rich caramel color (like the color of the unwrapped butterscotch candy

recipe continues

1. You can make the cake 1 day in advance; just tightly wrap in plastic once cool and keep at room temp. Make the frosting and frost the cake just before serving.
2. Most of the time, overmixing is a no-no in baked goods. But with this cake, the long whisking creates a cloudlike fudge texture that makes you think the Angels of Baking are singing to you.
3. If you don't want to buy whipping cream just to use it in this frosting, you can also use whole milk.

with a hair stuck on it at the bottom of a grandma's bag), about 6 minutes.

Move the caramel into the bowl of a stand mixer or other large bowl and let cool for 15 minutes. Using a stand mixer or hand mixer (this will only work with an electric mixer), sift in ½ cup powdered sugar and whisk on high until fully incorporated and silky. You can sift in more powdered sugar, 1 tablespoon at a time, until you like the consistency. I like it pretty thick, so I use the full 1½ cups of powdered sugar. If the frosting looks pebbly or

sandy, you can correct the texture by slowly whisking in more cream, 1 tablespoon at a time, until smooth.

Pour the frosting onto the cake right away, and smooth it across the top, letting extra frosting drip down the sides. If you want, you can create organic swirls and shapes using an offset spatula for more texture. Sprinkle with ¼ teaspoon of flaky sea salt to finish.

FLOOFY FUNFETTI CAKE

Serves 12; makes 1 cake
Total time: 1½ hours

Three years ago, I was on a trip with my best group of lady friends to Lake Arrowhead, and I wanted to make a cake to celebrate one of their sort-of-kind-of-almost birthdays. I came equipped with candles, boxed cake mix, and all the secret ingredients that go along with it.

As I haphazardly tossed together my batter, I realized . . . I hadn't brought a cake pan. I just assumed that the Airbnb would have one . . . Rookie mistake. So I grabbed a stainless-steel sauté pan and baked it right in there. It stuck like crazy, so I just plopped the frosting on it, splatted some sprinkles on top, shoved the candles in, and brought it over to the coffee table. We ate it with spoons right out of the pan and it's one of my favorite cake memories.

Cake

1 (15.25 ounce) box of Funfetti cake mix

1 (5.9 ounce) box of vanilla instant pudding

1 cup full-fat sour cream, room temp

4 large eggs, room temp

½ cup canola oil

½ cup water

½ cup sprinkles, plus extra for the top of the cake

Frosting

½ cup (1 stick) unsalted butter, room temp

1 (8 ounce) package of cream cheese, room temp

1½ cups powdered sugar, sifted and divided, plus more to taste

¼ teaspoon salt

1 teaspoon vanilla extract

Preheat the oven to 350°F. Lightly coat a 9 x 13-inch metal cake pan with cooking spray and line with parchment paper (see illustration on page 185).

TO MAKE THE CAKE: Using a stand mixer or a hand mixer, beat together the cake mix, instant pudding, 1 cup sour cream, 4 eggs, ½ cup canola oil, and ½ cup water for 5 minutes.

Fold in ½ cup sprinkles and then pour the batter into the cake pan. Use a spatula to flatten it out and bang the pan a few times on the counter to remove any air bubbles.

Bake until the cake doesn't jiggle when you shake it, and a cake tester (or toothpick) stuck through the center comes out clean, 30 to 35 minutes.

Allow the cake to cool completely before frosting.

TO MAKE THE FROSTING: Using a stand mixer or hand mixer, beat together ½ cup butter and 8 ounces cream cheese until fluffy, about 2 minutes. Add 1 cup sifted powdered sugar and beat until fully incorporated; use a spatula to scrape down the sides as needed. Add ¼ teaspoon salt and 1 teaspoon vanilla, followed by another ½ cup powdered sugar. Beat until very light and fluffy, about 3 minutes. Add extra powdered sugar to taste.

Remove the cake using the parchment wings and frost away! Finish the cake with even! more! sprinkles!

recipe continues

TIPS + TIMING

1. The unfrosted cake can be wrapped tightly in plastic wrap and stored at room temp for 1 day. Whipped cream cheese frosting can be made a day in advance and kept in the fridge in an airtight container. Frost the cake up to 2 hours in advance of serving.
2. If you like a super-thick frosting you can keep adding powdered sugar, up to 4 cups.
3. If you wanna jazz up your frosting, try adding:
   - **FRUITY:** 1 tablespoon pulverized freeze-dried strawberries
   - **CHOCOLATEY:** 1 tablespoon cocoa powder and 1 tablespoon cacao nibs
   - **EXTRA SPRINKLY:** 2 tablespoons sprinkles right into the frosting!
   - **BOOZY:** 1 teaspoon after-dinner digestif like pear schnapps or brandy
   - **MAPLEY:** a teaspoon or two of pure maple syrup

RAINBOW COOKIE ICEBOX CAKE

Serves 6 to 8; makes 1 loaf cake

Total time: 45 minutes + OVERNIGHT REFRIGERATION

A traditional icebox cake (chilled layers of whipped cream and boxed wafer cookies) is a Feldman family favorite and the number one choice for all birthday celebrations. Maybe it's because the tradition started with my dad and his two siblings growing up in the Bronx, all having summer birthdays, and my bubbe didn't want to turn the oven on? Maybe it's because they're easy and she was not at all a baker? Or maybe it's just because it's delicious. We'll never know why it stuck, but I'm happy it did.

My love for an icebox cake is only exceeded by my devotion to that New York bakery staple, the Italian rainbow cookie. Thus the rainbow cookie/icebox cake cake mash-up was born.

> "I rate this cake a 100 out of 5."
> —my friend's five-year-old

1 quart heavy whipping cream

3 tablespoons sugar

⅛ teaspoon salt

1 teaspoon vanilla extract

Green, yellow, and red food coloring

1 teaspoon almond extract

2 tablespoons seedless raspberry jam

½ cup (3 ounces) semi-sweet chocolate, chopped and melted

1 tablespoon cocoa powder

2 boxes of Nabisco Famous Chocolate Wafers (or other thin, crisp chocolate cookies)

Flaky sea salt, to finish

In a stand mixer or with hand beaters, whip 1 quart cream with 3 tablespoons sugar and ⅛ teaspoon salt into soft peaks. (If using a stand mixer, cover the top of the mixer with a large dish towel for the first minute to prevent splashing as the cream whirls around the bowl.)

Once soft peaks have formed, add 1 teaspoon vanilla and whip until stiff peaks form, about 3 minutes.

Divide the whipped cream evenly into four bowls.

To the first bowl, add 6 drops of green food color, 2 drops of yellow food color, and 1 teaspoon almond extract. Fold to incorporate.

To the second bowl, add 6 drops of red food color and 2 tablespoons raspberry jam. Fold to incorporate.

To the third bowl, add 9 drops of yellow food color. Fold to incorporate.

To the fourth bowl, add ½ cup melted semi-sweet chocolate and 1 tablespoon cocoa powder. You know what to do. (The chocolate layer may look a little marbled, and that's okay!)

Line a standard loaf pan with plastic wrap. Make sure that your wrap is long enough to cover the loaf pan once it's full.

Place a layer of wafers (use whole wafers and fill in with broken wafers) in the bottom of the pan, then spread with a layer of half the chocolate whipped cream.

Add another layer of wafers and half the pink whipped cream, followed by another layer of wafers and the rest of the pink whipped cream.

Follow with a layer of wafers and a layer of yellow whipped cream and repeat, then a layer of wafers and a layer of green whipped cream and repeat.

recipe continues

End with a layer of wafers, a layer of chocolate whipped cream, and a final layer of wafers. Note: The loaf pan will be quite full and runneth over. Don't worry. No one has ever been mad at too much icebox cake.

Cover tightly with the extra plastic wrap and refrigerate overnight. Pop the pan upside down and use a butter knife to release the plastic wrap. Unwrap, slice, and serve sprinkled with flaky sea salt.

TIPS + TIMING

1. Make and refrigerate 1 to 3 days in advance. The cake needs to set at least overnight.
2. Don't skimp on the whipped cream—the cookies will expand and you wanna see all those layers!
3. If you can't find the thin, crisp chocolate wafer cookies, you can always use chocolate wafer sandwich cookies or split Oreos.

The caramel and chocolate sauces can both be made up to a week in advance and stored in airtight containers in the fridge. Warm in the microwave before using. The whipped cream can be made up to 4 hours in advance and stored in the fridge. Assemble the sundaes just before serving.

THE MESSIEST ICE CREAM SUNDAES

Makes 6 glorious sundaes
Total time: 50 minutes (includes cooling time)

Dipping your spoon into a sundae and pulling up a perfect bite of chewy caramel, vanilla bean ice cream, chocolate sauce, and lightly sweetened whipped cream with crunchy, salty walnuts has got to be one of the most satisfying spoonfuls of all time. This is my personal favorite iteration, but I encourage you to try different ice creams and different toppings to make it your own. Keep in mind that the ice cream is important. It's the foundation, so get one that you really like. Perhaps pick up a few different pints a week before your party and do a taste test. It's a joyous activity and a great story to tell at your dinner party!

Caramel Sauce

1 cup sugar

½ cup water

12 tablespoons (1 stick plus 4 tablespoons) unsalted butter, cubed

¼ cup heavy whipping cream

2 teaspoons vanilla extract

½ teaspoon salt

Chocolate Sauce

½ cup heavy whipping cream

8 tablespoons (1 stick) unsalted butter

¼ cup light corn syrup

¼ cup powdered sugar

¼ teaspoon salt

9 ounces bittersweet chocolate, chopped

1 teaspoon vanilla extract

Whipped Cream

2 cups heavy whipping cream

¼ cup sugar

2 teaspoons vanilla extract

¼ teaspoon salt

Sundaes

1 cup caramel sauce (store-bought or make your own)

3 pints vanilla ice cream (I like Häagen-Dazs, McConnell's, or Tillamook)

1 cup chocolate sauce (store-bought or make your own)

4 cups whipped cream (store-bought or make your own)

1 cup chopped walnuts

6 cocktail cherries

TO MAKE THE CARAMEL SAUCE: In a medium pot over medium heat, whisk together 1 cup sugar and ½ cup water until the sugar is fully dissolved, about a minute. Cook, undisturbed, until the mixture turns golden brown, around 9 minutes.

BE CAREFUL! This mixture goes from happy and golden to burning quickly, so watch it as it cooks.

Once you're happy with the color, remove the pan from the heat and whisk in the butter cubes 1 tablespoon at a time. Whisk in ¼ cup heavy whipping cream, 2 teaspoons vanilla, and ½ teaspoon salt. Set aside for 15 minutes to thicken before using.

TO MAKE THE CHOCOLATE SAUCE: Bring ½ cup heavy whipping cream, 1 stick of butter, ¼ cup corn syrup, ¼ cup powdered sugar, and ¼ teaspoon salt to a boil in a small pot over medium heat and cook for about 5 minutes. Remove from the heat and whisk in the chopped bittersweet chocolate and 1 teaspoon vanilla. Cool for 15 minutes before serving.

TO MAKE THE WHIPPED CREAM: In a large bowl, combine 2 cups whipping cream, ¼ cup sugar, 2 teaspoons vanilla, and ¼ teaspoon salt and freeze the bowl for 5 minutes. Beat, using a hand mixer, on low speed for a minute, followed by the highest speed for another minute. The cream should be set in stiff peaks.

TO MAKE THE SUNDAES: Lay down a piece of parchment paper on your work surface for easy cleanup. Divide the caramel sauce into six glasses. Use the back of a spoon to coat the inside of each glass with the caramel. Freeze the cups for 5 minutes. Then scoop ice cream into the glasses and top with chocolate sauce. Smother the chocolate sauce with whipped cream, sprinkle generously with chopped walnuts, and, of course, finish with a cocktail cherry.

THIN MINT PUDDING PIE

Serves 6 to 8; makes 1 pie
Total time: 3 hours (including 2 hours of chilling time)

Growing up I had a friend, Sarah, whose mom made the best chocolate pudding pie. Every time I make one, it's an attempt to re-create the unadulterated joy I experienced every time I got my hands on a slice of that pie.

Recently, I had an extreme hankering for Thin Mints. But every time I creeped up to a grocery store, hoping to find a Girl Scout Cookie table outside, there was none to be found. So I decided to mash up the flavors of Thin Mints with the classic chocolate pudding pie to satisfy my craving and it worked like a charm. You can easily omit the mint, swap out the Oreo cookie bottom for any cookie of your choice, and have infinite pies at your fingertips.

Crust
24 Oreo cookies
4 tablespoons (½ stick) unsalted butter, melted
¼ teaspoon salt

Pudding
1 large egg, room temp
2 cups whole milk
¼ cup sugar
3 tablespoons cornstarch
¼ teaspoon salt
1 cup (6 ounces) chopped semi-sweet chocolate
½ teaspoon mint extract

Cream Topping
1 cup heavy whipping cream
2 tablespoons sugar
½ teaspoon vanilla extract
⅛ teaspoon salt
Extra crushed cookies, to finish

Preheat the oven to 350°F.

TO MAKE THE CRUST: In a food processor, pulse the 24 Oreos until finely ground. Add 4 tablespoons melted butter and ¼ teaspoon salt and pulse to combine. (You can also do this without a food processor by crushing the Oreos in a resealable plastic bag and mixing everything in a bowl.) The crumbs should be very small and should feel well-saturated with butter, like wet sand. Pour the mixture into a pie tin and spread evenly across the bottom and up the sides of the pan. Apply pressure to condense the cookie crumbs. Bake for 10 minutes. Set aside to cool.

TO MAKE THE PUDDING: In a medium pot, whisk together 1 egg, 2 cups whole milk, ¼ cup sugar, 3 tablespoons cornstarch, and ¼ teaspoon salt over medium-high heat. Whisk constantly until the pudding starts to boil, about 5 minutes, then reduce the heat to medium-low and continue whisking until the pudding thickens, another 2 to 3 minutes. Take the pot off the heat and add in the 1 cup chocolate and ½ teaspoon mint extract. Whisk until the chocolate is fully melted

and then pour the pudding into the pie shell. Smooth the top with an offset spatula or silicone spatula and immediately press plastic wrap onto the surface of the pudding. (Don't worry, it won't melt!)

Refrigerate until the pudding is fully set, at least 2 hours; overnight is ideal.

Just before serving, whip up the topping.

TO MAKE THE CREAM TOPPING: In a stand mixer with a whisk attachment or in a large bowl using hand beaters (or with a whisk), whisk 1 cup heavy whipping cream, 2 tablespoons sugar, ½ teaspoon vanilla, and ⅛ teaspoon salt until stiff peaks form.

Remove the plastic wrap from the pie and spread the whipped cream evenly over the top. Serve topped with some crushed cookies!

Tips + Timing

1. The pie and whipped cream can be made a day in advance and stored separately in the fridge. Cover the pie with plastic wrap and store the whipped cream in an airtight container. Spread the whipped cream on the pie just before serving.
2. If you overwhip the cream, have no fear! Just whip in a bit more cream by hand to thin it out.

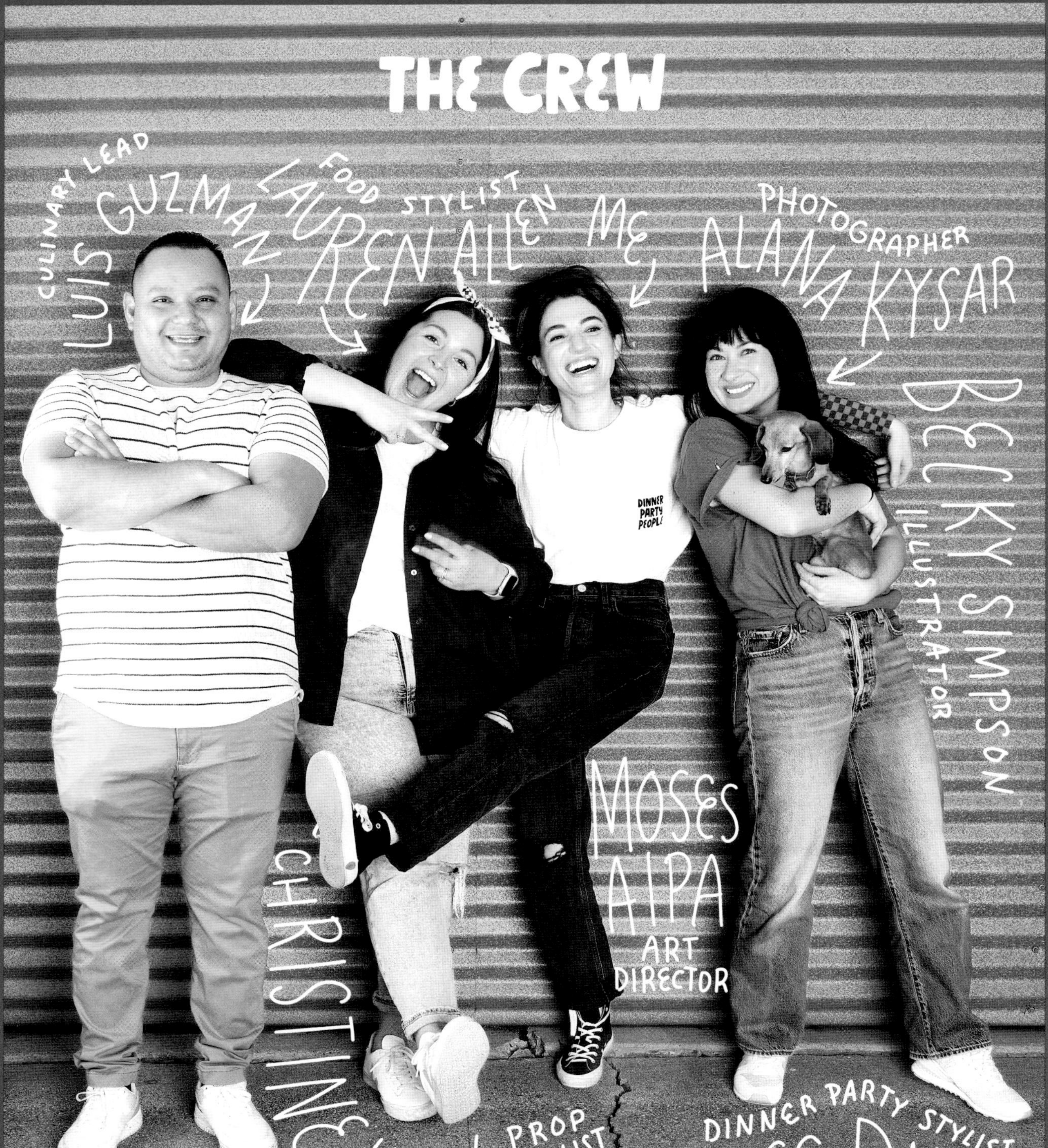
THE CREW
CULINARY LEAD
LUIS GUZMAN
FOOD STYLIST
LAUREN ALLEN
ME
PHOTOGRAPHER
ALANA KYSAR
BECKY SIMPSON
ILLUSTRATOR
DINNER PARTY PEOPLE
MOSES AIPA
ART DIRECTOR
CHRISTINE KELLY - PROP STYLIST
DINNER PARTY STYLIST
JESS DAMUK
MAX RAPPAPORT - DINNER PARTY STYLE ASSIST

Acknowledgments

To Alana, the greatest champion I could ever ask for. She encouraged me to make this book, she shot the whole thing, tested recipes, kept me organized, and was the wind behind my sails the entire time. You are the best of the best. And thank you to Moses for letting me come over all the time, for letting me steal Alana to shoot, and most importantly for creative directing. The fact that you both waited to move until we shot this book brings me to tears (in the best way).

To my partner, Andy*, who has encouraged me to tackle anything I've ever dreamed up. King of the spreadsheet, avid rejector of complaints, and #1 taste-tester. Thank you for being my partner in life. I love you big-time.

To Jordan, who helped me shape the proposal, made an enormous list of titles with me, added her magical words to the intro, and has been one of my biggest advocates and best pals since high school. I love you so much and I wish we could dine together every single week. Thank you for giggling when I thought it would be a good idea to specify that laughing till your cheeks hurt meant face cheeks and not butt cheeks.

To Lily, for helping me restructure all the good parts about how to make your dinner parties sing, for finding and sharing the world's best agent, and for being one of my favorite humans ever.

To my momma, Jeri, who came up and recipe tested with me whenever I needed and is the greatest wing woman of all time. And to my glorious dad, Andy F*, who let her leave him for prolonged stretches of time. Thank you for teaching me to think outside the box. And for supporting all this craziness.

To Nicole, the greatest agent of all time. (I wonder how many books mention how great you are, Nicole?!?!) A fierce advocate for what I thought was right for the book and a great problem-solving partner.

To Stephanie, for telling me that no one knows who the Honeycomb Guy is, for fixing all my bonkers grammar, and for quilting this book into reality. Every one of your notes was perfect and I am so thankful for you. Me want Honeycomb.

To my set family—Alana, Lauren, Luis, Christine, Jess, Max, and Kris—you made the photo shoot such a fun and joyous experience and I'm so grateful for all your hard work!

To my recipe-testing saints: Alexander, Kelly, Lily, Erin, Graham, Taylor W., Matthew, Sam, Tessa, Taylor R., Jonna, Kylie, Lydia, Eli, Ice, Hannah (my MVP), Nora, Dan, Michael, Thomas, Eileen, Abby, Danny, Max, Sarah, Susan, Kate, Kris, Camille, and Joanna.

To Andy M* for helping keep me organized; Julia D. for farmers' market runs and testing all the things in disturbing quantities; Sascha F. for reading/editing the pages over and over again; Kelly D. for helping pack, unpack, and cheerlead and for making yourself available when I needed help the most; Molly Y. for being such a curious brainstormer and sister in brisket; and Justin N. for helping wordsmith the front matter while being the busiest person on the planet.

To everyone who came to a dinner party, thank you for letting me highlight your beautiful faces!

To my sister cousin, Nora, and her husband/ my newish cousin, Dan, THANK YOU FOR

---

* I know, a lot of Andys.

LETTING ME SHOOT THIS BOOK IN YOUR HOME! I love you both so much and am forever grateful for your love and support even at my most pathetic. I hope looking at this book in the future brings back great memories of all the dinners shared at your home. Wanna party?

To Rachel and Carl, my second set of parents, who let me shoot the dinner party scenes in their beautiful home and yard. Your home has been the only consistent house I've ever known and being able to immortalize it in the book is incredibly special for me. P.S. I still owe you money to fix the table.

To the OG Cinema and Spice crew—Julianna, Mika, and Ilan: without all our production ridiculousness I seriously doubt I would have ever ended up writing a cookbook. I'm thankful for your friendship every day.

To the support of E.A.T. You will always and forever be my main squeezes. Having you two as my support system makes my life so so so much better.

To the brands that supported the photo shoot for this book: Mociun, Great Jones, Staub, Our Place, OXO, East Fork Pottery, Block Shop Textiles, Whitebark Workwear, Upstate, Las Jaras, Marshallberg Farm, Mepra, nail artist Meagan Knight, and Gozney. I am so proud to represent your products!

AND to anyone who reads this, likes it, tells a friend, buys an extra copy, shares a recipe on social, and/or hosts monthly dinners: THANK YOU for making all this time and effort worthwhile and for supporting me—I am forever grateful.

Tools for Your Kitchen

Let me preface this by saying that you should 100 percent use what you have and not run out and get every item on this list. But if you're looking to make your life easier, these kitchen tools will be extremely handy.

Baking Sheets/Pans: Use baking sheets/pans that are nonstick to prevent your hard work from falling apart in the final moments. (OXO makes a great variety!) Swap them out if they become warped or are no longer nonstick.

Blender/Immersion Blender: For sauces and soups and smoothies, if you're into that sort of thing.

Cake Tester: C'mon, don't stick a knife or a chopstick into your beautiful cake and poke a giant hole in it! A metal cake tester costs like two dollars and you'll never need another one. Alternatively, you can use a toothpick, but it's not quite as effective.

Cast-Iron Skillet: For searing steaks (page 79) or even making pancakes (page 173), nothing comes close to the perfect, even heat of a cast-iron skillet. You only need one, and get a big one so you can do just about anything in it. This isn't an item you need to spend serious $ on. Just get the standard Lodge brand, and you'll be very happy. This is an item you never want to put in the dishwasher. And read up a bit on how to season it!

Cheesecloth: Only necessary if you want to make the cream cheese in the book!

Cutting Boards: Get a big, heavy wooden cutting board for everyday chopping/cooking and use the heck out of it. It's sturdier and safer than thin, light boards. (I like Boos brand.) I also keep a large, dishwasher-safe plastic cutting board around for anything meat-related. If your cutting boards are slipping and sliding on your counter when you use them, dampen a paper or kitchen towel and lay it under the board.

Fine-Mesh Strainers: I keep a large one for rinsing rice, straining stocks, and washing produce, and a small one for straining cocktails, dusting cakes with powdered sugar, finishing cocoa with cinnamon, and other small tasks.

Fish Spatula: For flipping and flopping fish and for general everyday use. It's so slender and pliable that it's my go-to spatula for almost everything—just don't use it on nonstick pans since it's metal.

Food Processor: These are expensive, but you basically never have to replace them, and they mince, chop, blend, slice, grate, knead, and do your dishes (I wish!). It's a kitchen hero. Get one with a 10-cup capacity or bigger, and make sure it comes with disks for all your shredding/grating needs.

Garlic Press: For when you're too lazy to use a Microplane zester.

High-Sided (Sauté) Pan: For making a pasta dish, like the rigatoni (page 76), or spicy sausage pasta (page 65), this pan is a game-changer, as it's large enough to fit the pasta and the sauce without spills.

Knives: Get one or two chef's knives that feel good in your hands, and a sharp bread knife. All other knives are a bonus. I like Miyabi and Togiharu. Make sure to never put these knives in your dishwasher—and get them professionally sharpened every once in a while.

Ladle: The number of times I go to a friend's house and they don't have a ladle astounds me. Want soup? You'll need a ladle.

Large Nonstick Pan: Essential for pan-seared salmon (page 71), crispy tacos (page 155), and a zillion other projects where you're worried about sticking. Wash this pan by hand to extend its life.

Mandoline: A very handy tool for thinly slicing veggies and, less conveniently, for removing the tips of your fingers. You can also purchase cut-resistant gloves to protect the ol' hands.

Mixers: You only need a stand mixer if you bake A TON. I bought a deeply discounted KitchenAid stand mixer as a gift to myself when I started culinary school in 2012 and it's still with me today. Otherwise, a hand mixer will do any of the jobs in this book, and it's a much more cost-effective route.

Mixing Bowls: A set of three nesting bowls and a large tempered glass bowl for dough.

Parchment Paper or Silicone Baking Mats: If you don't have a nonstick baking sheet, use parchment paper. If you're a better person than I and want to take the eco-friendly route, silicone baking mats are going to be your MVP.

Rasp Grater/Microplane Zester: This little sucker is so much handier than you would think. Grated cheese? Done. Minced garlic? Done. Lemon zest? Done. Just don't grate off your fingers. When it starts to get dull (which it will after a few years), replace it.

Salad Spinner: It's not essential, but it makes washing and drying greens and herbs much, much faster and easier. I use mine almost daily, even though it lives in a cabinet over the fridge.

Stockpots: They're immensely useful for pasta dishes, multitasking, and straining stocks. If you have the space for two, it's super-handy to have an extra one lying around. You can get them very inexpensively at restaurant-supply stores.

Whisk: For making salad dressings and sauces and for looking cool.

Common Ingredients

These are super-common ingredients that you will need to make these recipes and probably already have on hand. I'm including suggestions for brands I especially like. When you finish up a bottle of your usual olive oil or jar of mustard, try finding one of these! You can, without a doubt, make amazing meals without fancy/costly ingredients, *but* the quality of your ingredients will make cooking something delicious much easier.

Boxed Cake Mix: I'm a Betty Crocker girl. It's moist, reliable, and tastes like childhood. In this book I use both Betty Crocker Devil's Food and Betty Crocker Funfetti.

Butter: Everything in the book was tested with Kerrygold salted or unsalted butter. For the price point it has the best deep, rich flavor and creaminess. If you want a really indulgent salted butter for slathering on bread, my favorite is Beurre de Baratte Doux. It's so expensive, but it'll change your life.

Canned Tomatoes: Bianco DiNapoli has my whole heart. Their canned tomatoes are balanced with an assertive tomatoey flavor, and they're super vibrant. If you can't find them, I also like San Marzano, Cento, or Mutti.

Chickpeas: For a tender, more fresh-tasting canned chickpea, try Westbrae or Bush's. Bush's are pretty salty, so you may want to add less salt to the recipe.

Chocolate: When you want smooth, velvety melted chocolate, opt for blocks, or fèves (bean-shaped discs), over chips. I like Guittard, Callebaut, and Valrhona. Bittersweet and semi-sweet can be used interchangeably.

Dried Pasta: The best dried pastas have only two ingredients: durum wheat and water. I love the brand Rustichella d'Abruzzo, but De Cecco is always a reliable classic. Don't forget to heavily salt the pasta water! The best dried pasta in the world won't save you if you forget to salt the water.

Eggs: Large eggs are standard for this book. I usually get organic, pasture-raised eggs because they have a bright orange yolk and make me feel good about myself, but do they taste all that different? Hard to say.

Flour: I always use King Arthur Flour. It's high quality and consistent. In this book I use their unbleached all-purpose flour, bread flour, and whole wheat flour.

Greek Yogurt: I always get a full-fat (5%) Greek yogurt, something so thick you could hold the container upside down and nothing would fall out.

Honey: If you have the option to buy local honey, you should! In the grocery store I find the most reliably delicious honeys are wildflower and orange blossom. If your honey crystallizes, run hot water over a very well-sealed jar until it begins to liquefy.

Mayo: Hellmann's/Best Foods (the same brand, sold under two different names depending on the region) is always the safest route. I do also like the mild sweetness of Vegenaise but would not look to other alternative brands.

Mustard: For yellow I like Plochman's. For a classic Dijon or stone-ground I love Maille, but I'm also a strong supporter of Grey Poupon (greatest commercials of all time).

Olive Oil: My everyday favorites are: Graza Olive Oil, Philippos Classic Extra-Virgin Olive Oil, California Olive Ranch 100% California Extra Virgin Olive Oil (do not get the global blends), and Enzo Organic Extra Virgin Olive Oil Bold. For finishing I love Le Mignole Olio Extra Vergine Di Oliva but it's $$$$$$, so use it sparingly—like a tiny drizzle on your hummus, for example.

Parmesan Rind: The rind is the protective layer on the outside of a parm wheel, and while it's hard and not ideal for consuming, it is ideal as a flavoring agent for soups. It doesn't matter what brand you get. When you work your way to the edge of your piece of parm, keep the rind! Also, when you see rinds being sold at the store, grab them because they last in the fridge for months.

Salt: I always have three salts on hand: Diamond kosher salt (for pasta water or anything using lots of salt), La Baleine French fine sea salt (for regular seasoning), and Maldon flaky sea salt (for finishing).

Sausage: If you have a local butcher, try a house-ground variety. Always read the ingredients in the sausage to make sure the flavors match what you're going to be making. My two favorite precooked store brands are Seemore Sausage—the La Dolce Beet-a is a classic in our house—and Aidells, which makes a variety of tasty options; I like the Italian and Cajun-style andouille.

Spices: Keep your spices for about a year and then treat yourself to new ones. I have seen so many people hoarding twenty-year-old spices that it's no longer surprising. My favorite brands are Burlap & Barrel, La Boîte, Diaspora Co., and Simply Organic.

Sprinkles: Use what you've got, but if you want to go on a shopping spree, I love my Williams Sonoma Dessert Sprinkle Mix. They bring the party.

Sugar: When I say "sugar" in the book, I always mean granulated sugar. I use C&H Pure Cane Sugar or Domino because they're inexpensive and easy to find. You will also see powdered sugar, light brown sugar, and its coarser cousin, turbinado, which can be interchanged with demerara.

Tahini: I always use Soom or Har Bracha. Look for one without much separation (could be an indication of age) and always mix it up really well before using. Tahini can be stored unopened for at least a year, and once opened it's good for a few months.

Tomato Paste: Always go tube over can. The tube can hang out in the fridge until you need it again, and the can always gets wasted. Cento or Mutti are both great.

Tomato Sauce: Rao's Homemade is the only sauce for me. For this book I use marinara and arrabiata. I am often inspired to make my own sauce, and then when I'm done with it I always think, "I wish I had just used Rao's."

Vinegar: For everyday staple vinegars, I use Napa Valley Naturals by Stonewall Kitchen. For a funky red wine vinegar, Camino makes a saucy number. And if you want fun flavored vinegars, I have a crush on Tart Vinegar.

Yeast: Saf-Instant is fast-acting and easy to use, perfect for any recipe that asks for instant or active dry yeast. You can store it in the fridge or freezer—no need to thaw before using.

Index

Note: Page references in *italics* indicate photographs.

A

Agua Fresca, *xxxii, 2*
Aioli, *28, 29*
Amaro Nonino
    Paper Plane, xxxii, 3
Ambiance, xxi
Aperol
    Paper Plane, xxxii, 3
Appetizers
    Athena's Dip Situation, 16–17, *19*
    creating cheese boards, 22–23
    Fancy Marinated Olives with Warm
        Feta, *12, 13*
    Hot Dog Soup (but Really Sausage),
        14–15, *15*
    Lemony Paprika Lentil Soup, 20–21, *21*
    Radishes Dipped in Honey-Fennel
        Butter, *24, 25*
    Ridiculously Smooth and Hilariously
        Easy Hummus, 26, *27*
    Smoked Paprika Potato Crisps with
        Aioli, *28, 29*
    Snackies—by Aristotle, 8, *9*
    Spiced Herby Yogurt Sauce, *10,* 11
    Tart Apple Butternut Squash Soup,
        30–31, *31*
Apple, Tart, Butternut Squash Soup,
    30–31, *31*
Apricot(s)
    Be-Your-Own-Bubbe (BYOB) Jewish
        Brisket, 41–42, *43*
    and Coconut Rice, Golden, *112,* 113
Arugula
    Carole King Salad, 95–96, *97*
    A Very Adult Salad (a.k.a. Grapies
        and Greenies), *134,* 135–36
Avocado(s)
    Andy-Approved Kale Salad, 104, *105*
    Carole King Salad, 95–96, *97*
    Crema, *163,* 165
    Fish-Fry Tacos with Smoky Mayo,
        156–57, *157*
    Super-Crunchy Green Salad, *102,*
        103

B

Babka-*Ish* Monkey Bread, *184,* 185–86
Bacon, Crispy Oven, and Anything
        Goes Buttermilk Pancakes,
        173–74, *175*
Bagels and Lox with Homemade Cream
        Cheese, 170–72, *171*
Baking sheets/pans, 226
Bars, Pink Lemonade, 206, *207*
Basil
    Dipping Magic, *56,* 57
    Party Pesto, *126,* 127
    Pizza Sprinkles, 153
Beans
    Black, Honey-Jalapeño, 167
    Braised Garlicky Eggplant with
        Chickpeas and Tomatoes, *38,*
        39–40
    chickpeas, buying, 229
    Green, Shallot Compote, *130,* 131
    Hot Dog Soup (but Really Sausage),
        14–15, *15*
    Ridiculously Smooth and Hilariously
        Easy Hummus, 26, *27*
    That Salad with the Herby Dressing
        (a.k.a. A Chopped Salad), *92,*
        93–94
Beef
    Be-Your-Own-Bubbe (BYOB) Jewish
        Brisket, 41–42, *43*
    Cozy Winter Night Borscht, 47–48,
        49
    Diner-Style Smash Burgers, 53–54, *55*
    Juicy Kofta with Lemon Coriander
        Yogurt, 67–68, *69*
    Perfect Seared Rib Eye, *78, 79*–80
    Your New Favorite Herby Meatballs,
        84, 85–86
Beets
    Cozy Winter Night Borscht, 47–48, *49*
Beurre Blanc, 72
Black Pepper
    Cacio e Pepe Mac and Cheese, *44,*
        45–46
    and Parm Phyllo, Veggie Pot Pie
        with, 81–82, *83*
Blender/immersion blender, 226
Borscht, Cozy Winter Night, 47–48, *49*

Bourbon
    Manhattan, 4
    Paper Plane, xxxii, 3
Branzino, Foolproof Lemon and Fennel,
    60, 61–62
Breads
    Babka-*Ish* Monkey, *184,* 185–86
    Fluffy Everything Pita Clouds, 106–9,
        107
    Olive Oil–Drenched Sourdough, *124,*
        125
Broccolini
    Charred Lemon, *118,* 119
    Pan-Crisped Sausage with Lemon
        Herb Veggies, *50,* 51–52
Burgers, Diner-Style Smash, 53–54,
    55
Butter
    Beurre Blanc, 72
    Bistro Compound, *78,* 79
    Brown, and Sage RKTs, *190,* 191
    buying, 229
    Honey-Fennel, Radishes Dipped in,
        24, 25

C

Cabbage
    Fish-Fry Tacos with Smoky Mayo,
        156–57, *157*
    Garlicky, with Whole-Grain Mustard,
        110, *111*
    Smoky Spicy Seared Fish Tacos, *155,*
        158–59
    Super-Crunchy Green Salad, *102,*
        103
Cacio e Pepe Mac and Cheese, *44,*
    45–46
Cake mix, boxed, 229
Cakes
    Coffee, Clara's, 187–88, *189*
    Floofy Funfetti, *212,* 213–14
    Fudgy Chocolate, with Salted
        Caramel Frosting, *208,* 209–10
    Lemon, Sisterhood of the Traveling,
        198, 199–200
    Rainbow Cookie Icebox, 215–16,
        217

Cake tester, 226
Campari
    Negroni, 4
Caramel
    Frosting, Salted, Fudgy Chocolate
        Cake with, *208,* 209–10
    Sauce, *218,* 219
Carrot(s)
    Babies, Roasted, *98,* 99
    Veggie Pot Pie with Parm and Black
        Pepper Phyllo, 81–82, *83*
Cast-iron skillet, 226
Cauliflower
    Roasted Veg Parade, 128, *129*
Cheese
    Andy-Approved Kale Salad, 104, *105*
    Cacio e Pepe Mac and, *44,* 45–46
    Carole King Salad, 95–96, *97*
    Cream, Homemade, 170–72, *171*
    creating cheese boards, 22–23
    Diner-Style Smash Burgers, 53–54,
        55
    Fancy Marinated Olives with Warm
        Feta, 12, *13*
    A Frittata for All Seasons, *176,*
        177–79
    Glorious Spicy Sausage Pasta, *64,*
        65–66
    Honey-Drizzled Zucchini Fritters,
        140, 141
    Parmesan rinds, 230
    Pizza Sprinkles, 153
    Rigatoni with Confit Tomatoes and
        Burrata, 76–77, *77*
    Roasted Tomato and Burrata
        Eggplant Parm, 34–37, *35*
    Spicy Soppressata Pizza, *149,* 151
    That Salad with the Herby Dressing
        (a.k.a. A Chopped Salad), *92,*
        93–94
    Veggie Pot Pie with Parm and Black
        Pepper Phyllo, 81–82, *83*
    A Very Adult Salad (a.k.a. Grapies
        and Greenies), *134,* 135–36
    Wine-Drunk Onion and Fennel Pizza,
        152–53
    World's Best Oven Fries with Parsley
        and Parm, 138, *139*
Cheesecloth, 226
Chickpeas
    buying, 229
    Ridiculously Smooth and Hilariously
        Easy Hummus, 26, *27*

That Salad with the Herby Dressing
    (a.k.a. A Chopped Salad), *92,*
    93–94
and Tomatoes, Braised Garlicky
    Eggplant with, *38,* 39–40
Chipotle Mayo, Smoky, *163,* 164
Chocolate
    Babka-*Ish* Monkey Bread, *184,* 185–86
    buying, 229
    Cake, Fudgy, with Salted Caramel
        Frosting, *208,* 209–10
    Churro Hot, *194,* 195
    Not Your Grandma's Pinwheel
        Cookies, 201–2, *203*
    Oops, I Forgot Dessert! Choco-
        Dipped Fruit, 192, *193*
    Rainbow Cookie Icebox Cake,
        215–16, *217*
    Sauce, *218,* 219
    Thin Mint Pudding Pie, 220–21, *221*
Churro Hot Chocolate, *194,* 195
Cilantro
    Athena's Dip Situation, 16–17, *19*
    Avocado Crema, *163,* 165
    Lemon Coriander Yogurt, 67, *69*
    Smoky Spicy Seared Fish Tacos, *155,*
        158–59
    Sort-of-Kind-of Cochinita Pibil,
        160–62, *161*
    Spiced Herby Yogurt Sauce, *10,* 11
Cinnamon
    Churro Hot Chocolate, *194,* 195
    Clara's Coffee Cake, 187–88, *189*
Cochinita Pibil, Sort-of-Kind-of,
    160–62, *161*
Cocktails
    Campari Lemonade, 3
    Extra-Fun French 75, 4
    Manhattan, 4
    Negroni, 4
    Not-So-Sweet Strawberry Daiquiri,
        1, 5
    Paper Plane, *xxxii,* 3
    The Versatile Margarita, *xxxii,* 5
    Xtra-Limey Piña Colada, *xxxii,* 3
Coconut
    and Apricot Rice, Golden, *112,* 113
    Butter, 106–9
    Xtra-Limey Piña Colada, *xxxii,* 3
Coffee Cake, Clara's, 187–88, *189*
Compound Butter, Bistro, *78,* 79
Cookies, Pinwheel, Not Your
    Grandma's, 201–2, *203*

Cream Cheese, Homemade, 170–72,
    171
Crema, Avocado, *163,* 165
Crème Fraîche, Dilly Horseradish, 116,
    117
Cucumbers
    A Simple Bistro Salad, 90–91, *91*
    Super-Crunchy Green Salad, *102,*
        103
    That Salad with the Herby Dressing
        (a.k.a. A Chopped Salad), *92,*
        93–94
Cutting boards, 226

D

Daiquiri, Not-So-Sweet Strawberry,
    1, 5
Date-Pistachio Salsa Verde Sauce, 71
Desserts
    Babka-*Ish* Monkey Bread, *184,*
        185–86
    Brown Butter and Sage RKTs, *190,*
        191
    Churro Hot Chocolate, *194,* 195
    Clara's Coffee Cake, 187–88, *189*
    Floofy Funfetti Cake, *212,* 213–14
    Fudgy Chocolate Cake with Salted
        Caramel Frosting, *208,* 209–10
    Juicy Fruit Greek Yogurt Panna
        Cotta, *204,* 205
    The Messiest Ice Cream Sundaes,
        218, 219
    Not Your Grandma's Pinwheel
        Cookies, 201–2, *203*
    Oops, I Forgot Dessert! Choco-
        Dipped Fruit, 192, *193*
    Orange Dream Granita, 196, *197*
    Pink Lemonade Bars, 206, *207*
    Rainbow Cookie Icebox Cake,
        215–16, *217*
    Sisterhood of the Traveling Lemon
        Cake, *198,* 199–200
    Thin Mint Pudding Pie, 220–21, *221*
    You Don't Have to Make, 182–83
Dill
    Brown Rice That Doesn't Suck, 114,
        115
    Dilly Horseradish Crème Fraîche,
        116, *117*
    -Lemon Sauce, 71
Dinner parties
    ambiance and tips, xxi

checklist for, xxxi
choosing menu items, xxii–xxiii
four steps to, xviii
overcoming challenges of, xv
psychological benefits, xiv–xv
recipe notes, xxix
sample menus, xxiv–xxviii
three styles of, xviii, xix
timeline, xx
Dips
　Aioli, *28, 29*
　Athena's Dip Situation, 16–17, *19*
　Basil Dipping Magic, *56, 57*
　Lemony Herby Yogurt, *140,* 141
　Ridiculously Smooth and Hilariously
　　Easy Hummus, 26, *27*
　Spiced Herby Yogurt Sauce, *10,* 11
Dough, Same-Day, *146,* 147–48
Drinks. *See also* Cocktails
　Agua Fresca, *xxxii,* 2
　Churro Hot Chocolate, *194,* 195
　Sparkling Ginger Limeade, 2

E

Eggplant
　Braised Garlicky, with Chickpeas and
　　Tomatoes, *38,* 39–40
　Parm, Roasted Tomato and Burrata,
　　34–37, *35*
Eggs
　A Frittata for All Seasons, *176,* 177–79
　large, for recipes, 229

F

Fennel
　Carole King Salad, 95–96, *97*
　-Honey Butter, Radishes Dipped in,
　　24, 25
　and Lemon Branzino, Foolproof, *60,*
　　61–62
　and Wine-Drunk Onion Pizza, 152–53
Fine-mesh strainer, 226
Fish
　Bagels and Lox with Homemade
　　Cream Cheese, 170–72, *171*
　Foolproof Lemon and Fennel
　　Branzino, *60,* 61–62
　-Fry Tacos with Smoky Mayo, 156–57,
　　157
　Pan-Seared Salmon for Any Mood,
　　70, 71

Smoky Spicy Seared, Tacos, *155,*
　158–59
Fish spatula, 226
Flour, 229
Food processor, 226
French 75, Extra-Fun, 4
A Frittata for All Seasons, *176,* 177–79
Fritters, Honey-Drizzled Zucchini, *140,*
　141
Fruit. *See also specific fruits*
　Agua Fresca, *xxxii,* 2
　Carole King Salad, 95–96, *97*
　Choco-Dipped, Oops, I Forgot
　　Dessert!, 192, *193*
Funfetti Cake, Floofy, *212,* 213–14

G

Garlic
　Aioli, *28,* 29
　Athena's Dip Situation, 16–17, *19*
　Braised Garlicky Eggplant with
　　Chickpeas and Tomatoes, *38,*
　　39–40
　Garlicky Cabbage with Whole-Grain
　　Mustard, 110, *111*
　Gremolata, 122, *123*
　Party Pesto, *126,* 127
Garlic press, 226
Gin
　Extra-Fun French 75, 4
　Negroni, 4
Ginger Limeade, Sparkling, 2
Granita, Orange Dream, 196, *197*
Grapefruit
　Pink Lemonade Bars, 206, *207*
Grapies and Greenies (a.k.a. A Very
　Adult Salad), *134,* 135–36
Grater, 227
Green Beans, Shallot Compote, *130,*
　131
Gremolata, 122, *123*

H

Herbs. *See also specific herbs*
　Lemony Herby Yogurt, *140,* 141
　Spiced Herby Yogurt Sauce, *10,* 11
　Your New Favorite Herby Meatballs,
　　84, 85–86
Honey
　buying, 229
　-Drizzled Zucchini Fritters, *140,* 141

-Fennel Butter, Radishes Dipped in,
　24, 25
-Jalapeño Black Beans, 167
Spicy Soppressata Pizza, *149,* 151
Horseradish Dilly Crème Fraîche, 116,
　117
Hot Chocolate, Churro, *194,* 195
Hot Dog Soup (but Really Sausage),
　14–15, *15*
Hummus, Ridiculously Smooth and
　Hilariously Easy, 26, *27*

I

Icebox Cake, Rainbow Cookie, 215–16,
　217
Ice Cream Sundaes, The Messiest, *218,*
　219
Immersion blender, 226
Ingredients, 229–30

J

Jam, Caramelized Onion, 73, *75*

K

Kale Salad, Andy-Approved, 104, *105*
Knives, 226
Kofta, Juicy, with Lemon Coriander
　Yogurt, 67–68, *69*

L

Ladle, 227
Lemon
　Broccolini, Charred, *118,* 119
　Cake, Sisterhood of the Traveling,
　　198, 199–200
　Campari Lemonade, 3
　Coriander Yogurt, 67, *69*
　-Dill Sauce, 71
　and Fennel Branzino, Foolproof, *60,*
　　61–62
　Gremolata, 122, *123*
　Lemony Herby Yogurt, *140,* 141
　Pink Lemonade Bars, 206, *207*
Lentil Soup, Lemony Paprika, 20–21, *21*
Lettuce
　Carole King Salad, 95–96, *97*
　A Simple Bistro Salad, 90–91, *91*
　Super-Crunchy Green Salad, *102,*
　　103

Lettuce (cont.)
    That Salad with the Herby Dressing
        (a.k.a. A Chopped Salad), 92,
        93–94
Lime
    Sparkling Ginger Limeade, 2
    The Versatile Margarita, xxxii, 5
    Xtra-Limey Piña Colada, xxxii, 3
Lox and Bagels with Homemade Cream
    Cheese, 170–72, 171

M

Main dishes. See also Pizza; Tacos
    Anything Goes Buttermilk Pancakes
        and Crispy Oven Bacon, 173–74,
        175
    Bagels and Lox with Homemade
        Cream Cheese, 170–72, 171
    Be-Your-Own-Bubbe (BYOB) Jewish
        Brisket, 41–42, 43
    Braised Garlicky Eggplant with
        Chickpeas and Tomatoes, 38,
        39–40
    Cacio e Pepe Mac and Cheese, 44,
        45–46
    Cozy Winter Night Borscht, 47–48,
        49
    Crispy-Crispy Turkey Thighs with
        Caramelized Onion Jam, 73–74,
        75
    Diner-Style Smash Burgers, 53–54,
        55
    Foolproof Lemon and Fennel
        Branzino, 60, 61–62
    A Frittata for All Seasons, 176,
        177–79
    Glorious Spicy Sausage Pasta, 64,
        65–66
    Juicy Kofta with Lemon Coriander
        Yogurt, 67–68, 69
    Pan-Crisped Sausage with Lemon
        Herb Veggies, 50, 51–52
    Pan-Seared Salmon for Any Mood,
        70, 71
    Peel 'n' Eat Shrimp with "I'd Eat This
        on a Shoe" Basil Dipping Magic,
        56, 57–58
    Perfect Seared Rib Eye, 78, 79–80
    Rigatoni with Confit Tomatoes and
        Burrata, 76–77, 77
    Roasted Tomato and Burrata
        Eggplant Parm, 34–37, 35

Veggie Pot Pie with Parm and Black
    Pepper Phyllo, 81–82, 83
Your New Favorite Herby Meatballs,
    84, 85–86
Mandoline, 227
Manhattan, 4
Margarita, The Versatile, xxxii, 5
Marshmallows
    Brown Butter and Sage RKTs, 190,
        191
    Churro Hot Chocolate, 194, 195
Mayo
    buying, 229
    Smoky Chipotle, 163, 164
Meatballs, Your New Favorite Herby,
    84, 85–86
Menus
    The Birthday Dinner, xxvi
    Bistro Night, xxiv
    Casual Herby Salmon, xxviii
    Easy Soup Night, xxvi
    Fancy Pants Salmon, xxviii
    Frittata Night, xxvii
    The Godfather (+ Funfetti), xxvi
    how to choose, xxi–xxiii
    Ideal Burger Night, xxv
    Kofta Platter, xxv
    Lemon & Dill Salmon, xxviii
    Lower East Side Night, xxvii
    Mediterranean Summer Dinner,
        xxiv
    Midwinter Stew Party, xxvi
    Mix 'n' Match Pasta Night, a.k.a.
        Garlic Breath Party, xxvii
    Old Jewish Lady Night, xxv
    Pancake Night, xxvii
    Pi Day, xxvi
    Pizza Night, xxiv
    Pretending It's Autumn in LA, xxv
    Sheet Pan Dinner, xxvii
    Steakhouse Night, xxv
    Summer Shrimp Fest, xxv
    Taco Night, xxiv
    Ugly But Delicious Vegetarian
        Dinner, xxvi
Microplane zester, 227
Mixers, 227
Mixing bowls, 227
Monkey Bread, Babka-Ish, 184,
    185–86
Mushrooms
    Veggie Pot Pie with Parm and Black
        Pepper Phyllo, 81–82, 83

Mustard
    buying, 229
    Whole-Grain, Garlicky Cabbage with,
        110, 111

N

Negroni, 4
Nonstick pan, 227
Noshes/appetizer recipe list, vi
Nuts. See also Pecans
    Clara's Coffee Cake, 187–88, 189
    The Messiest Ice Cream Sundaes,
        218, 219
    Party Pesto, 126, 127
    Pistachio-Date Salsa Verde Sauce, 71

O

Olive Oil
    buying, 230
    –Drenched Sourdough, 124, 125
Olives, Fancy Marinated, with Warm
    Feta, 12, 13
Onion(s)
    Brown Rice That Doesn't Suck, 114,
        115
    Caramelized, Jam, 73, 75
    Everything Bagel Seasoning, 106–9
    Quickled, 163, 166
    Wine-Drunk, and Fennel Pizza,
        152–53
Orange Dream Granita, 196, 197
Oregano
    Pizza Sprinkles, 153

P

Pancakes, Anything Goes Buttermilk,
    and Crispy Oven Bacon, 173–74,
    175
Panna Cotta, Juicy Fruit Greek Yogurt,
    204, 205
Paper Plane, xxxii, 3
Paprika
    Lentil Soup, Lemony, 20–21, 21
    Smoked, Potato Crisps with Aioli,
        28, 29
Parchment paper, 227
Parsley
    Athena's Dip Situation, 16–17, 19
    Brown Rice That Doesn't Suck, 114,
        115

Gremolata, 122, *123*
and Parm, World's Best Oven Fries with, 138, *139*
Pistachio-Date Salsa Verde Sauce, 71
Pasta
Cacio e Pepe Mac and Cheese, *44,* 45–46
dried, 229
Rigatoni with Confit Tomatoes and Burrata, 76–77, *77*
Sausage, Glorious Spicy, *64,* 65–66
Peaches
Carole King Salad, 95–96, *97*
Pears
Carole King Salad, 95–96, *97*
Peas
Carole King Salad, 95–96, *97*
Veggie Pot Pie with Parm and Black Pepper Phyllo, 81–82, *83*
Pecans
Candied, *134,* 135
Carole King Salad, 95–96, *97*
Pink Lemonade Bars, 206, *207*
A Very Adult Salad (a.k.a. Grapies and Greenies), *134,* 135–36
Peppers
Honey-Jalapeño Black Beans, 167
Pan-Crisped Sausage with Lemon Herb Veggies, *50,* 51–52
Roasted Veg Parade, 128, *129*
Smoky Chipotle Mayo, *163,* 164
Pesto, Party, *126,* 127
Phyllo, Parm and Black Pepper, Veggie Pot Pie with, 81–82, *83*
Pie, Thin Mint Pudding, 220–21, *221*
Piña Colada, Xtra-Limey, *xxxii,* 3
Pineapple
Xtra-Limey Piña Colada, *xxxii,* 3
Pine nuts
Party Pesto, *126,* 127
Pink Lemonade Bars, 206, *207*
Pinwheel Cookies, Not Your Grandma's, 201–2, *203*
Pistachio-Date Salsa Verde Sauce, 71
Pita Clouds, Fluffy Everything, 106–9, *107*
Pizza
basics, 144
Same-Day Dough, *146,* 147–48
Spicy Soppressata, *149,* 151
Sprinkles, 153
stone and peel, 144

Wine-Drunk Onion and Fennel, 152–53
Pork. *See also* Bacon; Sausage(s)
Sort-of-Kind-of Cochinita Pibil, 160–62, *161*
Your New Favorite Herby Meatballs, *84,* 85–86
Potato(es)
Cozy Winter Night Borscht, 47–48, *49*
Crisps, Smoked Paprika, with Aioli, *28,* 29
Latke-Style Smashed, with Dilly Crème Fraîche, 116–17, *117*
Pan-Crisped Sausage with Lemon Herb Veggies, *50,* 51–52
Sour Cream Mashed, 100, *101*
Veggie Pot Pie with Parm and Black Pepper Phyllo, 81–82, *83*
World's Best Oven Fries with Parsley and Parm, 138, *139*
Pot Pie, Veggie, with Parm and Black Pepper Phyllo, 81–82, *83*
Prunes
Be-Your-Own-Bubbe (BYOB) Jewish Brisket, 41–42, *43*
Pudding Pie, Thin Mint, 220–21, *221*

Q

Quickled Onions, *163,* 166
Quickled Radishes, *163,* 166

R

Radishes
Carole King Salad, 95–96, *97*
Dipped in Honey-Fennel Butter, *24,* 25
Quickled, *163,* 166
A Simple Bistro Salad, 90–91, *91*
Sort-of-Kind-of Cochinita Pibil, 160–62, *161*
Rainbow Cookie Icebox Cake, 215–16, *217*
Rasp grater, 227
Recipe notes, xxix
Rice
Brown, That Doesn't Suck, 114, *115*
Golden Coconut and Apricot, *112,* 113
Rice Krispies treats. *See* RKTs
RKTs, Brown Butter and Sage, *190,* 191

Rum
Not-So-Sweet Strawberry Daiquiri, *1,* 5
Xtra-Limey Piña Colada, *xxxii,* 3
Rye
Manhattan, 4

S

Sage
and Brown Butter RKTs, *190,* 191
Yogurt, Roasted Squash with, 122, *123*
Salads
Carole King, 95–96, *97*
Green, Super-Crunchy, *102,* 103
Kale, Andy-Approved, 104, *105*
A Simple Bistro, 90–91, *91*
That, with the Herby Dressing (a.k.a. A Chopped Salad), *92,* 93–94
A Very Adult (a.k.a. Grapies and Greenies), *134,* 135–36
Salad spinner, 227
Salmon, Pan-Seared, for Any Mood, *70,* 71
Salsa Verde Sauce, Pistachio-Date, 71
Salt, 230
Sauces
Avocado Crema, *163,* 165
Beurre Blanc, 72
Bistro Compound Butter, *78,* 79
Caramel, *218,* 219
Chocolate, *218,* 219
Lemon Coriander Yogurt, 67, *69*
Lemon-Dill, 71
Party Pesto, *126,* 127
Pistachio-Date Salsa Verde, 71
Smoky Chipotle Mayo, *163,* 164
Special, 53
Yogurt, Spiced Herby, *10,* 11
Sausage(s)
buying, 230
Hot Dog Soup (but Really Sausage), 14–15, *15*
Pan-Crisped, with Lemon Herb Veggies, *50,* 51–52
Pasta, Glorious Spicy, *64,* 65–66
Spicy Soppressata Pizza, *149,* 151
Sauté pan, 226
Seasoning, Everything Bagel, 106–9
Seeds
Everything Bagel Seasoning, 106–9
Party Pesto, *126,* 127

Shallot Compote Green Beans,
    130, 131
Shrimp, Peel 'n' Eat, with "I'd Eat
    This on a Shoe" Basil Dipping
    Magic, *56,* 57–58
Side dishes. *See also* Salads
    Brown Rice That Doesn't Suck,
        114, *115*
    Charred Lemon Broccolini, *118,* 119
    Fluffy Everything Pita Clouds,
        106–9, *107*
    Garlicky Cabbage with Whole-
        Grain Mustard, 110, *111*
    Golden Coconut and Apricot Rice,
        112, 113
    Honey-Drizzled Zucchini Fritters,
        140, 141
    Latke-Style Smashed Potatoes
        with Dilly Crème Fraîche,
        116–17,
        117
    Olive Oil–Drenched Sourdough,
        124, 125
    Party Pesto, *126,* 127
    Roasted Carrot Babies, *98,* 99
    Roasted Squash with Sage Yogurt,
        122, *123*
    Roasted Veg Parade, 128, *129*
    Shallot Compote Green Beans,
        130, 131
    Sour Cream Mashed Potatoes,
        100, *101*
    World's Best Oven Fries with
        Parsley and Parm, 138, *139*
Silicone baking mats, 227
Smoked Paprika Potato Crisps with
    Aioli, *28,* 29
Snackies—by Aristotle, 8, *9*
Soppressata Pizza, Spicy, *149,* 151
Soups
    Cozy Winter Night Borscht, 47–48,
        49
    Hot Dog (but Really Sausage),
        14–15, *15*
    Lemony Paprika Lentil, 20–21, *21*
    Tart Apple Butternut Squash,
        30–31, *31*
Sour Cream Mashed Potatoes, 100,
    101
Sourdough, Olive Oil–Drenched, *124,*
    125
Spatula, fish, 226
Special Sauce, 53

Spices, 230
Spinach
    Athena's Dip Situation, 16–17, *19*
Sprinkles
    buying, 230
    Floofy Funfetti Cake, *212,* 213–14
    Not Your Grandma's Pinwheel
        Cookies, 201–2, *203*
Squash
    Butternut, Tart Apple Soup, 30–31,
        31
    A Frittata for All Seasons, *176,*
        177–79
    Honey-Drizzled Zucchini Fritters,
        140, 141
    Roasted, with Sage Yogurt, 122,
        123
St. German
    Extra-Fun French 75, 4
Stock, Veg, 132, *133*
Stockpots, 227
Strainer, fine-mesh, 226
Strawberry(ies)
    Daiquiri, Not-So-Sweet, *1,* 5
    Juicy Fruit Greek Yogurt Panna
        Cotta, *204,* 205
Sugars, 230
Sundaes, The Messiest Ice Cream,
    218, 219

T

Tacos
    Fish-Fry, with Smoky Mayo,
        156–57, *157*
    Smoky Spicy Seared Fish, *155,*
        158–59
    Sort-of-Kind-of Cochinita Pibil,
        160–62, *161*
Tahini
    buying, 230
    Ridiculously Smooth and
        Hilariously Easy Hummus,
        26, *27*
Tequila
    The Versatile Margarita, *xxxii,* 5
Thin Mint Pudding Pie, 220–21, *221*
Toast. *See* Sourdough
Tomato(es)
    canned, 229
    Carole King Salad, 95–96, *97*
    and Chickpeas, Braised Garlicky
        Eggplant with, *38,* 39–40

Confit, and Burrata, Rigatoni with,
    76–77, *77*
Glorious Spicy Sausage Pasta, *64,*
    65–66
paste, 230
Roasted, and Burrata Eggplant
    Parm, 34–37, *35*
sauce, 230
That Salad with the Herby
    Dressing (a.k.a. A Chopped
    Salad), *92,* 93–94
Tools, kitchen, 226–27
Tortillas. *See* Tacos
Turkey
    Thighs, Crispy-Crispy, with
        Caramelized Onion Jam,
        73–74, *75*
    Your New Favorite Herby
        Meatballs, *84,* 85–86

V

Vegetables. See also specific
    vegetables
    A Frittata for All Seasons, *176,*
        177–79
    Pan-Crisped Sausage with
        Lemon Herb Veggies, *50,*
        51–52
    Roasted Veg Parade, 128, *129*
    Veggie Pot Pie with Parm and
        Black Pepper Phyllo, 81–82,
        83
    Veg Stock, 132, *133*
Vermouth
    Manhattan, 4
    Negroni, 4
Vinegar, 230

W

Walnuts
    Clara's Coffee Cake, 187–88,
        189
    The Messiest Ice Cream Sundaes,
        218, 219
Whipped Cream, *218,* 219
Whisk, 227
Wine
    buying for parties, xxi
    -Drunk Onion and Fennel Pizza,
        152–53
    Extra-Fun French 75, 4

Y

Yeast, 230
Yogurt
    Braised Garlicky Eggplant with
        Chickpeas and Tomatoes, *38,*
        39–40
    Greek, buying, 229

Greek, Panna Cotta, Juicy Fruit,
    204, 205
Lemon Coriander, 67, *69*
Lemony Herby, *140,* 141
Sage, Roasted Squash with, 122,
    123
Sauce, Spiced Herby, *10,* 11

Z

Zester, 227
Zucchini Fritters, Honey-Drizzled,
    140, 141

NATASHA FELDMAN is a culinary-school dropout, chef, and the creator of *Nosh with Tash*—a YouTube series turned TV show that teaches viewers to cook in a fun, nonfussy, and approachable way. Natasha hosts cooking shows for outlets like Food Network, MGM, and Huffington Post; contributes to national news programs and magazines; and teaches private classes for aspiring cooks and corporate clients. She lives in Los Angeles with her husband and fluffy dog, Malone.